THE FOLLY
OF EMPIRE

WHAT GEORGE W. BUSH COULD LEARN
FROM THEODORE ROOSEVELT
AND WOODROW WILSON

JOHN B. JUDIS

A LISA DREW BOOK

SCRIBNER
NEW YORK   LONDON   TORONTO   SYDNEY

A LISA DREW BOOK/SCRIBNER
1230 Avenue of the Americas
New York, NY 10020

For information about special discounts for bulk purchases,
please contact Simon & Schuster Special Sales:
1-800-456-6798 or business@simonandschuster.com

DESIGNED BY ERICH HOBBING

Text set in Adobe Garamond

Manufactured in the United States of America

1   3   5   7   9   10   8   6   4   2

Library of Congress Cataloging-in-Publication Data is available.

ISBN 0-7432-6127-5

For Jorgen Dragsdahl and David Moberg

A new age has come which no man may forecast. But the past is the key to it; and the past of America lies at the center of modern history.

—Woodrow Wilson,
Preface to *The Harper's Encyclopedia of the United States*, 1901

CONTENTS

At noon, October 18, 2003, President George W. Bush landed in Manila as part of a six-nation Asian tour. Because officials were concerned about a terrorist attack on the embattled islands, the presidential airplane, *Air Force One,* was shepherded into Philippine air space by F-15s. Bush's speech to the Philippine Congress was delayed by what one reporter described as "undulating throngs of demonstrators who lined his motorcade route past rows of shacks."[1] Outside the Philippine House of Representatives, several thousand more demonstrators greeted Bush, and several Philippine legislators staged a walkout during his twenty-minute speech.

In his speech, Bush took credit for America transforming the Philippines into "the first democratic nation in Asia." Said Bush, "America is proud of its part in the great story of the Filipino people. Together our soldiers liberated the Philippines from colonial rule. Together we rescued the islands from invasion and occupation." And he drew an analogy between America's attempt to create democracy in the Philippines and its attempt to create a democratic Middle East through invading and occupying Iraq in the spring of 2003: "Democracy always has skeptics. Some say the culture of the Middle East will not sustain the institutions of democracy. The same doubts were once expressed about the culture of Asia. These doubts were proven wrong nearly six decades ago, when the Republic of the Philippines became the first democratic nation in Asia."

After a state dinner, Bush and his party were bundled back onto *Air Force One* and shunted off to the president's next stop, Thailand. The Secret Service had warned Bush that it was not safe for him to remain overnight in the "first Democratic nation in Asia."

As many Philippine commentators remarked afterward, Bush's rendition of Philippine-American history bore very little relation to fact. True, the

United States Navy under Admiral George Dewey had ousted Spain from the Philippines in the Spanish-American War of 1898. But instead of creating a Philippine democracy, President William McKinley annexed the country and installed a colonial administrator. The United States then fought a brutal war against the same Philippine independence movement it had encouraged to fight Spain. The war dragged on for fourteen years. Before it was over, about 120,000 American troops were deployed and more than 4,000 died; more than 200,000 Filipino civilians and soldiers were killed.[2] And the resentment against American policy was still evident a century later during George W. Bush's visit.

The Filipinos were not the only ones to rue the American occupation. Before he was assassinated in September 1901, McKinley himself had come to have doubts about it. He told a friend, "If old Dewey had just sailed away when he smashed that Spanish fleet, what a lot of trouble he would have saved us."[3] By 1907, Theodore Roosevelt, who had earlier championed the war and occupation, recognized the United States had made a mistake in annexing the Philippines. After Woodrow Wilson became president, he and the Democrats backed Philippine independence, but were thwarted by Republicans who still nurtured dreams of American empire. Only in 1946, after reconquering the Philippines from Japan, did the United States finally grant independence—and even then it retained military bases and special privileges for American corporations.

As for the Philippines' democracy, the United States can take little credit for what exists, and some blame for what doesn't. The Philippines were not the first Asian country to hold elections. And the electoral machinery the U.S. designed in 1946 provided a veneer of democratic process beneath which a handful of families, allied to American investors and addicted to payoffs and kickbacks, controlled Philippine land, economy, and society. The tenuous system broke down in 1973 when Ferdinand Marcos had himself declared president for life. Marcos was finally overthrown in 1986, but even today Philippine democracy is more dream than reality. Three months before Bush's visit, beleaguered Philippine president Gloria Macapagal Arroyo had survived a military coup; and with Islamic radicals and communists roaming the countryside, the Philippines are perhaps the least stable of Asian nations. If the analogy between America's "liberation" of the Philippines and of Iraq were to hold true, the United States can look forward to four decades of occupation, culminating in an outcome that is still far from satisfactory. Such an outcome would not redound to the credit of the Bush administration, but instead to the "skeptics" who charged that the Bush administration had undertaken the invasion of Baghdad with its eyes wide shut.

Politicians often rewrite history to their own purposes, but, as Bush's analogy to Iraq suggested, there was more than passing significance to his revision of the history of the Spanish-American War. It reflected not just a distorted picture of a critical episode in American foreign policy but a seeming ignorance of the important lessons that Americans drew from this brief and unhappy experiment in creating an overseas empire. If Bush had applied these lessons to the American plans for invading Iraq and transforming the Middle East, he might have proceeded far more cautiously. But as his rendition of history showed, he was either unaware of them or had chosen to ignore them.

The Spanish-American War and its aftermath represented a turning point in American foreign policy. Until the 1890s, the United States had adhered to George Washington and Thomas Jefferson's advice to stay out of "foreign entanglements." America had expanded over the continent and sought to prevent new foreign incursions into the hemisphere, but it had avoided Europe's growing struggle for empire in Asia and Africa. Now, by going to war against Spain in the Pacific and the Caribbean, and by establishing what it thought of as a stepping-stone to the China market, the United States had abandoned its own splendid isolation and thrown itself into the worldwide struggle.

To take this momentous step, the United States had discarded its historic opposition to imperialism. Founded as a result of an anti-colonial war against the British, the United States had sought to expand westward by adding new states and citizens that enjoyed equal rights with those that existed. Americans had stood firmly against acquiring overseas people and territories that would be ruled from afar. But by taking over the Spanish empire, America had become the kind of imperial power it had once denounced. It was now vying with Great Britain, France, Germany, Russia, and Japan for what Theodore Roosevelt called "the domination of the world."[4]

American proponents of imperialism argued that the country needed colonies to bolster its military power and to find markets for its capital, but they also believed that by expanding overseas, the United States was fulfilling its historic mission to transform the world in its image. The United States had been founded by descendants of emigrants from Protestant Britain and Holland who viewed their new land as a "city on a hill" that would initiate the "new Israel" and the Kingdom of God on Earth. Well after the glow of Puritan conviction dimmed, Americans still believed that they had a unique or special millennial role in transforming the world—not necessarily into a replica of early Christian communities, but into states and countries that shared America's commitment to liberty and democracy.

Roosevelt, McKinley, and the other proponents of an American imperialism insisted that by annexing other countries, Americans would, in McKinley's words, "civilize and Christianize" them. Said McKinley of the Philippines in October 1900, "Territory sometimes comes to us when we go to war in a holy cause, and whenever it does the banner of liberty will float over it and bring, I trust, blessings and benefits to all people."[5] Their convictions were echoed by a prominent historian who had recently become president of Princeton. In 1901, Woodrow Wilson wrote in defense of the annexation of the Philippines:

> The East is to be opened and transformed, whether we will it or not; the standards of the West are to be imposed upon it; nations and peoples who have stood still the centuries through are to be quickened and to be made part of the universal world of commerce and of ideas which has so steadily been a-making by the advance of European power from age to age.[6]

America, the proponents of imperialism argued, would acquire an overseas empire of its own, and through careful administration and the defeat of backward, or "savage," resistance movements, lay the basis for the spread of liberty and democracy throughout the world. "God's hand," Indiana senator Albert Beveridge declared in 1900, "is in . . . the movement of the American people toward the mastery of the world."[7]

The two presidents who figured out that America's experiment with imperialism wasn't working were, ironically, Theodore Roosevelt and Woodrow Wilson. Roosevelt was an enthusiastic supporter not only of the Spanish-American War, in which he enlisted, but of the subsequent American takeover of the Spanish empire. Said Roosevelt in April 1899, "If we do our duty aright in the Philippines, we will add to that national renown which is the highest and finest part of national life, and will greatly benefit the people of the Philippine islands, and above all, we will play our part well in the great work of uplifting mankind."[8] Yet after he became president in September 1901, his enthusiasm for overseas expansion noticeably waned. Urged to take over the Dominican Republic, he quipped, "As for annexing the island, I have about the same desire to annex it as a gorged boa constrictor might have to swallow a porcupine wrong-end-to."[9] Under Roosevelt, America's colonial holdings actually shrunk. And after the Russo-Japanese War in 1904, Roosevelt changed America's diplomatic posture from competitor with the other imperialist powers in dominating the world to mediator in their growing conflicts.

Woodrow Wilson had initially cheered the American takeover of the Spanish empire, although not as lustily as Roosevelt and McKinley. When he became president in 1913, he boasted that he could transform Latin America, if not the rest of the world, into constitutional democracies in America's image. Proclaiming his opposition to Mexican dictator Victoriano Huerta, Wilson promised that he was "going to teach the South American republics to elect good men."[10] But Wilson discovered in Mexico that attempts to instill American-style constitutional democracy and capitalism through force were destined to fail. And not just to fail, but to spark a nationalist, anti-American backlash that would threaten American security during World War I. In Mexico, Wilson came to understand in practice what he had written in his theories of government—that "self-government is not a thing that can be 'given' to any people."[11]

Like Roosevelt, and many European leaders, Wilson had also believed that imperialism was contributing to a higher, more pacific civilization by bringing not only capitalist industry but also higher standards of morality and education to what had been barbarous regions. Wars would be fought, but primarily between uncivilized nations, or between them and civilized countries. Eventually, war would disappear. But as Wilson learned from the outbreak of World War I, the struggle for colonies had precipitated a savage and destructive war between the imperial powers themselves.

World War I turned Wilson not only against German militarism but against the structure of world politics and economics that the imperial struggle for colonies had sustained. The only way to prevent future war, he concluded, was to dismantle the structure itself. During the war and in the peace negotiations that followed, Wilson attempted to put America and the world on a new footing—one that would prevent future wars. Wilson's plan included self-determination for former colonies, an open trading system to discourage economic imperialism, international arms reduction, and a commitment to collective security through international organizations—what is now sometimes referred to as "multilateralism." Wilson continued to believe that the United States had a special role to play in the world. But he now believed that it could best play that role by getting other nations to work with it to effect a global transformation.

Wilson failed to get either the other victors from World War I or the Republican-controlled Senate in the United States to agree to his plan for a new world order. His Republican successors organized international disarmament conferences but ignored the structure of imperialism that was fueling a new arms race. They called for an "open door" in world markets, but protected America's prosperity behind high tariff walls. They played a small, but real, part in fulfilling the prediction of a new world war that Wilson had made in Pueblo, Colorado, in September 1919, on the eve of the vote on the League of Nations.

Franklin Roosevelt, who had served under Wilson, saw the onset of World War II as a vindication of Wilson's approach. Roosevelt and Harry Truman attempted to craft a new "community of power" based upon Wilsonian principles. It was embodied in organizations such as the United Nations and the International Monetary Fund and in treaties such as the General Agreement on Tariffs and Trade. This approach helped prevent a new world war and depression, but it did not succeed exactly as Wilson, Roosevelt, or Truman initially envisaged. After the war, the British and French refused to give up their colonies without a fight, and the Soviet Union fueled a Cold War by attempting to restore, and build upon, the older czarist empire in eastern Europe and southern and western Asia.

During the Cold War, the United States used Wilson's approach to create a "community of power" against the Soviet Union—chiefly through the creation of the North Atlantic Treaty Organization (NATO), a new type of alliance that encouraged the defense and spread of democratic principles. That aspect of American foreign policy proved to be remarkably successful. But outside of western Europe and Japan, American policymakers often believed that they had to choose between maintaining America's opposition to imperialism and colonialism and opposing the Soviet

Union in the Cold War. They opposed anti-imperialist movements in southeast Asia, the Mideast, and Latin America because they believed that their victory would aid the Soviet Union. That led to the catastrophic war in Vietnam and to serious setbacks in the Caribbean, Central America, and the Mideast. American policy-makers discovered once more that when America took the side of the imperial powers or acted itself as an imperial power, it courted disaster and even defeat.

The end of the Cold War created the conditions for finally realizing the promise of Wilson's foreign policy. With the collapse of the Soviet empire and the dissolution of western Europe's empires, one key aspect of the age of empire—the struggle for world domination among great powers—was over. What remained were the conflicts that imperialism had instigated or suppressed in the regions that the great powers had dominated. These were evident in the Mideast, South Asia, the Taiwan Straits, the Korean peninsula, the Balkans, and the Caribbean. The great powers could now, as Wilson had hoped, form a "community of power" to manage and resolve these remaining conflicts.

The administrations of George H. W. Bush and Bill Clinton understood the new opportunity that existed. When Iraq invaded and annexed Kuwait in August 1990, Bush built a powerful coalition through the United Nations Security Council to drive Saddam Hussein's forces out of the Gulf kingdom. Clinton worked through NATO to protect the independence of Bosnia and the autonomy of Kosovo from a Serbia bent upon reestablishing its own version of hegemony over peoples that had suffered centuries of ethnic conflict under the Ottoman and Austro-Hungarian empires. Under Clinton, the nations of the world also founded a new World Trade Organization to move toward open markets.

These years represented a triumph of Wilsonianism and of the lessons that America had learned from the Spanish-American War, two world wars, and the Vietnam War. But these lessons were entirely lost on the administration of George W. Bush that took office in January 2001. Like the Republicans of the 1920s, the Bush Republicans were determined to forget rather than build upon the past. The new Bush administration was composed primarily of two factions that were deeply hostile to the tradition of Wilson, Franklin Roosevelt, and Truman. The nationalists, as they were called, were only willing to support American overseas intervention when it met a strict test of national interest and didn't involve ceding control to international organizations or coalitions. Their policies, wrote Condoleezza Rice, who would become George W. Bush's national security adviser, "proceed from the firm ground of the national interest, not from the interests of an illusory international community."[12]

The neoconservatives were the second and third generation of the former socialists and liberals who had moved to the right during the 1960s. They declared their admiration for the Theodore Roosevelt of the 1890s and for America's first experiment with imperialism. Some, like *Wall Street Journal* editorial page editor Max Boot, called on the United States to "unambiguously . . . embrace its imperial role," while others preferred terms like "American hegemony."[13] Like the nationalists, they scorned international institutions and the Wilsonian idea of a community of power. But unlike them, they strongly advocated using America's military and economic power to transform countries and regions in America's image. They were a throwback to the Republican imperialists who had agitated for the United States to occupy and annex the Philippines at the turn of the last century.

Well before the September 11, 2001, attack by Osama bin Laden's al-Qaeda organization, both factions had advocated overthrowing Iraq's Saddam Hussein, but they were restrained by natural caution and by the public's reluctance to support a war against an adversary that didn't directly threaten the United States. September 11 provided them with the grounds to convince the public of a potential Iraqi threat, while America's easy victory in Afghanistan in the fall of 2001 nourished an illusion that America could do whatever it wanted in the world. Both the nationalists and neoconservatives came to believe that they could invade Iraq, overthrow Saddam, and quickly install a regime that was friendly to the United States, while sending a signal to terrorists and neighboring autocracies that their days were numbered. The McKinley administration had acquired similar illusions after its quick victory over Spain in 1898. And while McKinley had dreamed of civilizing and Christianizing, the Bush administration dreamed of liberating and democratizing not just Iraq but the entire Mideast.

Just as in the Philippines in 1900, Mexico in 1913, or South Vietnam in 1961, things didn't turn out as American policy-makers had hoped. America's invasion and occupation of Iraq—a perfect imitation of an earlier imperialism—awakened dormant Iraqi nationalism. After a quick march across the desert to Baghdad, American forces found themselves besieged in a bloody and seemingly interminable occupation. In the Middle East, the invasion and occupation were seen as confirmation of bin Laden's charge that the United States was bent on exploiting the region's resources and imposing its culture. Instead of curtailing the "war on terror," as Bush had promised, the war in Iraq brought a new wave of recruits. Instead of encouraging a democratic transformation, it reinforced the rule of neighboring autocracies.

History is not physics. The study of the past doesn't yield unalterable laws that allow one to predict the future with the same certainty that a physicist can chart the trajectory and velocity of a falling object. But historical experiences do yield lessons that convince peoples and their leaders to change their behavior to avoid expected, and undesired, consequences. America's initial experiment with imperialism in the late nineteenth and early twentieth centuries yielded these kinds of lessons. Under Theodore Roosevelt and Woodrow Wilson, and later under a succession of presidents from Franklin Roosevelt to Bill Clinton, these experiences convinced Americans to change their attitude toward imperial conquest and toward nationalism in countries like the Philippines and Iraq.

But as America entered the twenty-first century, this history appeared to have been forgotten or revised in the interests of a new nationalism and neoconservatism. Only a president deeply ignorant of the past and what it teaches could journey to the Philippines in 2003 and declare that a century ago Americans had "liberated the Philippines from colonial rule." America's decision to invade and occupy Iraq wasn't, of course, a direct result of this misreading of the past. If Bush or Vice President Dick Cheney or Deputy Secretary of Defense Paul Wolfowitz, the administration's leading neoconservative, had been aware of the brutal war America had fought in the Philippines, or of Wilson's misadventures in Mexico, or of the blighted history of Western imperialism in the Mideast, they might still have invaded Iraq. But they also might have had second or even third or fourth thoughts about what Bush, echoing Beveridge and the imperialists of a century ago, would call "a historic opportunity to change the world."[14]

CHAPTER ONE

An Empire of Liberty:
The Framework of American Foreign Policy

In their first hundred years as a nation, Americans were preoccupied with their own continent. America's foreign policy was principally concerned with removing Mexicans and Indians from lands that American settlers coveted. James Bryce wrote in *The American Commonwealth* in 1888, "The only one principle to which people have learnt to cling in foreign policy is that the less they have of it the better."[1] In 1889, the *New York Sun,* the precursor of the current neoconservative daily, advocated that the diplomatic service be abolished altogether. Americans, of course, wanted to trade with other countries, but they recoiled at the thought of becoming involved in their quarrels.

In the 1890s, however, the world and its quarrels came to America. Americans were suddenly forced to deal with the rapid growth of European and Japanese imperialism. Between 1876 and 1914, one quarter of the world was divvied up among these imperial powers.[2] During these years, Great Britain increased its territories by 4 million square miles, France by 3.5 million, and Germany by more than a million. By 1900, Britain had 50 colonies, France 33, and Germany 13.[3] Over 90 percent of Africa was colonized, 98.9 percent of Polynesia, and 56.5 percent of Asia.[4]

As the British economist J. A. Hobson argued in his 1902 book, *Imperialism,* much of this new competition for colonies was driven by economics. Faced with Britain's domination of the world's shipping and banking and America's high tariff walls, European countries and Japan sought colonies in order to gain guaranteed markets and outlets for investment and to obtain raw materials that they could not extract at home. As France, Russia, Germany, and Japan established protectorates and colonies, they walled them off from economic competition. That aroused understandable fear among

American businesses, banks, and farms that had become increasingly dependent on exports and on overseas capital investments. By the 1890s, it looked as if the China market, which was assumed to be a future source of untold riches, might eventually be closed off to American business.

Europe and Japan's scramble for colonies was also driven by a combustible mixture of nationalism and militarism. In the late nineteenth century, the possession of colonies became an important measure of prestige and power for newly formed states like Germany and Italy and for older empires like the Russian, Ottoman, or Austrian that were threatened with disintegration. The Germans insisted that their colonial possessions should reflect their growing economic and military power in relation to Britain and France. The French sought overseas colonies to overcome the humiliation of their defeat in the Franco-Prussian War of 1871. This kind of competition fueled a massive naval arms race and a succession of wars, contributing finally to the outbreak of World War I.

Americans could look on the Franco-Prussian War dispassionately, but as the first major war broke out in China in 1894, and as German warships began to penetrate the Pacific and patrol the South American coast, they begin to reconsider their historic isolation. In 1890, the Naval Policy Board warned that

> there are not wanting indications that [America's] comparative isolation will soon cease to exist, and that it will gradually be replaced by a condition of affairs which will bring this nation into sharp commercial competition with others in every part of the world. . . . In the adjustment of our trade with a neighbor we are certain to reach out and obstruct the interests of foreign nations.[5]

Forced finally to look outward, Americans began a fifty-year-long debate about what kind of foreign policy the country should adopt. At its center was the question of how the United States should respond to the growth of this new imperialism. Should it maintain its traditional opposition, borne of the American Revolution, to colonial conquests? Should it seek, as the young Theodore Roosevelt advised, to compete with the imperial powers by acquiring colonies of its own? Or should it aggressively attempt, as Woodrow Wilson would later advocate, to dismantle the global structure of imperialism?

In deciding what policies to pursue, Americans, like their European cousins, drew upon a sense of their own national mission and purpose. This was often expressed in quasi-religious or moral terms. The proponents of an American imperialism insisted it would lead to the "redemption of the world." They claimed it was "America's duty to educate the Filipinos and uplift and Christianize them." They argued that "the great civilized peoples have today at their command the means of developing the decadent nations of the world." The opponents of imperialism, on the other hand, warned against a "war of selfish ambition" and the "temptation of conquest." And they defended the opposition to imperialism as "the grandest triumph of the democratic idea."

Sophisticated historians might dismiss these kind of statements about civilization, Christianity, and democracy as bombast. Foreign policy, they might argue, is always about power and money, not morals and religion. But a particular conception of America's mission in the world has consistently shaped Americans' understanding of geopolitics and economics. It has been central to the American debate over imperialism and empire. It provided the basis on which Americans rejected acquiring colonies, and later, it was modified, and perhaps twisted, to justify America's acquiring colonies. Most recently, it was used by the Bush administration to justify its decision to invade and occupy Iraq.

A PECULIAR CHOSEN PEOPLE

Americans' sense of mission predates the debate over imperialism. It originated with the dissenting Protestants from England and Holland who landed on the Atlantic Coast in the seventeenth century. These Puritans brought with them a set of beliefs about the New World and its mission. It was refined and given new substance by the American Revolution, the westward expansion, and the Indian wars, and was then invoked to justify and condemn different responses to the growth of European imperialism. It has long since lost its conscious connection to biblical passages, and provides a framework by which Americans of different faiths or no faith think about the country's foreign policy.

There are two interrelated concepts that make up this framework of belief. While the precise content of these concepts has changed over the centuries, the overall relation between them and their importance to American foreign policy has endured:

Americans as the "chosen people": The first settlers from Puritan England saw themselves as "chosen people" who had made a mutual "covenant" with God and who would have a special role in establishing a "new Israel." As one prominent Connecticut clergyman put it in 1777, "We in this land are, as it were, led out of Egypt by the hand of Moses."[6] Over the next 225 years, this concept has kept recurring, whether in its original religious form or in a more modern, secular guise. In 1900, during the Senate debate over imperialism, Albert Beveridge would declare that God "has marked the American people as His chosen nation to finally lead in the redemption of the world."[7] In 1917, Woodrow Wilson called America "the greatest hope and energy of the world."[8] Bill Clinton's secretary of state Madeleine Albright regularly described the United States as "the indispensable nation." And in his 2002 State of the Union address, George W. Bush declared that the United States had "been called to a unique role in human events."[9]

Americans as having a moral or religious mission: As the "chosen people" in their "unique role," Americans have seen themselves as having a special mission in the world. Jefferson envisioned Americans forging an "empire of liberty," Jacksonian Democrats talked of "manifest destiny," and Franklin Roosevelt and later Ronald Reagan spoke of a "rendezvous with destiny." The mission is, above all, religious or moral in nature and defined as a struggle between good and evil and for redemption and salvation. In 1919, arguing for the ratification of the treaty establishing the League of Nations, President Woodrow Wilson declared, "For nothing less depends upon this decision, nothing less than the liberation and salvation of the world."[10] George W. Bush called on America in his 2002 State of the Union address to defeat an "axis of evil." He declared in November 2003 that "the advance of freedom is the calling of our time. It is the calling of our country. . . . We believe that liberty is the design of nature. We believe that liberty is the direction of history."[11]

In *White Jacket*, Herman Melville's narrator summed up Americans' view of themselves and their mission: "And we Americans are the peculiar, chosen people—the Israel of our time; we bear the ark of the liberties of the world. . . . God has predestined, mankind expects great things from our race. . . . The rest of the nations must soon be in our rear. . . . Long enough have we been skeptics with regard to ourselves, and doubted whether, indeed, the political Messiah had come. But he has come in *us*, if we would be given utterance to his promptings. And let us always remember that with ourselves, almost for the first time in the history of the earth, national selfishness is unbounded philanthropy; for we cannot do a good to America, but we give alms to the world."[12]

Over the centuries, Americans have changed their idea of who the chosen people are. In the seventeenth century, it was the members of the scattered Protestant communities along the East Coast of North America. With the Revolution, and the nation's founding, the chosen people became Americans, but the term "American" sometimes referred in fact only to white Christian Anglo-Saxons. In *Our Country*, his best-selling argument in 1885 for imperialism, Josiah Strong wrote that God is "preparing in our Anglo-Saxon civilization the die with which to stamp the peoples of the earth."[13] Only after World War II did the term "Americans" come to have the full-throated multiethnic, multiracial connotation that it currently has.

The specific idea of *mission* has also changed. Before the Revolution, the mission was defined by the dissenting Protestantism of the early settlers. America's mission was *millennial*: it was to create a thousand-year-long Kingdom of God on Earth, a new Israel, that would resemble the early Christian communities that the Puritans admired and that would combat the influence of the papal Antichrist. After the Revolution, many Americans moved from a primarily religious conception of the Kingdom of God on Earth to what historian Nathan Hatch called "civil millennialism."[14] They talked of America as founding what Jefferson called an "empire of liberty." In the nineteenth century, many Americans talked of spreading civilization in lands dominated by savages, and in the twentieth century of spreading democracy to nations controlled by fascism and communism.

Americans have changed their idea of the mission to adapt to changing economic, political, and military circumstances. This is where the interplay of ideal and interest figures. Sometimes the conception of mission has served primarily as a rationalization for pursuing less than noble interests, such as ousting the Sioux from the Black Hills of South Dakota in order to make room for gold prospectors. Other times, such as during America's recent intervention in the Balkans, ideal has appeared to drive interest. But at crucial junctures in American history, in the late eighteenth and late nineteenth century and even in the early twenty-first century, Americans have earnestly sought a happy marriage of America's mission with the immediate interests of its citizens.

Finally, the *means* by which Americans thought they could accomplish their mission has changed. In 1630, John Winthrop, who would later become governor of Massachusetts, told his fellow émigrés aboard the *Arabella* that they were going to establish a "city on the hill" that would transform the world by example. In the nation's first two decades, George Washington and Thomas Jefferson would insist that the United States steer clear of old-world conflicts and alliances. Throughout most of the nineteenth century Americans would take their advice, and would seek to transform the world through continental expansion. Only at the end of the nineteenth century, faced with the rise of European imperialism, would Americans begin to consider actively transforming the world outside their hemisphere. Over the next four decades, Americans would debate whether to concern themselves with affairs in Europe and Asia. Finally, during World War II, Americans would assume world leadership.

Looked at over seven key periods—with the definition of the seventh still under contention—the different components of the American framework would look something like the table on the opposite page.

The United States is not the first or only nation in the world to believe that it had a special role to play in transforming the world. So did imperial Rome, Napoleonic France, Victorian Britain, Wilhemine and Nazi Germany, and the Soviet Union. But these countries' sense of mission eventually ran afoul of the reality they sought to transform. They had to abandon their visions, whether as a result of devastating military defeat or gradual economic decline. America, too, has periodically had to modify its visions in the face of new circumstances and adversaries. But what distinguishes America today is that it has not had to abandon its millennial hopes. A string of victories in major wars, coupled with an almost unbroken rise in the national standard of living, has strengthened Americans' conviction of their exceptionalism.

Not all Americans have adhered to this view of themselves and their nation. It is not a genetic inheritance like height or eye color, but rather an understanding that is passed down from generation to generation by parents, teachers, ministers, politicians, and what is now called the media. But

Period	Mission	Adversary	Means
Pre-Revolutionary, Colonial America (1600–1776)	Kingdom of God on Earth	Papal Antichrist	Example as "city on the hill"
Revolutionary and founding era (1776–1815)	Empire of liberty	Old-world tyranny, monarchy, and empire	Example, continental expansion without entangling alliances
Jacksonian America (1815–1848)	Christian civilization	Savages or "children"	Example, continental expansion without entangling alliances
Imperial America (1898–1908)	Christian civilization	Barbarians and savages	Overseas expansion without entangling alliances
Wilsonian internationalism (1914–1919 and 1939–1946)	Global democracy, four freedoms	Autocracy, imperialism, and fascism	International organization and alliances
Cold War liberalism (1946–1989)	Global democracy	Communism	International organizations and alliances
Post-imperialism with remnants of imperialism (1989–)	Global democracy, third way?	International terrorism, rogue states?	International organizations, unilateral action?

dissent itself has taken place within what might be awkwardly described as the framework of the framework. There was an original strand of American Protestantism that preached withdrawal and separation. In theological terms, it held a "premillennial" rather than "postmillennial" vision of the future—that the world would end and Jesus would come and spirit away the saved *before* the millennium. Some prominent Puritan clerics, including Increase Mather, took this view.[15] So did the Disciples of Christ when Ronald Reagan was growing up, and the Reverend Jerry Falwell, one of the founders of the modern Christian right. There has been a strand of American foreign policy that corresponds to this theological outlook. It counsels isolation from what Thomas Jefferson called the "exterminating havoc" of the Old World.[16] It sees Americans as chosen and as having a mission, but the mission is one of saving themselves while the rest of the world wallows in sin or is consumed by destruction. It doesn't see the rest of the world as potential converts to the American example, but as hardened sinners whom it is best to avoid. Its pessimistic view of the world outside America and of Americans' obligation to save themselves from it could be seen vividly in the isolationism of the 1930s. It would reappear among some Republicans in the 1990s and even in the statements of George W. Bush. But in the span of American history, this premillennial vision has usually taken second place to that of the postmillennial.

CIVIL MILLENNIALISM

As Ernest Tuveson argues in *Redeemer Nation,* the origins of America's millennial framework go back to the Protestant Reformation and to its linear and progressive view of history.[17] English Puritans read the New Testament's "Revelation of St. John" to mean that the millennium—interpreted by most medieval clerics to be a purely symbolic event—would actually occur before the end of history as a result of the triumph of the forces of Good over Evil in the Battle of Armageddon. After this glorious victory, human beings would enjoy a thousand years of the Kingdom of God on Earth. Out of this theological conviction, English Puritans embraced the social or political objective of creating the Kingdom of God on Earth—first as a religious community and then as a nation and world dedicated to life, liberty, and the pursuit of happiness.

The English Puritans believed that the Reformation, by overthrowing the papal Antichrist, had begun the process that would culminate in the millennium. The next step would be the overthrow of England's Catholic monarchy and the creation of an English republic shaped by the principles of primitive Christianity. But Oliver Cromwell's New Model Army did not succeed in getting rid of the English monarchy. After Cromwell's fall, the Puritans increasingly rested their hopes for establishing the kingdom of God on their American co-religionists, who had fled England to establish religious communities in the New World. The Puritan poet George Herbert wrote:

> *Religion stands tip-toe in our land*
> *Ready to pass to the American strand.*

The Pilgrims and Puritans who landed in North America believed that they were founding a "new Israel" that would serve as the site of the millennium. Cotton Mather described New England as "the spot of Earth, which the God of Heaven spied out . . . as the center of the future Kingdom."[18] In the mid-eighteenth century, Jonathan Edwards, the leader of the Great Awakening, spoke of "the dawning, or at least a prelude, of that glorious work of God, so often foretold in Scripture, which in the progress and issue of it, shall renew the world of mankind. . . . Many things . . . make it probable that this work will begin in America."[19]

By the time of the Revolution, many Americans were moving from a primarily religious conception of the Kingdom of God on Earth to "civil millennialism." Americans' view of the millennium became secular, but it also became defined in peculiarly American terms. The breakdown of feudal-era social stratification in the New World reinforced the belief of dissenting Protestants that all people were equal before God and led to belief in the liberty and equality that Jefferson expressed in the Declaration of Independence.[20] The revolution against British rule led Americans to advocate the elimination of feudal servitude *and* independence from foreign rule by the "antichrist of British tyranny."[21]

Americans would later expand their understanding of liberty. Democracy and human rights would also be included. But this basic version of American civil millennialism has remained remarkably intact from the American Revolution to today. In 1942, during World War II, Franklin Roosevelt would urge Americans to be true to their "divine heritage. We are fighting, as our fathers have fought, to uphold the doctrine that all men are equal in the sight of God. . . . This is the conflict that day and night now pervades our lives. No compromise can end that conflict. There never has been—there never can be—successful compromise between good and evil." In November 2003, George W. Bush, defending the invasion of Iraq, would say, "Liberty is both the plan of Heaven for humanity, and the best hope for progress here on Earth."

AN EMPIRE FOR LIBERTY

America's founders saw the continental nation they had created as an "American empire." Washington spoke of a "rising American empire," and Jefferson of an "empire for liberty" and an "empire of liberty."[22] Theodore Roosevelt, Indiana senator Albert Beveridge, and some current proponents of imperialism would claim that they were following in Washington and Jefferson's footsteps—Beveridge would describe Jefferson as "the first imperialist"—but their conception of empire was fundamentally different from that of the founders.[23]

Washington and Jefferson adapted the classical theory of the cycle of empires to America's millennial vision. America would be the next and, perhaps, the last stop in the cycle of great empires, succeeding Great Britain. Bishop George Berkeley, better known for his solipsistic theory of knowledge, had voiced this theory in his "Verses on the Prospect of Planting Arts and Learning in America":

> *Westward the course of empire takes its way;*
> *The four first acts already past,*
> *A fifth shall close the drama with the day;*
> *Time's noblest offspring is the last.*

Washington, Jefferson, and other founders believed that the United States would grow and surpass its predecessors in size and population by expanding across the North American continent. But in expanding, it would create new states and citizens that enjoyed the same liberty and self-government as the old. As reflected in the Northwest Ordinance of 1787, Washington and Jefferson conceived of an American empire as a very large federated nation made up of equal states and citizens. They condemned the idea of an empire based on a powerful core state ruling over colonies and subject peoples. Indeed, Jefferson envisaged the world of nations on the model of a nation of equal individuals, writing to Madison in 1789 that "I know but one code of morality for man whether acting singly or collectively."[24]

The founders explicitly rejected empires based on conquest and distant rule. In 1777, poet Timothy Dwight, who was then serving as chaplain to the Army of the Potomac and would later become the president of Yale, contrasted the European idea of conquest with the American view of "empire . . . on Freedom's broad basis":

> *To conquest, and slaughter, let Europe aspire,*
> *Whelm nations in blood, and wrap cities in fire . . .*
> *A world is thy realm: for a world be thy laws,*
> *Enlarg'd as thine empire, and just as thy cause;*
> *On Freedom's broad basis, that empire shall rise,*
> *Extend with the main, and dissolve with the skies.*[25]

In 1780, the Reverend Samuel Cooper told the Massachusetts legislature, "Conquest is not indeed the aim of these rising states; sound policy must ever forbid it. We have before us an object more truly great and honorable. We seem called by heaven to make a large portion of this globe a seat of knowledge and liberty, of agriculture, commerce, and arts, and what is more important than all, of Christian piety and virtue."[26] In 1788, John Jay, the president of the Continental Congress, told the French envoy that America's Constitution was "inconsistent with the passion for conquest."[27]

ENTANGLING ALLIANCES

Americans believed their revolution would serve as a "city on the hill" for all the nations of the world. Declared Yale president Ezra Stiles, "This great American revolution, this recent political phenomenon of a new sovereignty arising among the sovereign powers of the earth, will be attended to and contemplated by all nations."[28] And in the wake of the French Revolution in 1789, some Americans became convinced that they had actually sparked a world revolution. When the French revolutionary Edmond Charles Genet, dubbed Citizen Genet, landed in America in 1793, he won widespread support for plans to attack the Spanish and British empires. Americans would actually furnish foot soldiers for this worldwide revolution. In 1794, theologian David Austin predicted that the millennium itself would occur in 1796![29]

Washington, however, recognized that the new nation was still extraordinarily weak and could barely defend its own frontier, let alone get involved in a European war. He opposed any alliance with France and opted for a strategy of noninterference in European affairs that implicitly acknowledged Britain's superior navy. In his Farewell Address in 1796, Washington said, "The great rule of conduct for us in regard to foreign nations is, in extending our commercial relations to have with them as little *political* connection as possible." He warned against "permanent inveterate antipathies against particular nations and passionate attachments for others."

Jefferson and John Quincy Adams both reaffirmed Washington's foreign policy. In his first inaugural address, Jefferson warned against "entangling alliances." In 1821, John Quincy Adams, serving as James Monroe's secretary of state, rejected pleas that the United States intervene on behalf of the Greek revolutionaries. Adams rejected "going abroad in search of monsters to destroy," urging instead that America "commend the general cause by the countenance of her voice and the benignant sympathy of her example."[30] Washington, John Quincy Adams, and Jefferson were making a judgment that given America's military and economic weakness, it had nothing to gain and everything to lose from involving itself in Europe's quarrels. Except for Jefferson at moments of extreme antipathy toward Europe, they weren't rejecting the framework, they were insisting that the way America would transform the world was by example, not by active intervention. Said Washington in his Farewell Address, "It will be worthy of a free, enlightened, and at no distant period a great nation to give to mankind the magnanimous and too novel example of a people always guided by an exalted justice and benevolence."

CIVILIZATION AND BARBARISM

During most of the nineteenth century, the main focus of American foreign policy was on westward expansion and on the Indian wars. (Americans fought the War of 1812 partly or even primarily to end British support for the Indians in what was then the Northwest.) Indians were driven off their lands; many were killed, and some were even enslaved. In 1820, for instance, 125,000 Indians lived east of the Mississippi River. By 1844, only 30,000 remained, and most of those lived in the northern Lake Superior region.[31] Both Democrat Andrew Jackson and Whig president William Henry Harrison made their reputations primarily as Indian fighters.

The brutal wars of conquest—often motivated by land speculation and the quest for gold—appeared to contradict America's historic mission, but Americans invented an elaborate rationale to justify them, and it later provided a justification for imperialism. Missouri senator Thomas Hart Benton and other proponents of westward expansion described the Western settlers in terms that were borrowed from the Puritan emigration to North America. Although it was often land speculators and mineral prospectors who led the way, Benton described the settlers as the "children of Israel" who "entered the promised land, with the implements of husbandry in one hand and the weapons of war in the other."[32] In 1846, writer, editor, and land speculator William Gilpin declared that "the untransacted destiny of the American people is to subdue the continent."[33] The settlers and land speculators were fulfilling America's historic mission.

To justify the removal of the Indians from the land, Benton and others grafted onto the millennial theory of history the Enlightenment theory of stages of civilization. According to this theory, races—of which the bulk of white Americans were thought to be "Anglo-Saxons"—passed through different stages from savagery to barbarism to civilization. America's mission was to spread civilization in the face of barbarism and savagery. That could mean lifting up and converting the barbarians or savages, as Jefferson proposed to do for the Native Americans. Or it could mean killing or removing them if they resisted the spread of civilization. That was the tack taken by Andrew Jackson.

The settlers and land speculators in the frontier lands in Kentucky, Tennessee, Georgia, and Mississippi were not interested in civilizing the Indians. They wanted their land. To justify Indian removal, Andrew Jackson, who began his career as a land speculator, Benton, and other champions of westward expansion modified the Enlightenment theory of civilization. They construed the theory not as a ladder of development but as a static description of different stages of development. Some races, including Indians, would never progress from savage to civilized. Indians, Jackson's secretary of war Lewis Cass declared, would not exchange their lives for "the stationary and laborious duties of civilized societies."[34] Instead, if allowed to flourish, they could potentially drag civilized peoples down to their level, or even destroy them. In a Senate speech in 1846, Benton outlined the choices that faced the white settlers and their savage foes: "Civilization or extinction has been the fate of all people who have found themselves in the track of advancing whites; civilization, always the preference of the advancing whites, has been pressed as an object, while extinction has followed as a consequence of its resistance."[35]

Benton's ethics, and those of the proponents of Indian removal, were a departure from those of Jefferson and the Enlightenment. In his statement on equality in the Declaration, Jefferson assumed the ethical principle of the Golden Rule—that each human being is equally worthy of respect and not to be considered a means to someone else's end, or a colonial subject to do with as a conqueror pleases. But for Benton, Jackson, and Cass, the Indians were expendable as human beings because they stood in the way of the march of white civilization. The moral principles that governed behavior among whites did not govern behavior between whites and Indians. Theirs was a utilitarianism that justified injustice if it advanced civilization. After Herbert Spencer's application of a pre-Darwinian theory of evolution to sociology and history, these kinds of arguments would become extremely popular among defenders of imperialism, but Americans were already using them to defend their tactics in the Indian wars.

To make their case that Indians were unredeemable, the proponents of Indian removal cast them as less than human, or less than human adults. The Indians, historian Francis Parkman wrote, were "man, wolf, and devil, all in one."[36] To justify their view of Indians as "savages," Parkman and others cited Indian violence against whites, particularly women and children, although, in fact, settlers had provoked much of the violence and had acted with equal brutality against the Indians themselves. As president, Jackson addressed Indians in his communications as "my children." But Jackson's relationship to them was similar to that between God and his subjects. They would not become fathers themselves, but would always remain children.

The first application of this new version of the framework came in justifying the war against Mexico. The Americans who had settled in Texas declared their independence from Mexico in 1836. That commenced twelve years of intermittent war between the settlers and Mexico. In 1845, the new president, James Polk, got involved. Polk was interested not just in acquiring Texas from Mexico but also the lands to the west, which would eventually provide a commercial gateway to the Pacific. Polk precipitated a war with Mexico in 1846. With a force of 7,000, Polk wildly underestimated what would be necessary to expel the Mexicans. On the eve of war, a New York poet, reflecting the Polk administration's optimism, predicted that the Mexicans would be chanting, "The Saxons are coming, our freedom is nigh."[37] But the war took three years and more than 100,000 men: 1,712 Americans were killed, 4,102 wounded, and 11,155 died of disease.[38] In the end, the United States won from Mexico not only Texas, but what would become the states of New Mexico, Arizona, and California.

Many prominent Whigs, including Henry Clay and a young Abraham Lincoln, denounced war and annexation as an unjustified act of conquest. Albert Gallatin, who had been Jefferson's secretary of the treasury, wrote Congress in 1846:

> Your mission was to be a model for all other governments and for all other less-favored nations, to adhere to the most elevated principles of political morality, to apply all your faculties to the gradual improvement of your own institutions and social state, and by your example to exert a moral influence most beneficial to mankind at large. Instead of this, an appeal has been made to your worst passions; to cupidity; to the thirst of unjust aggrandizement by brutal force; to the love of military fame and false glory; and it has even been tried to pervert the noblest feelings of your nature.[39]

But Polk and the Jacksonian Democrats carried the day by invoking the same kind of arguments that had been used to justify the Indian wars. Mississippi senator Robert Walker, who became Polk's secretary of the treasury, urged Americans to rejoice that "our kindred race, predominated over that fair country, instead of the colored mongrel race, and barbarous tyranny, and superstitions of the Mexican."[40] John L. O'Sullivan, the editor of the *United States Magazine and Democratic Review,* who coined the term "manifest destiny" to justify America's westward expansion, wrote, "The Mexican race now sees, in the fate of the aborigines of the north, their own inevitable destiny. They must amalgamate and be lost, in the superior vigor of the Anglo-Saxon race, or they must inevitably perish."[41]

THE AVOIDANCE OF POSSESSIONS

While the United States was eager to expand over the North American continent, Americans had little interest in absorbing Latin America or lands across the waters. President James Monroe declared his Monroe Doctrine in 1823, but the United States depended on the British navy to keep other European powers from staking new claims in Latin America. In 1864, during the Civil War, when the French installed Austrian Archduke Maximilian as emperor of Mexico, the United States protested vigorously, but had to rely on Mexican rebels to force Maximilian to abdicate three years later.

After the Civil War, some American statesmen and politicians did believe that the United States should emulate the British and acquire overseas possessions, but the great majority viewed the temptations of the new imperialism through the prism of Jefferson's concept of an empire for liberty and Washington and Jefferson's warning to avoid Europe's quarrels. During Ulysses Grant's presidency, the Senate turned down an administration plan to annex Santo Domingo. In 1877, Grant's secretary of state, Hamilton Fish, rejected a request from Samoan tribal chiefs to annex the island. In 1883, Chester Arthur's secretary of state, Theodore Frelinghuysen, turned down an offer of two Haitian harbors. "The policy of this government," Frelinghuysen explained, "has tended toward the avoidance of possessions disconnected from the main continent."[42]

American planters in Hawaii favored annexation of the islands, and some congressmen who later opposed the annexation of the Philippines favored it in the case of Hawaii, because they thought it would eventually become a state on a par with others, but a majority in Congress rejected annexation because it reeked of colonialism. Taking Hawaii, President Grover Cleveland declared in 1893, was "a perversion of our nation's mission. The mission of our nation is to build up and make a greater country out of what we have instead of annexing islands."[43]

But the pressures were growing on American officials to modify the framework in the light of changes in the United States and in the world. American administrations worried about getting shut out of the China market. They also had to respond to incursions from European powers and Japan. The Harrison administration stared down Germany over the Pacific island of Samoa, which was on the trade route between the western United States and Australia; Cleveland's administration had to worry about Germany and Japan's ambitions in Hawaii and about British encroachments on Venezuela. Cleveland's secretary of state Richard Olney worried that "the struggle now going on for the acquisition of Africa might be transferred to South America. . . . With the powers of Europe permanently encamped on American soil, the ideal conditions we have thus far enjoyed cannot be expected to continue."[44]

Like a storm that gathers in the far horizon and steadily approaches until it darkens the sky, the struggle for colonies that had embroiled Europe since 1871 was beginning to threaten the insularity of the United States. Americans who had preferred to look inward and to lead by example were being forced to look outward. Most statesmen and politicians still resisted the temptation to acquire colonies for the United States, but beginning in the late 1880s, a loose network of intellectuals and political officials had begun to argue for what would become an American version of imperialism. Their arguments, relying on the precedent of the Indian wars, would attempt to modify, but also remain consistent with, the framework that had governed American foreign policy since the nation's founding. And in 1898, they would win the most important convert of all, the president of the United States.

CHAPTER TWO

America's Imperial Moment

In November 1896, Republican William McKinley defeated Democrat William Jennings Bryan in a climactic campaign that pitted the promise of industrialization against populist demands for free silver. There was barely mention of foreign policy. But as he took office, McKinley could not avoid the growing public concern about the harsh measures that Spain was taking against the rebels in Cuba who were trying to win their independence. There was growing clamor to intervene, but McKinley's position was initially no different from that of the Cleveland administration: sympathy with the rebels but unwillingness to aid them with troops. And the thought of seizing Cuba for the United States was out of the question. Said McKinley in his inaugural address:

> Our diplomacy should seek nothing more and accept nothing less than is due us. We want no wars of conquest; we must avoid the temptation of territorial aggression. War should never be entered upon until every agency of peace has failed; peace is preferable to war in almost every contingency. Arbitration is the true method of settlement of international as well as local or individual differences.

McKinley, like Cleveland, wanted no taint of an American imperialism or of entanglement with Europe's quarrels. Yet within eighteen months, McKinley had completely reversed himself. He had not merely gone to war with Spain, he had seized for America what remained of the Spanish empire in the Caribbean and in the Pacific. And he fought attempts by his critics in Congress to commit the United States to granting these possessions independence.

A host of prominent anti-imperialists—including Mark Twain, William

James, Jane Addams, Samuel Gompers, Charles W. Eliot, and Charles Francis Adams—tried to rally opposition against McKinley's policies, but Congress and the public went along. In December 1898, the Senate didn't even vote on a resolution by Missouri senator George G. Vest requiring that "under the Constitution of the United States no power is given to the Federal Government to acquire territory to be held and governed permanently as colonies."[1] In February 1899, it turned down by one vote a similar resolution by Georgia senator August O. Bacon promising independence to the Filipinos when they established a stable government.

Politicians and intellectuals who had once vigorously opposed the idea of America having overseas colonies suddenly changed their tune. Connecticut senator Orville Platt had originally opposed war with Spain. Afterward, he described the annexation of the Philippines to a journalist as the fulfillment rather than the betrayal of America's millennial mission: "Does not providence, does not the finger of God unmistakably point to the civilization and uplifting of the Orient, to the development of its people, to the spread of liberty, education, social order and Christianity there through agency of American influence."[2]

The change in American foreign policy occurred almost overnight, but the sudden shift was the product of economic and geopolitical pressures that had been building for decades and of a concerted effort by a group of intellectuals to promote a new foreign policy and understanding of America's mission. When the United States went to war and easily defeated Spain in the summer of 1898, it had the effect of suddenly removing the obstacles that had stood in the way of this new foreign policy. Captain Alfred T. Mahan, who would play a key role in this sudden conversion, wrote later of how a "seed of thought germinates when it falls upon mental soil prepared already to receive it."[3] It is important to understand how this process worked in the 1890s, because a very similar kind of overnight conversion would take place in the early twenty-first century.

THE BEST HOPE OF AMERICAN COMMERCE

Spurred by the Civil War, the United States rose in the late nineteenth century from being a primarily agricultural nation that imported more than it exported to become the world's leading industrial nation. By 1900, the U.S.

was producing 23.6 percent of the world's manufacturing goods compared to 18.5 percent for former leader Great Britain.[4] Reflecting America's growing strength, W. T. Stead, editor of the British magazine *Review of Reviews,* published a special issue in 1902 entitled "The Americanization of the World."[5]

In the past, America's focus had been on protecting its industries against imports. Now, as American overseas trade grew, American economists and business leaders came to believe that rising exports were a necessary ingredient of growth. After a financial panic in 1873, a recession in the early 1880s, and a deep depression that began in 1893 and didn't really end until 1901, they began to nourish hopes, sometimes wildly exaggerated, for expanded foreign trade, especially in the new China market.

In 1895, the National Association of Manufacturers was established to promote exports abroad, particularly with China. Whitelaw Reid, the Republican candidate for vice president in 1892, and the influential publisher of the *New York Tribune,* called China "the best hope of American commerce."[6] At the same time, American political and business leaders became increasingly worried about European and Japanese machinations in the region. Japan went to war with China in 1894 and laid claim to Formosa, Korea, and the Liaodung Peninsula. Russia, which had started to build the Trans-Siberian Railway, demanded that Japan transfer the Liaodung Peninsula to its care. Germany, France, and Britain demanded and got new concessions of their own from the doddering Chinese government. Fears that American business would be shut out of the China market by European and Japanese imperialism made business leaders more receptive to an aggressive, outward-looking foreign policy.

In the wake of the depression, several noted economists made the case for a foreign policy aimed at securing markets outside America's hemisphere. Perhaps the most important of these was Charles A. Conant, who would later become an adviser to the McKinley and Roosevelt administrations. In a series of books and articles, Conant argued that a glut of capital had caused the depression of the 1890s and that if the United States wanted to avoid future depressions of this severity, it would have to find investment outlets overseas. One possibility was an American imperialism. Wrote Conant, "The writer is not an advocate of 'imperialism' from sentiment, but does not fear the name if it means only that the United States shall assert their right to free markets in all the old countries which are being opened to the surplus resources of the capitalistic countries and thereby given the benefits of modern civilization."[7]

On the eve of the Spanish-American War, few business leaders shared even Conant's limited support for American imperialism. Most business leaders, fearing instability in the midst of the continued recession, opposed going to war against Spain. But Conant articulated, and gave substance to, the growing conviction of business leaders that one solution to American capitalism's continuing crises lay in the expansion of foreign markets and outlets for investment. The business leaders were not ready in the mid-1890s to back an American imperialism, but after the war with Spain, Conant's kind of argument would help convince many of them that it was the best way to protect and expand American foreign trade and investment.

SEA POWER

American military experts also began to worry about what would happen when America's expanding trade bumped up against the new European imperialism, whether in the Caribbean and South America or in the Pacific, where German and British ships were patrolling and were on the lookout for new colonies. One of the most influential theorists was Alfred Mahan, a graduate of West Point, who joined the faculty of the Naval War College in the fall of 1886 after an undistinguished career at sea. His encounters with British ships off the South American coast had convinced him that America's navy was woefully ill-equipped. But Mahan was not just concerned about the navy defending America's coastline. He reasoned that in the new era of imperialism and global economic competition, the navy had to function for the United States as it had for Britain—as the chief protector of its trading routes.

In an article in the *Atlantic Monthly* in 1890, Mahan argued that America's need for exports in a world of competing imperial powers meant that Americans "must now begin to look outward. The growing production of the country demands it." Mahan warned that "unsettled political conditions, such as exist in Haiti, Central America, and many of the Pacific Islands, especially the Hawaiian group, when combined with real military or commercial importance . . . involve dangerous germs of quarrels, against which it is at least prudent to be prepared."[8]

In his most famous book, *The Influence of Sea Power Upon History, 1660–1783,* Mahan attributed Britain's economic success to its network of colonies that provided ports and fueling stations that allowed its navy to protect its worldwide trade routes. Without colonies, Mahan warned, "the ships of war of the United States, in war, will be like land birds, unable to fly far from their own shores. To provide resting places for them, where they can coal and repair, would be one of the first duties of a government proposing to itself the development of the power of the nation at sea."[9]

THE EVANGELIZATION OF THE WORLD

In the 1880s and early 1890s, there was very little public interest in foreign policy, but some American intellectuals, attuned to what was happening across the Atlantic, were already attempting to come to terms with the new imperialism. Two of the key figures in laying these philosophical cornerstones were John Fiske and Josiah Strong.

In 1885, Fiske, a Harvard graduate who had become the principal exponent of Herbert Spencer's theory of Social Darwinism in the United States, wrote an essay for *Harper's* entitled "Manifest Destiny" that proved to be extremely influential. After it appeared, Fiske undertook a twenty-city lecture tour that included a visit to Washington on the invitation of the president, chief justice, and cabinet.[10] Fiske contended that the "English race," of which the United States would prove to be the principal agent, was destined to dominate the entire world during the twentieth century through colonizing other countries with its rapidly multiplying numbers. Over the next century, Fiske argued, nations will unite under Anglo-Saxon hegemony. "The time will come . . . when it will be possible . . . to speak of the United States as stretching from pole to pole," Fiske wrote.[11]

Fiske believed this imperial struggle would lead toward a millennium of peace and prosperity by civilizing the "barbarous races" and establishing such close economic interconnections among the industrial nations as to make war an "absurdity." "The economic competition will become so keen that European armies will have to be disbanded, the swords will have to be turned into ploughshares, and thus the victory of the industry over the military type of civilization will at last become complete," Fiske wrote.[12]

Josiah Strong, who was born in 1847, graduated, after the Civil War, from

Lyman Beecher's Lane Theological Seminary in Cincinnati, where he came under the influence of Beecher's millennialism. Strong became the Ohio representative of the Congregationalist Home Missionary Society and, later, the general secretary of the Evangelical Alliance, headquartered in New York. His views were highly representative of the Protestant awakening that began in the 1880s.[13] In 1886, Strong published *Our Country,* which became one of the best-selling nonfiction books of the nineteenth century. It sold 175,000 copies in a decade. (By contrast, *New Republic* founder Herbert Croly's influential book *The Promise of American Life,* published in 1910, would sell 7,500 copies in two decades.)

Like Fiske, Strong believed that the English-speaking peoples, or Anglo-Saxons, would be the agents of millennial change. Wrote Strong in *Our Country,* "It is chiefly to the English and American peoples that we must look for the evangelization of the world."[14] And America would be the key citadel of Anglo-Saxon influence. "America is to have the great preponderance of numbers and of wealth, and by the logic of events will follow the scepter of controlling influence."[15]

Strong's views deeply influenced Protestant clergy, missionaries, and parishioners who formed in the late nineteenth century an important political movement. The Student Volunteers for Foreign Missions adopted as its slogan Strong's promise of "the evangelization of the world in this generation." But Fiske and Strong, along with Mahan, also influenced an important group of political intellectuals who, in the 1890s, would attempt to develop a new foreign policy for America.

LAFAYETTE SQUARE

In the 1890s, a group of like-minded friends met frequently at historian Henry Adams's house on Lafayette Square in Washington, D.C. Massachusetts senator Henry Cabot Lodge had been Adams's graduate student at Harvard. Theodore Roosevelt, who had come to Washington in 1889 as civil service commissioner, was Lodge's closest friend. Brooks Adams, Henry's younger brother, was Lodge's brother-in-law. John Hay, Abraham Lincoln's former assistant and biographer and later McKinley's secretary of state, was Adams's neighbor. Cecil Spring-Rice, secretary of the British legation in Washington and later ambassador to the United States, had been the best man at Roosevelt's second wedding.[16]

The friends had extensive connections in the world of politics and letters. They met and corresponded with Whitelaw Reid of the *New York Tribune;* Walter Hines Page, the editor of the *Atlantic Monthly;* and Albert Shaw, the editor of the *American Review of Reviews.* Tom Reed, the Speaker of the House, would drop in on Adams's dinner parties. They were also acquainted with the earlier generation of intellectuals. The Adams brothers and Lodge knew Fiske from Harvard. In 1887, Roosevelt had been invited by Mahan to lecture at the Naval War College on the War of 1812 (about which he had written a history), and Roosevelt had in turn introduced Mahan and his book to Lodge. Roosevelt also knew and admired Josiah Strong and would introduce him to Mahan. Lodge, Roosevelt, and their friends weren't a faction, rather the hub of an influential political network. They didn't always agree with one another, but in the late 1890s, they closed ranks to have enormous influence on the country's foreign policy.

Theodore Roosevelt would eventually eclipse all of them in fame and influence, but in the early 1890s, Lodge was probably the more important political figure. The grandson of Federalist George Cabot, and the son of a wealthy Boston merchant, Lodge had graduated from Harvard in 1871 and had gone on to write a Ph.D. thesis under Adams on Anglo-Saxon law. Much of his scholarly and political writing would refer back to the prevailing arguments about Anglo-Saxon supremacy. In 1888, the young historian was elected to Congress and in 1892 to the Senate, rising quickly to become the leading force and then the chairman of the Foreign Relations Committee. In 1884, he met Roosevelt at the Republican convention, where they championed Republican reform, but where afterward, unlike the Republicans who came to be called "mugwumps," they reluctantly backed the regular Republican nominee.

In the 1880s and even early 1890s, the two men were not primarily concerned with foreign policy. Lodge wrote about George Washington and Alexander Hamilton, and Roosevelt began his romance with the West, culminating in his four-volume work, *The Winning of the West.* The two men shared a concern with Anglo-Saxon racial supremacy, manly character, patriotism, nationalism, and what Lodge (even before Roosevelt) called "national greatness." They worried that Americans, devoted to commerce, were losing their character and their commitment to national greatness, which they often identified with military power and success. In a children's book on America's heroes that they wrote together, they extolled "the stern and manly qualities which are essential to the well-being of a masterful race."[17] Roosevelt commented, "It is better for a nation to produce one [General Ulysses] Grant or one [Admiral David] Farragut than a thousand shrewd manufacturers."[18]

Lodge and Roosevelt's preoccupation with national greatness stemmed partly from the need many northerners felt after the Civil War to reaffirm the national union against sectionalism. It also arose from a concern that immigrants from southern and eastern Europe would prefer a hyphenated identity. But the two men were primarily looking across the Atlantic and making a statement about the need for America to assert its greatness in the face of the rising threat from European imperialism. They wanted, as Roosevelt put it, for America to "uphold [America's] interests in the teeth of the formidable Old World powers."[19]

Both Lodge and Roosevelt were deeply influenced by Brooks Adams's eccentric book *The Law of Civilization and Decay*, which began appearing in installments in 1894. According to Adams, nations oscillated historically between barbarism and civilization. Barbarians were warriors and conquerors who established empires. But once a barbarous people had risen to the heights of empire, "the combative instinct becomes unnecessary to the preservation of life, the economic supersedes the martial mind, being superior in bread-winning."[20] Eventually, highly civilized societies dominated by commerce and usury become soft and open to attack from martial societies and are conquered. And then the cycle begins anew.

Adams's theory jibed perfectly with Lodge and Roosevelt's concern with "stern and manly qualities" and with Roosevelt's assertion that "all the great masterful races have been fighting races."[21] According to Adams, the only way for civilized societies to avoid decay was to incorporate the martial spirit of the barbarian. Ancient Rome had done that, Adams argued, through its far-flung empire. Adams wrote that the "infusion of vitality which Rome ever drew from territories beyond her borders was the cause both of her strength and of her longevity."[22] The implication was clear: if the United States was to enjoy the longevity of Rome, it, too, would have to incorporate barbarians within it by developing an empire and colonies. And Roosevelt, Lodge, Hay, and Adams would hit upon the obvious conclusion: the United States should expand into Asia.[23]

By the mid-1890s, what had been separate strains of thought—Fiske's Social Darwinism, Strong's Millennialism, Mahan's geopolitics, Adams's theory of history, and Roosevelt and Lodge's preoccupation with national greatness—merged into a single powerful case for an American imperialism. In 1894, Lodge, echoing Mahan and Fiske, wrote:

> The modern movement is all toward the concentration of people and terri-tory into great nations and large dominions. The great nations are rapidly absorbing for their future expansion and their present defense all the waste places of the earth.* It is a movement which makes for civilization and the advancement of the race. As one of the great nations of the world, the United States must not fall out of the line of march.[24]

The new imperialism also acquired an advocate within the McKinley administration. When McKinley won the presidency, Lodge lobbied him to make Roosevelt the secretary of the navy—in those days, a position only slightly less important than the secretaries of war and state. McKinley initially demurred because he found Roosevelt "hotheaded and harum scarum," but after Lodge enlisted other close friends of the president, he finally consented to make Roosevelt the assistant secretary of the navy under John Long.[25] In what was then a small government, being assistant secretary afforded Roosevelt considerable access to McKinley. But it would take the Spanish-American War to boost Roosevelt and Lodge and their views into prominence—to turn what until then was a dissident current in

---

*The English settlers of the seventeenth century brought with them the idea, dating from the enclosure movement, that land that wasn't cultivated in the methods of what was then modern agriculture was "waste land." They then applied this idea to the lands on which the Indians lived. Theodore Roosevelt in *The Winning of the West* referred to these lands as "an unpeopled waste, the hunting ground of savages." The imperialist movement then applied the same con-cept to much of Asia and Africa, regarding it, in Lodge's terms, as the "waste places of the earth." See Patricia Seed, *American Pentimento* (Minneapolis, 2001), pp. 30ff. The concept reappears in the early twentieth century when Zionist émigrés describe Palestine, where more than 700,000 Arabs already lived, as a "land without people for a people without land"—the suggestion being that no one really lived there.

American politics into a majority sentiment fully backed by the McKinley administration.

WAR FEVER

Since 1895, Spain had been battling an independence movement in Cuba, as well as in its other possessions. In 1896, the Spanish responded with a vicious campaign of repression—forcing Cubans to leave their homes and be "reconcentrated" into newly constructed villages, where many of them died of starvation and disease. Roosevelt and Lodge began agitating for intervention, but the loudest voices came at this point from the Protestant press and from populist Democrats.

Protestant leaders, who were already hostile to Catholic Spain for barring missionaries from their colonies, denounced Spain's brutal repression of the Cubans and called on McKinley to intervene. If the United States were to go to war, one Methodist journal boasted, "every Methodist preacher will be a recruiting officer."[26] Populists and agrarians in the South and West, many of whom would later oppose any hint of American imperialism, identified with the rebel Cubans, most of whom were poor farmers. William Jennings Bryan would even raise a regiment to fight the Spanish.

McKinley's hand was finally forced by events that winter. He sent the battleship *Maine* to Havana's harbor partly as an attempt to appease his critics who were calling for war. But on February 15, the *Maine* blew up, killing 266 Americans. Investigations a century later would suggest the likelihood of an internal accident, but the Hearst and Pulitzer newspapers, locked in a circulation war, tried to outdo each other in blaming the Spanish for the deed and in calling for war. The Hearst *Journal* declared triumphantly, "The whole country thrills with war fever."[27]

Lodge, Roosevelt, and other expansionists fanned this sentiment. Lodge declared in the Senate, "I have no more doubt than that I am now standing in the Senate of the United States that that ship was blown up by a government mine, fired by, or with the connivance of, Spanish officials."[28] Lodge warned McKinley in March, "If the war in Cuba drags on through the summer with nothing done, we shall go down in the greatest defeat ever known."[29] McKinley, facing rising pressure within his own party as well as from Bryan Democrats, and worried about the effect of continued instability on the ailing economy, finally sent a declaration of war to Congress in April.

ILLUSIONS OF OMNIPOTENCE

The war itself lasted barely three months and was a triumph for an American military that had never fought outside the continent. American forces took not only Spain's Caribbean possessions but also Guam and the Philippines. There, Admiral George Dewey and the six-boat Asian fleet defeated the Spanish on May 1 in Manila Bay in a morning's battle. Four hundred Spaniards were killed in Manila, while one American was slightly wounded. On July 17, Spain's army in Santiago, Cuba, surrendered, and a week later General Nelson A. Miles took Puerto Rico with only three Americans lost. On July 22, Spain sued for peace.

The victory was greeted by euphoria. Dewey and Roosevelt, who had resigned from the administration to organize the First United States Voluntary Cavalry, dubbed the "Rough Riders," became national heroes. John Hay exulted over the "splendid little war." Banker Henry Higginson, who had opposed the war, told Lodge of the enthusiasm at his upper-class New York club. "I believe the whole country would enlist if need be," Higginson wrote.[30] And Lodge himself wrote Hay, "What a wonderful war it has been. What a navy we have got and what good fighters our soldiers are. Nothing but victory and at such small cost."[31] The *Washington Post* captured the broader public reaction in an editorial:

> A new consciousness seems to have come upon us—the consciousness of strength—and with it a new appetite, the yearning to show our strength. . . . The taste of empire is in the mouth of the people even as the taste of blood in the jungle. It means an imperial policy, the Republic, renascent, taking her place with the armed nations.[32]

The victory itself transformed American opinion and laid the groundwork for the McKinley administration's turn toward an imperial foreign policy. It swept away century-old doubts about American power and confirmed what Fiske, Strong, Lodge, Roosevelt, and the other expansionists had argued: that the United States could compete directly with, and even surpass, other major powers. America could transform the world not simply by example, but by its superior military power and industry. It could remake the world in its image.

But the victory also nourished what British political scientist Denis Brogan, in a 1952 essay, called Americans' "illusions of omnipotence."[33] In the early 1790s, the French Revolution coming on the heels of the American Revolution led some Americans to believe they could lead a worldwide revolution. In the 1840s, America's defeat of Mexico prompted similar visions of America's manifest destiny. So, too, the victory over Spain in 1898. This "American frame of mind," historian Richard Hofstadter wrote, "was created by a long history that encouraged our belief that we have an almost magical capacity to have our way in the world, that the national will can be made entirely effective, as against other peoples, at a relatively small price."[34]

Over the next three years, as the Congress and the country debated whether the United States should become an imperial power, Lodge, Roosevelt, Strong, and the other expansionists fed these illusions by adapting America's conquest of the Philippines to a new version of American millennialism. They conjured up images of a new American overseas empire while consistently ignoring or underestimating the obstacles that stood in the way—both from other imperial powers and from the indigenous peoples that they sought to subjugate in the name of higher civilization.

THE SEAT OF EMPIRE

The proponents of imperialism portrayed the war, and the decision to annex the Philippines, not merely as a turning point in American foreign policy but as a turning point in world history. In 1900, Strong published a new book, *Expansion Under New World Conditions,* in which he cited favorably a Columbia University professor's opinion that the war "was the most important historical event since Charles Martel turned back the Moslems" in A.D. 732.[35] America's acquisition of the Philippines, he argued, would accelerate the movement of the world toward a higher civilization. "The movement is upward and greater altitudes will surely be gained."[36] In immediate terms, Strong insisted that the American victory in the Philippines had opened the way to American hegemony in China. "Our possession of the Philippines has enormously increased our national prestige in China and throughout the East," he wrote. When Dewey won, "tens of thousands of the most intelligent Chinese all over the empire exclaimed: 'This means the salvation of China.' "[37] (In fact, barely eighteen months later, the Boxer Rebellion attempted to expel all "foreign devils," including Americans, from China.)

Lodge and Roosevelt claimed that America's victory would transform the nation's character. In a letter to his friend, British diplomat Cecil Spring-Rice, Roosevelt wrote, "I believe in the expansion of great nations. India has done an incalculable amount for the English character. If we do our work well in the Philippines and the West Indies, it will do a great deal for our character."[38] In the Senate debate over annexation, Lodge declared:

> The athlete does not win his race by sitting habitually in an armchair. The pioneer does not open up new regions to his fellow men by staying in warm shelter behind the city walls. . . . If a man has the right qualities in him, responsibility sobers, strengthens and develops him. The same is true of nations. The nation which fearlessly meets its responsibilities rises to the task when the pressure is upon it. I believe that these new possessions and these new questions, this necessity for watching over the welfare of another people, will improve our civil service, raise the tone of public life, and make broader and better all our politics.[39]

Brooks Adams refashioned his "law" to fit the new reality. In an essay "The Spanish War and World Equilibrium," Adams argued that the Spanish-American War was "premonitory"—it set the stage for the emergence of an Anglo-Saxon alliance between the United States and Great Britain that would dominate the world. Wrote Adams, "The prize at stake is now what has always been in such epochs the seat of commercial exchanges—in other words, the seat of empire. . . . For upward of a thousand years the social center of civilization has advanced steadily westward. Should it continue to advance it will presently cross the Atlantic and aggrandize America."[40]

The voices of the Lafayette Square group were amplified by Protestant evangelicals who, having cheered the liberation of Cuba and the Philippines, now suddenly embraced their colonization. The *Standard* called for the United States to practice "the imperialism of righteousness."[41] The *Missionary Journal* asked, in December 1899, "Has it ever occurred to you that

Jesus was the most imperial of imperialists?"[42] *The Interior* assured its readers that in establishing colonies, Americans were not acting like European exploiters, but acting in their special role as redeemers of the world: "By no possibility can we become oppressors. The work of emancipation has providentially been thrust upon us. . . . The question is, shall we back out of, and back down from, our responsibility and duty, and selfishly abandon peoples who are holding up their manacled hands to us and praying us not to desert them?"[43]

The thrill of victory made a convert of Lyman Abbott, a prominent Protestant cleric and editor of *The Outlook*. On the eve of the war, Abbott had initially opposed taking any territory. "What America wants is not territorial expansion, but expansion of civilization," he wrote. Six months later, he was trumpeting the new American imperialism:

> The radical difference between the expansionist and the continentalist— that is, between the one who believes that American ideas and institutions are good for the whole world and the one who thinks they are adapted only to the continent of North America—is not that the former is an imperialist and the latter a democrat, but that the former is a more radical, a more enthusiastic, and a more optimistic democrat than the latter.[44]

Business leaders, who experienced a boom at the war's beginning, also became ardent imperialists. They saw American possession of the Philippines as "stepping-stones" to the lucrative China market. Whitelaw Reid, whose paper was an important voice of Wall Street, wrote, "To extend now the authority of the United States over the great Philippine Archipelago is to fence in the China Sea and secure an almost equally commanding position on the other side of the Pacific—doubling our control of it and of the fabulous trade the Twentieth Century will see it bear. Rightly used, it enables the United States to convert the Pacific Ocean almost into an American lake."[45]

Perhaps the most influential voice for the new imperialism came from a brilliant young legislator and orator, Albert J. Beveridge. Born in 1862 to a modest farm family in Indiana, he became a lawyer in Indianapolis and a well-known Republican orator. In 1898, he ran successfully for the Senate and immediately became a leader of the imperialist faction in the Republican Party. He had first met Roosevelt when he spoke before the Republican Club in New York in February 1898, a week before the *Maine* blew up. Roosevelt said at the time that he "had never heard anyone expound the principles for which Abraham Lincoln lived and died more ably."[46]

Beveridge united all the religious, political, economic, historical, and psychological themes of the new imperialism. Campaigning in 1898, he declared:

> It is a glorious history God has bestowed upon his chosen people. Therefore in this campaign, the question is larger than a party question. . . . Shall the American people continue their march toward the commercial supremacy of the world? Shall free institutions broaden their blessed reign as the children of liberty wax in strength, until the empire of our principles is established over the hearts of all mankind?[47]

After he had toured the American-occupied Philippines in 1899, he invoked Jesus, "If this be imperialism, the final end will be the empire of the Son of Man."[48] In the Senate, he proclaimed America's mission to create a higher civilization against the opposition of savages: "It is destiny that the world shall be rescued from its natural wilderness and from savage men. Civilization is no less an evolution than the changing forms of animal and vegetable life. . . . In this great work the American people must have their part. They are fitted for the work as no people have ever been fitted; and their work lies before them."[49] Beveridge's speeches were widely reprinted and turned into pamphlets, and he himself rose in the ranks of the Republican Party.

PHILIPPINE REBELLION

In response, the opponents of the new American imperialism cited the principles that had underlain American foreign policy since the Revolution. In defending his resolution banning the government from acquiring colonies, Senator George Vest cited Jefferson's statement in the Declaration of Independence that "all governments derive their just powers from the consent of the governed."[50] William Jennings Bryan argued, "Once you admit that some people are capable of self-government and that others are not and that the capable people have a right to seize upon and govern the incapable and you make force—brute force—the only foundation of government and invite the reign of a despot."[51]

Businessman-economist Edward Atkinson warned that if the United States adopted an "imperial policy," it would bring itself "down to the level of the semi-barbarous states and nations of Continental Europe."[52] The program of the American Anti-Imperialist League, which Atkinson helped to found in 1898, stated, "The United States have always protested against the doctrine of international law which permits the subjugation of the weak by the strong. A self-governing state cannot accept sovereignty over an unwilling people."[53] Yale sociologist William Graham Sumner dismissed the promise to civilize the Filipinos: "We talk of civilizing lower races, but we have never done it yet; we have exterminated them."[54]

In countering these arguments, Beveridge, Lodge, and Roosevelt invoked America's experience with the Indians—not to demonstrate that Americans were capable of civilizing a savage people, but to argue for the limited application of the Declaration of Independence. Responding to Bryan, Beveridge said, "It is not true, as the Opposition asserts, that every race without instruction and guidance is naturally self-governing. If so, the Indians were capable of self-government." In the Senate debate on annexing the Philippines, Lodge, referring to America's subjugation of the Indians, argued that if anti-imperialists were right, "then our whole past record of expansion is a crime."[55] In a letter in 1900 accepting the vice presidential nomination, Roosevelt wrote that on Indian reservations "the army officers and civilian agents still exercise authority without asking the 'consent of the governed.' We must proceed in the Philippines with the same wise caution."[56]

McKinley, who had entered the war reluctantly, was the most important convert to the new imperialism. A week after Dewey's victory, he sent Congress a proposal to annex Hawaii, which both houses passed, even though few of the Democrats or Republicans believed then that Hawaii would eventually become a state. McKinley and Hay initially favored making the Philippines a protectorate—guaranteeing its independence from control by other imperial powers without annexing it—but by the fall, McKinley had decided to install an American military governor in the Philippines. With an American military government in place, McKinley, sounding very much like Roosevelt and Lodge, wrote a friend, "One of the best things we ever did was to insist upon taking the Philippines and not a coaling station or island, for if we had done the latter we would have been the laughing stock of the world. And so it has come to pass that in a few short months we have become a world power."[57] In his instructions to American negotiators who were meeting with the Spanish in Paris to decide on the fate of the Philippines, he declared that the war had "brought us new duties and responsibilities which we must meet and discharge as becomes a great nation on whose growth and career from the beginning the Ruler of Nations has plainly written the high command and pledge of civilization."[58]

In Boston in February 1899, he brushed aside the charge that the annexation of the Philippines had abrogated the principle of consent of the governed. "Did we need their consent to perform a great act for humanity? We had it in every aspiration of their minds, in every hope of their hearts," he declared, ignoring the war against American occupation that had already begun.[59] In a meeting later that year with Methodist Church leaders, McKinley explained how his thinking had evolved on the Philippines:

When I next realized that the Philippines had dropped into our laps I confess I did not know what to do with them. . . . I went down on my knees and prayed Almighty God for light and guidance more than one night. And one night late it came to me . . . that there was nothing left for us to do but to take them all, and to educate the Filipinos, and uplift and civilize and Christianize them, and by God's grace do the very best we could by them, as our fellow-men for whom Christ also died.[60]

McKinley was less sure what to do about Cuba. His initial declaration of war did not mention Cuban independence, but a coalition of populist Democrats and Republicans who were close to Cuban business leaders in New York inserted a commitment to Cuban independence into the declaration. After the American victory, however, McKinley acted as if he intended to occupy Cuba indefinitely, if not to annex it. He would not recognize the Cuban independence movement, and barred the Cubans from participating in victory celebrations. He installed a military government to rule the island. In his Annual Message to Congress in December 1898, he set numerous conditions on the removal of American forces, including "complete tranquility." The *London Chronicle* commented that "this is precisely the language that successive British governments have maintained about Egypt, with a result known to the world."

THE PHILIPPINE WAR

The anti-imperialists predicted that the annexation of the Philippines would "lead to the hell of war."[61] Harvard philosopher William James warned that annexation would destroy "the one sacred thing in the world, the spontaneous budding of a national life . . . we can destroy their old ideals, but we can't give them ours."[62] Sumner warned that "the most important thing which we shall inherit from the Spaniards will be the task of suppressing rebellions."[63] Andrew Carnegie predicted that the Americans who had enlisted "to fight the oppressor" would end up "shooting down the oppressed."[64] But the proponents of annexation dismissed them, citing wealthy Filipinos in Manila, according to McKinley biographer Margaret Leech, who had reported to the McKinley administration that there was minimal "nationalist sentiment" and who had predicted that Americans would be welcomed as liberators.[65] The anti-imperialists turned out to be entirely correct.

In the Philippines, a liberation army led by Emilio Aguinaldo had fought the Spanish for two years before the arrival of the Americans in 1898. Dewey had encouraged Aguinaldo, and Aguinaldo had responded by writing a constitution for the new Philippines modeled on the U.S. Constitution and drafting a Declaration of Independence for the island. The American consul in the Philippines and several generals who visited the island were optimistic about Aguinaldo's ability to establish an independent government, but McKinley, advised by upper-class Manilans and by military officials who viewed the Filipinos through the prism of the Indian wars, balked at granting the islands independence. Even before the Senate had ratified the treaty with Spain in February 1899, Indian war veteran General Ewell Otis, whom McKinley had appointed governor of the islands, had set about trying to suppress Aguinaldo and his forces.

The American occupation provoked a nationalist reaction. When Aguinaldo refused to surrender unconditionally, "the hell of war" broke out. It raged for three years and then dragged on for another four. As late as 1913, the United States was still fighting insurgents. Otis and the three governors who succeeded him were all veterans of the Indian wars, and in reports on the war, often referred to the Filipinos as "braves" or "Indians." And just as with the Indians, they claimed they were fighting savages. One of the generals who fought there told a Senate committee that the Filipinos thought independence was "something to eat." When pressed by the senators, he acknowledged that some of the Filipinos may want "absolute independence and somebody to take care of them" but "we are simply fighting children," which is exactly what Andrew Jackson said about his Indian foes.[66]

Just as they had done in the Indian wars, Americans also projected their own worst impulses onto their adversaries in order to justify the war itself. Otis charged, for instance, that the "insurgents" tortured Americans in a "fiendish fashion," burying them alive or castrating them, or even infecting them with leprosy.[67] None of these claims were later verified, but American forces used these spurious claims to justify torturing and killing Filipino prisoners. Americans had criticized the Spanish "reconcentration" policies in Cuba, but American forces used the same tactics against the Filipinos, burning down villages and forcing women and children into unsafe and unsanitary camps. Worst of all, Americans committed massacres. Reported F. A. Blake, from the International Red Cross, after a visit, "American soldiers are determined to kill every Filipino in sight." Blake reported seeing "horribly mutilated Filipino bodies, with stomachs slit open and occasionally decapitated."[68]

Journalists reported that instead of welcoming the American invaders, most Filipinos resented the American occupation. Phelps Whitemarsh, a former missionary who became a journalist, reported, "Everywhere one finds the same old hatred toward Americans, the same hope and belief in ultimate independence. With the exception of a mere handful, too insignificant, every Filipino is an *insurrecto* and wishes to drive the Americans from the islands."[69] Journalist George Kennan, the great-uncle of the diplomat, visited and found "deep-seated and implacable resentment of American rule":

> We have offered them many verbal reassurances of benevolent intentions; but at the same time, we have killed their unresisting wounded; we hold 1,500 to 2,000 in prison . . . and we are resorting directly or indirectly to the Spanish inquisitorial methods . . . that the present generation of Filipinos will forget these things is hardly to be expected.[70]

But there was no cable television in 1901 to beam photographs of American atrocities around the world. Otis cabled to Washington that there was a "warm welcome" for American rule. "Inhabitants rejoiced at deliverance and welcome with enthusiastic demonstrations arrival of our troops."[71] In response, McKinley congratulated Otis on his "victory over the forces of barbarism in the Philippines."[72]

CUBAN RESENTMENT

America's occupation of Cuba followed a different, but no less treacherous, trajectory. McKinley appointed Roosevelt's friend General Leonard Wood as the military governor. Wood, a veteran of the Indian wars, opposed Cuban independence. Wood commented to McKinley, "We are dealing with a race that has been steadily going down for a hundred years and into which we have got to infuse new life."[73] Wood, along with upper-class Cubans and allies in the administration, advocated annexation. So did Mahan and other imperialists. But some Republican imperialists, as well as anti-imperialist Democrats, were leery of annexing multiracial Cuba for fear it would someday claim statehood under the principles of the Northwest Ordinance. Whitelaw Reid described the idea of a Cuban state as "humanitarianism run mad, a degeneration and degradation of the homogeneous, continental Republic of our pride."[74]

By 1900, McKinley's secretary of war, Elihu Root, was also worried that an American attempt to deny Cuban independence could provoke the same kind of revolt that the United States was facing in the Philippines. Root, taking the advice of James Harrison Wilson, a top military commander in Cuba, proposed to turn Cuba into a protectorate rather than a colony. He bought off the liberation forces, and proposed independence only on the condition that Cubans accept an "amendment" drafted by Connecticut senator Orville Platt that gave the United States the right to intervene in the case of Cuban unrest and to maintain naval bases on the island.

Wood and other proponents of annexation saw the wisdom of Root's solution. Wood wrote to Roosevelt in 1900, "There is, of course, little or no independence left Cuba under the Platt amendment."[75] Just to make sure, Wood also limited the Cuban franchise to well-to-do property owners in order to rule out the "revolutionary element." Wood and Root also took steps to ensure that Cuba's economy was entirely dependent on the U.S., selling off Cuban land to American buyers, while refusing to extend credit to Cuban small farmers whose land had been devastated during the war.[76]

Root's strategy for informal control, dubbed by its opponents "neo-imperialism," would become popular later—to be used by the United States in Latin America and the Middle East and by the British in the Middle East. In Cuba, it did prevent the kind of war that occurred in the Philippines, but it sowed distrust and resentment, beginning with the first elections in 1900, which, to Wood's consternation, were won by Cuban nationalists. Historian Jules Benjamin writes, "The U.S. presence created a resentment among many elements of the post-independence generation of Cubans which was to give popular opinion a strong anti-U.S. bias. Since each Cuban president had to make his peace with the United States, none of them was able to avoid for very long the accusation of having betrayed the nation. Hence, Cuban governments never achieved true legitimacy, and the more they depended on the United States for the indispensable tools of stability (such as recognition, loans, and sugar quotas) the less legitimate they became."[77] Continued American domination of the Cuban economy and government fueled popular resentment that continued for five decades, and finally gave rise to Cuban revolutionary Fidel Castro.

The McKinley administration, to its credit, championed America's commitment to a more aggressive, outward-looking foreign policy—one that accurately reflected the country's growing industrial strength and the threat that European and Japanese imperialism posed to its security and prosperity. As McKinley recognized, what happened to the Philippines and the division of China had a direct bearing on American prosperity, if not security. But the policy that McKinley adopted was an American version of European imperialism. McKinley's version involved the United States in a brutal, shameful war in Asia and destabilized the Caribbean for much of the next century. By aquiescing in high tariff walls, it encouraged Europe to create closed trading blocs in defense, which would contribute eventually to the outbreak of World War I. Theodore Roosevelt, who became president in September 1901 when McKinley was assassinated, had helped inspire this new policy and its millennial credo, and it would now fall to him and his successors to undo the damage it had caused.

CHAPTER THREE

Theodore Roosevelt
and the Heel of Achilles

Theodore Roosevelt, whose face adorns Mount Rushmore along with George Washington, Thomas Jefferson, and Abraham Lincoln, is one of America's most popular presidents. There have been four major biographies of Roosevelt published in the last fifteen years—compared to one for Woodrow Wilson, a president of equal, if not greater, accomplishment. In the 1980s, there were two best-selling portraits of Roosevelt's family and early life. But much of Roosevelt's fame and popular acclaim rests on the larger-than-life figure he created as a "rough rider" and as the champion of American imperialism. That's too bad, because Roosevelt was a much more complex figure than many of his admirers would acknowledge.

Roosevelt played a critical, and not particularly praiseworthy, role in the initial launch of American imperialism. A successful author before he had become a national politician, Roosevelt promoted a pseudo-scientific racism and an ideal of the warrior male to justify the Indian wars and later American imperialism. Elements of what Roosevelt thought and wrote during this period would reappear in the darkest corners of twentieth-century political ideology. Along with Lodge and Mahan, Roosevelt prodded McKinley into annexing the Philippines and installing a military government in Cuba. In the war's aftermath, he promoted a halcyon, and unrealistic, view of world imperialism; and he led the Republican campaign to brand the critics of the U.S. imperialism as cowardly and treasonous. As president, Roosevelt backed the suppression of the Filipino rebels and covered up and excused atrocities committed by American troops.

Yet Roosevelt, like other great American presidents, was able to learn from experience. During his two terms in office and his later career with the Progressive Party, Roosevelt tempered his racial views and lost his enthusiasm for the broader imperial project he had helped to initiate. He was still willing to defend British imperialism in Egypt or India, but he was no longer eager to back an imperial role for America in Asia. Roosevelt came to understand that in becoming a world power, the United States could not simply emulate Europe. It would have to develop a foreign policy that was not only consistent with its sense of millennial purpose, but that took account of, and tried to avert, the dangerous conflicts that European imperialism was beginning to spawn. He set American foreign policy on the course it would adopt under Wilson and Franklin Roosevelt.

Theodore Roosevelt's life is a history in miniature of the rise and fall of America's imperial project. And it also shows the importance of the framework—and its underlying millennial content—to the development of American foreign policy. Roosevelt is sometimes portrayed as the representative of pagan militarism or the will to power in contrast with the pious and priestly Wilson, but Roosevelt was no less pious than Wilson; and Protestant millennialism played as much a role in his thinking as it did in Wilson's.[1] The main themes that converge in Roosevelt's call for an American imperialism in the 1890s—an ideal of manliness that could best be fulfilled in righteous war; the triumph through war and social evolution over barbarism or savagery; and the central role of white American racial bloodlines in this struggle—have their basis in his religious training, and his special understanding of the American millennial framework.

MUSCULAR CHRISTIANITY

Roosevelt was born in 1858 in New York. His father, Theodore Sr., was a wealthy New York businessman and Republican political leader who might have run for high office one day had he not died in 1878 when he was only forty-six. Young Theodore's mother, Martha Bulloch Roosevelt, was raised by slaveholders in Georgia on land from which the Cherokees had been driven. Roosevelt admired his mother's family for its courage in the Revolutionary and Civil Wars, but he wrote little in praise of his perpetually ailing mother, who spent her later years at the kind of upper-class watering holes that the young Roosevelt despised. By contrast, Roosevelt idolized his father. He was, he wrote in his *Autobiography*, "the best man I ever knew. He combined strength and courage with gentleness, tenderness and great unselfishness."[2]

Theodore Roosevelt Sr. was a "big powerful man" who was active at once in business, politics, religion, and charity.[3] He was a follower of the "muscular Christianity" that was first propounded by Charles Kingsley and Thomas Hughes in England and championed by Thomas Wentworth Higginson and Phillips Brooks in the United States. Muscular Christians combined a commitment to the Social Gospel (Hughes and Kingsley were Christian Socialists) with a concern for healthiness, manliness, athletic ability, and courage in battle. (Higginson became famous as the author of "Onward Christian Soldiers.")[4] Theodore Roosevelt Sr. imparted this outlook to his sickly son, who was afflicted with asthma. He bought his son exercise equipment and sent him on camping trips, and the young Roosevelt successfully fought through his own illnesses. He became a man of considerable strength and endurance, and an impassioned advocate of what he called "the strenuous life."

Roosevelt's life can be seen as a series of ordeals in which he sought to prove his own manliness.[5] In 1881, after leaving Columbia Law School without a degree, Roosevelt was elected to the New York State Assembly, where he served for four years. When he arrived in Albany, he found his manhood repeatedly questioned by opposition legislators and the Democratic press. With his high voice and upper-class manners, he was lampooned as a "weakling," a "Jane-dandy," "the exquisite Mr. Roosevelt," and even as "Oscar Wilde." Roosevelt threatened to fight his detractors, but he only finally overcame this reputation when he turned himself into a Western cowboy and ranchman.

Roosevelt's love of the West and of the prairie life was undoubtedly sincere, but his was also a deliberate political makeover of a kind that is now familiar in American politics. After returning from the Badlands in 1884, he boasted to the *New York Tribune*: "It would electrify some of my friends who have accused me of presenting the kid-glove element in politics if they could see me galloping over the plains, day in and day out, clad in a buckskin shirt and leather chaparajos, with a big sombrero on my head."[6] In his travel books, Roosevelt wrote of hunting buffalo and facing down murderous Indians. He became known in New York political circles as the "Cowboy of the Dakotas."

Like many children who grew up during the Civil War, Roosevelt saw war itself as the ultimate test of manliness. ("Thank God for the iron in the blood of our fathers, the men who upheld the wisdom of Lincoln, and bore sword or rifle in the armies of Grant!" Roosevelt later exclaimed.)[7] That view of war was probably reinforced inadvertently by Roosevelt's own father. Worried about his wife's failing health, Theodore Roosevelt Sr. had paid $300 to avoid serving in the Civil War. That remained a source of great shame to him and to his son and may have contributed to the importance that Theodore Roosevelt attached to war and to his own military service in the Spanish-American War. "No qualities called out by a purely peaceful life stand on a level with those stern virile virtues which move the men of stout heart and strong hand who uphold the honor of their flag in battle," Roosevelt declared.[8]

A distinction between the virile, robust, muscular, warlike, and fearless man and the effete, soft, weak, and cowardly man would become a prism through which Roosevelt would judge not just individuals but also nations and races. The "martial virtues" were good in themselves, but also essential to a nation or a race's success in the struggle for survival. "For it is only through strife, through hard and dangerous endeavor, that we shall ultimately win the goal of true national greatness," Roosevelt wrote.[9] Roosevelt warned repeatedly of "a certain softness of fiber in civilized nations, which, if it were to prove progressive, might mean the development of a cultured and refined people quite unable to hold its own in those conflicts through which alone any great race can ultimately march to victory."[10]

Roosevelt's father raised his children to put religion at the center of their social understanding. On Sundays, he dropped them at Sunday school on his way to teaching Sunday school himself. When they returned home, they were expected to write a summary of the day's sermon. Later that day, he led them and other families in a prayer meeting. And in the evening and on holidays, he would sometimes take his oldest son with him to visit the orphans at the Newsboy's Lodging House.[11] Charles Loring Brace, who founded the Children's Aid Society, said of Theodore Roosevelt Sr.'s work with him and at the Lodging House, "Undoubtedly the great impelling power of his life was a sense of duty, essentially implanted by his Christian belief."[12]

Theodore followed his father's lead. His letters to him almost invariably include some reference to religious observance. When he went to Harvard, he regularly attended sermons by Phillips Brooks, and he would later follow his father's example by teaching Sunday school. And he was deeply influenced by the political ideology of muscular Christianity. Over the decades, it flowed into the larger stream of the Social Gospel, which stressed the creation of the Kingdom of God at home through progressive and moral reform and abroad through missionary activity and imperialism.* (The proponents of muscular Christianity and the Social Gospel were quick to adapt their own views to the Social Darwinian theory of the struggle for survival.) Josiah Strong and Lyman Abbott, the editor of *Outlook,* could both trace their religious outlook back to Kingsley, Hughes, Higginson, and Brooks. Roosevelt became one of the leading proponents of this view. After he left office in 1909, he would become a regular columnist for Abbott's *Outlook.*

Roosevelt, like his closest friend, Lodge, was also acutely conscious of the Puritan roots of his own political and social convictions. He wrote a biography of Oliver Cromwell, to whom, one English friend commented, "he felt a certain affinity."[13] He described "the epoch of the [English] Puritans" as "the beginning of the great modern epoch of the English-speaking world—infinitely its greatest epoch" and Cromwell's movement "the first of the great movements which, marching along essentially the same lines, have produced the English-speaking world as we at present know it."[14]

One of Roosevelt's favorite fictional heroes was Greatheart, the warrior who guided the Pilgrims to the Celestial City in John Bunyan's *Pilgrim's Progress.* Bunyan himself had fought in Cromwell's army and modeled Greatheart after the Lord Protector. Roosevelt often compared his father to Greatheart. Fusing muscular and millennial Protestantism, he also compared America's mission to that of Greatheart:

> We gird up our loins as a nation with the stern purpose to play our part manfully in winning the ultimate triumph; and therefore we turn scornfully aside from the paths of mere ease and idleness, and with unfaltering steps tread the rough road of endeavor, smiting down the wrong and battling for the right, as Greatheart smote and battled in Bunyan's immortal story.[15]

---

*In England as well as the United States, many of the proponents of muscular Christianity became champions of the new imperialism. In *Imperialism,* J. A. Hobson writes, "From the muscular Christianity of the last generation to the imperial Christianity of the present day it is but a single step."

And of course, he compared his own role to that of Greatheart. In a speech to the Bible Society sometime in the late 1890s, Roosevelt said, "If we read the book aright, we read a book that teaches us to go forth and do the work of the Lord in the world as we find it. . . . That kind of work cannot be done except by a man who is neither a weakling nor a coward, by a man who, in the fullest sense of the word, is a true Christian, like Greatheart, Bunyan's hero."[16] Roosevelt saw himself, like Greatheart, as both warrior *and* priest, and he saw his task, like Greatheart's, as guiding others to the Kingdom of God on Earth.

TEUTONIC BLOODLINES

While he was a student at Harvard, Roosevelt became enthralled with the British historian Thomas Macaulay, who attributed English superiority to its Teutonic heritage. Bored with his classes at Columbia Law School, Roosevelt discovered historian John Burgess, who, like Macaulay, taught that the Teutonic peoples, who had settled in England and migrated to America, had developed "the most modern and the most complete solution of the whole problem of political organization." The Teutonic nations were also destined "to carry the political civilization of the modern world into those parts of the world inhabited by unpolitical and barbaric races."[17] Roosevelt became a leading proponent of this racial theory of history, which had first become popular in the United States in the 1840s. In his first book, *The War of 1812,* he even explained the standoff in the war as the result of two equally accomplished branches of the Teutonic race vying against each other.[18]

But in his analysis of the American West, Roosevelt would add a new wrinkle to Burgess's theory. In the 1880s, Roosevelt produced a succession of books describing and analyzing the American West, including *Hunting Trips of a Ranch Man, Ranch Life and the Hunting Trail,* a *Life of Thomas Hart Benton,* and the first two volumes of his four-volume history *The Winning of the West.* The latter, which became a bestseller, was the crowning glory of Roosevelt's years as an author. The historian Frederick Jackson Turner called it "a wonderful story, most entertainingly told."[19] But *The Winning of the West* was also based upon the kind of racial theories that would later surface in German Nazism. And it defended actions by American soldiers that later generations would have labeled "war crimes." *The Winning of the West* was a paean to the darker side of the American past.

In the life of Benton and *The Winning of the West*, Roosevelt explained how, through waging continual war with the Indian "savages" on the frontier, the English settlers produced a racial strand that was superior even to the Teutonic English. Wrote Roosevelt:

> There sprang up in conquered southern Britain, where its name had been significantly changed to England, that branch of the Germanic stock which was in the end to grasp almost literally worldwide power, and by its overshadowing growth to dwarf into comparative insignificance all its kindred folk. . . . The English race . . . has a perfectly continuous history. . . . [The American movement was the] crowning and greatest achievement of a series of mighty movements.[20]

The key was subjugating rather than adapting to the natives. While the Germans who migrated into Latin Europe adapted to the larger population, the Germans who traveled to England "exterminated or assimilated the Celts of Britain." When they journeyed to America, they outdid themselves by simply exterminating or removing the native Indian population. "In America, there was very little, instead of very much, assimilation," Roosevelt wrote approvingly. Killing off the Indians accomplished three important objectives: it toughened the American spirit; it preserved the Teutonic bloodlines; and it made the world more civilized by eliminating savages.[21]

Like the antebellum proponents of Indian removal, Roosevelt explained away the worst Indian massacres. He wrote of Sand Creek, for instance, where in 1864 several hundred noncombatant Cheyenne women and children were slaughtered by the U.S. cavalry, that it was "on the whole as righteous and beneficial a deed as ever took place on the frontier."[22] Like Jackson or Benton, he justified these kinds of massacres by portraying the Indians themselves as less than human. Indians, he wrote, have an "inhuman love of cruelty for cruelty's sake."[23] Their life was "but a few degrees less meaningless, squalid and ferocious than that of the wild beasts."[24]

But he principally justified the extermination of the Indians on the grounds that it advanced the progressive march of civilization. His was a utilitarianism of the sword. Killing savages made the world more civilized. Wrote Roosevelt, "The most ultimately righteous of all wars is a war with savages, though it is apt to be also the most terrible and inhuman. The rude fierce settler who drives the savage from the land lays all civilized mankind under a debt to him. . . . It is of incalculable importance that America, Australia and Siberia should pass out of the hands of their red, black and yellow aboriginal owners, and become the heritage of the dominant world races."[25]

The work's ideological power came from its fusing together the main theories of history and race that had been swirling around the American psyche for a century: the theory of Anglo-Saxon superiority, Bishop Berkeley's "course of empire," Jacksonian manifest destiny with its reformulation of the Declaration of Independence to justify Indian removal and extermination, and, finally, Puritan millennialism:

> The American frontiersmen warred to make this wilderness the heart of the greatest of all republics; they obeyed the will of no superior; they were not urged onward by any action of the supreme authorities of the land; they were moved only by the stirring ambitions of a masterful people, who saw before them a continent which they claimed as their heritage. The Americans succeeded, the British failed; for the British fought against the stars in their courses, while the Americans battled on behalf of the destiny of the race.[26]

Roosevelt's thesis in *The Winning of the West* was later compared to Turner's *The Frontier in American History*, but the two men were making very different points about the role of the frontier. Turner argued that the possibility of westward expansion had made possible America's yeoman democracy, based on the diffusion of property ownership. His hero was the farmer, not the hunter.[27] Turner worried that with the closing of the frontier, America would evolve into the kind of urban-class society that Jefferson had warned against. Roosevelt wasn't concerned with the economics and social organization of the frontier, but with the virile, martial character that the settlers and hunters acquired in fighting the Indians for possession of the land. His frontier was a whetstone on which the Teutonic character honed its already-formed blade. The frontier didn't make Americans fundamentally different from their ancestors, but it made them stronger and therefore better.

Roosevelt was worried that the frontier's closing would deprive Americans of a needed opportunity to build character through war. For Roosevelt, writes Richard Slotkin in *Gunfighter Nation,* "the closing of the frontier doesn't mean the end of economic opportunity but the loss of those elements in national life that made Americans virile and vigorous, stimulated their taste and aptitude for competition, and gave them a strong and unifying sense of racial solidarity."[28] Along with Brooks Adams, Roosevelt worried that with the absence of battle, Americans would grow soft and overcivilized and unable to defend themselves against a new "masterful race" that still carried within the fighting qualities of the barbarian. And like Adams, he came to see the solution in America's expansion overseas. Through imperialism, Americans would once again have to fight savages for the sake of a higher civilization.

THE IMPERIAL INSTINCT

Ever since Roosevelt published his *Autobiography,* in which he insinuated that he had manipulated McKinley into ousting Spain from the Philippines, historians have debated how much of a role Roosevelt actually played in the war plans.[29] Some historians, including Margaret Leech and H. Wayne Morgan, have argued that McKinley acted largely on his own initiative.[30] But what is clear is that by the mid-1890s, Roosevelt, working frequently with Lodge, had begun to take a large role in arguing for a more active, and, finally, an imperialist, foreign policy.

During the Cleveland administration, while he was still serving as New York's police commissioner, Roosevelt and Lodge mounted a campaign to pressure the administration to annex Hawaii and to go to war, if necessary, with Britain over Venezuela's boundary. In August 1895, he wrote Lodge, "Personally I rather hope the fight will come soon. The clamor of the peace faction has convinced me that the country needs a war. Let the fight come if it must. I don't care whether our seacoast cites are bombarded or not; we would take Canada."[31]

In March 1897, Roosevelt joined the McKinley administration as assistant secretary of the navy. He continued to hope for, he wrote a friend, "a general national buccaneering expedition to drive the Spaniards out of Cuba, the English out of Canada."[32] "I should welcome almost any war, for I think this country needs one," he wrote another friend in 1897.[33] In September, while his superior, Secretary of the Navy John Long, was on vacation, he lobbied McKinley at dinner to prepare for war with Spain. He also continued to support the annexation of Hawaii—"in the interests of the white race," he wrote James Bryce that same month.[34] In a letter to his brother-in-law William Clowes in January 1898, he lamented "the queer lack of imperial instinct that our people show."*[35] When the *Maine* blew up the next winter, he advocated going to war in cabinet meetings, and through pressure from the Senate got Admiral George Dewey appointed the head of the Pacific squadron. On February 25, with Long once more absent, Roosevelt sent orders to Dewey to be ready to attack the Spanish in Manila.

But while Roosevelt was sanguine about going to war, he was initially cool to the idea of annexing any territory except for Hawaii. While McKinley opposed recognizing the Cuban insurgents, Roosevelt wrote a friend in April 1898 that he thought it was a "mistake . . . to follow the policy of intervening without recognizing independence."[36] Roosevelt also initially favored merely retaining a coaling station in Luzon without annexing the Philippines. But soon after his return in the summer of 1898, he joined Lodge in championing the annexation of the Philippines and in defending the McKinley administration's ambiguous position in the Caribbean, including the draconian rule by his friend Leonard Wood, whom McKinley had appointed to govern Cuba.

Roosevelt, like others in Washington, was clearly swept up in the enthusiasm for American power created by the "splendid little war." He caught the millennial spirit of the times and became entranced with the image of Amer-

---

*In his letter accepting the Republican nomination as vice president in 1900, Roosevelt would later insist that he was not in favor of "imperialism." "The simple truth is that there is nothing even remotely resembling 'imperialism' or 'militarism' involved in the present development of that policy of expansion which has been part of the history of America from the day when she became a nation. These words mean absolutely nothing as applied to our present policy in the Philippines; for this policy is only imperialistic in the sense that Jefferson's policy in Louisiana was imperialistic. . . ." (TR to Wolcott, Sept. 15, 1900). Roosevelt was one of the most skilled politicians in American history, and by 1900 he was well aware that "imperialism" had become a loaded term in American politics. Details aside, it conjured up practices that were common to the Old World, not the New. So Roosevelt adopted the tactic of describing himself as an "expansionist" rather than an "imperialist" and of arguing tendentiously that there was no difference between the Louisiana Purchase and the annexation of the Philippines. Beveridge took the opposite tack, arguing that America had always been "imperialist" and that Jefferson had been an imperialist. But in Roosevelt's private correspondence, and in his actual assessment of European policies, it is clear that he had formed a favorable opinion of the actual practice of imperialism.

ica as the star of empire. But Roosevelt was also aroused by the violent opposition to American rule in the Philippines and by popular unrest in Cuba. Instead of viewing these insurgents through the prism of America's own revolution against colonialism, he viewed them through the prism of the Indian wars. They were savages, not revolutionaries, and they had to be defeated on behalf of civilization.

In a series of speeches, Roosevelt defended the new American imperialism. He argued that the expansion of America overseas was simply an extension of American expansion over the continent. "The parallel between what Jefferson did with Louisiana and what is now being done in the Philippines is exact," he declared.[37] The only difference was America's opponent was not the Creeks or the Seminoles but Aguinaldo's rebels. Neither was capable of self-government. In a speech given on Lincoln's Birthday in New York just after the Filipinos rioted to protest the American occupation, Roosevelt said:

> It is, I am sure, the desire of every American that the people of each island, as rapidly as they show themselves fit for self-government, shall be endowed with a constantly larger measure of self-government. But it would be criminal folly to sacrifice the real welfare of the islands, and to fail to do our own manifest duty, under the pleas of carrying out some doctrinaire idea which, if it had been lived up to, would have made the entire North American continent, as now found, the happy hunting ground of savages. It is the idlest of chatter to speak of savages as being fit for self-government.[38]

Roosevelt dismissed arguments by anti-imperialists that the annexation of the Philippines violated the Declaration's commitment to rule by the "consent of the governed." The principles that applied to white emigrants from Europe did not apply to Native Americans, nor to Filipinos. Jefferson's "doctrine of the 'consent of the governed,'" Roosevelt wrote, "was not held by him or by any other sane man to apply to the Indian tribes in the Louisiana territory which he thus acquired."[39]

The American counsel in Manila, as well as Dewey, had praised Aguinaldo's leadership, but Roosevelt repeatedly dismissed him as a savage, comparing him to the Indians America had fought and killed. Roosevelt said, "The reason which justifies our having made war against Sitting Bull also justifies our having checked the outbreaks of Aguinaldo and his followers."[40] Roosevelt wrote in accepting the nomination as vice president in 1900, "To grant self-government to Luzon under Aguinaldo would be like granting self-government to an Apache reservation under some local chief."[41] Roosevelt insisted that the United States must "stamp out" the insurrection in the Philippines in the same way it had stamped out the Indian uprisings.[42]

Roosevelt tied together all the themes of the prior decades, including strength and manliness and national greatness. Speaking in Chicago in April 1899, he warned Americans that "the nation that has trained itself to a career of unwarlike and isolated ease is bound, in the end, to go down before other nations which have not lost the manly and adventurous qualities. If we are to be a really great people, we must strive in good faith to play a great part in the world. . . . We cannot avoid the responsibilities that confront us in Hawaii, Cuba, Puerto Rico, and the Philippines."[43]

He invoked "international honor." "If we drove out a medieval tyranny only to make room for savage anarchy, we had better not have begun the task at all," Roosevelt said. "Some stronger manlier power would have to step in and do the work and we would have shown ourselves weaklings, unable to carry to successful completion the labors that great and high-spirited nations are eager to undertake." The war was part of America's millennial mission. "Is America a weakling, to shrink from the world work of the great world-powers? No. The young giant of the West stands on a continent and clasps the crest of an ocean in either hand. Our nation, glorious in youth and strength, looks into the future with eager eyes and rejoices as a strong man to run a race."[44]

THE CAUSE OF PEACE

In the essay "Expansion and Peace" that he published in December 1899, Roosevelt framed his defense of American and European imperialism in the context of a larger theory of civilization that recalled John Fiske's essay on "Manifest Destiny."[45] According to Roosevelt, history was moving on two different tracks. War between civilized countries was becoming "rarer and rarer," while wars between civilized and barbarous nations were continuing, or even increasing as the civilized powers sought to expand their reach:

On the border between civilization and barbarism war is generally normal because it must be under the conditions of barbarism. Whether the barbarian be the Red Indian of the frontier of the United States, the Afghan on the border of British India, or the Turkoman who confronts the Siberian Cossack, the result is the same. In the long run civilized man finds he can keep the peace only by subduing his barbarian neighbor; for the barbarian will yield only to force, save in instances so exceptional that they may be disregarded. [46]

These wars between civilized and barbarous powers contributed to international progress because, by extending civilization (whether by eliminating or civilizing barbarians), the civilized powers increased the scope of world peace. "Every expansion makes for peace," Roosevelt wrote. "This has been the case in every instance of expansion in the present century, whether the expanding power were France or England, Russia or America." By this logic, imperialism was all to the good. And America's conquest of the Philippines, and the brutal war it was fighting against the insurgents, was in the ultimate interests of world peace:

This county will keep the islands and will establish therein a stable and orderly government, so that one more fair spot of the world's surface shall have been snatched from the forces of darkness. Fundamentally, the cause of expansion is the cause of peace. With civilized powers there is but little danger of our getting into war. . . . In North America, as elsewhere throughout the entire world, the expansion of a civilized nation has invariably meant the growth of the area in which peace is normal throughout the world. [47]

There were, of course, skeptics like William Graham Sumner, Edward Atkinson, and Paul Reinsch in the United States, who warned that imperialism could further war and strife in the world. In *World Politics at the End of the Nineteenth Century*, which was published in 1900, University of Wisconsin political scientist Reinsch warned that the "idea of world empire" could "ultimately lead to a world conflict." [48] Similarly, British economist J. A. Hobson, writing in 1902, warned that imperialism brought in its wake "militarism, oligarchy, bureaucracy, protection" and was "the supreme danger of modern national states." [49]

And by the beginning of the twentieth century, there were abundant signs that they were right. Germany's victory in the Franco-Prussian War—and its annexation of Alsace-Lorraine—had sown the seeds of war on the continent. In 1894, France allied itself with Russia against Germany and Austria. Under Kaiser Wilhelm II, Germany had decided to challenge Britain for world supremacy, initiating a naval arms race in 1898 and contesting Britain's hold over southern Africa. In China, the great powers had also begun to quarrel over the spoils of the Sino-Japanese War, leading to the Russo-Japanese War in 1904. But young Roosevelt was oblivious to the danger of a major war among the great powers that would draw in the United States. Given "the great progressive, colonizing nations" of England and Germany, he wrote in December 1899, "there is but little danger of our getting into war."

In the wake of two world wars, Roosevelt's essay appears to be the height of folly. And it certainly is. But it was not simply a case of making erroneous predictions based on false or incomplete information, or even of the kind of wishful thinking that led Roosevelt in April 1900 to declare that "the insurrection in the Philippine Islands has been overcome."[50] In the late 1890s, Roosevelt, like many Americans, was held captive by the millennial fires that America's "splendid little war" had kindled. And this burning vision of the future clouded his understanding of the present.

To Roosevelt's credit, however, he came to realize that he was harboring illusions. "We have continually to accommodate ourselves to conditions as they actually are and not as we would wish them to be," Roosevelt wrote in 1907.[51] But this realization came after having served as president for two terms, and after witnessing the loss of American hopes in the Pacific and the deterioration of the peace in Europe.

POINTLESS WAR

In 1899, in the wake of Roosevelt's speech on "The Strenuous Life," William James wrote of his former Harvard student in a Boston newspaper:

> Although in middle life, as the years age, and in a situation of responsibility concrete enough . . . [Roosevelt] is still mentally in the Sturm und Drang period of early adolescence, treats human affairs, when he makes speeches

about them, from the sole point of view of the organic excitement and difficulty they may bring, gushes over war as the ideal condition of human society, for the manly strenuousness which it involves, and treats peace as a condition of blubberlike and swollen ignobility, fit only for huckstering weaklings, dwelling in the gray twilight and heedless of the higher life.[52]

There was considerable truth to James's characterization. Roosevelt was a perpetual adolescent, and his enthusiasm for war resembled that of a child who had grown up in wartime playing toy soldiers. In Roosevelt's mind, it seemed, the English cannonballs that fell on "seacoast cities" would demolish a few wharf-side facilities but not affect the populace. Mark Twain called Roosevelt "clearly insane . . . and insanest upon war and its supreme glories."[53] But as Twain would lament, Roosevelt defied his own critics. He was a dour moralist but also a man of great joy and wit. He was capable of great heartlessness but also of compassion. (As he said of his father, he could combine strength with gentleness.) He was sometimes foolish in his enthusiasms but could also be extraordinarily sober in his judgments. And as he showed as president, he was capable of tempering his millennial idealism with a realistic grasp of the obstacles that America faced in the new century.

Even before Roosevelt's first term had ended, he had abandoned his enthusiasm for the glory of war and his theory that civilized countries would not go to war against each other but only against barbarous countries. In February 1904, war broke out between Russia and Japan over who would control Korea and Manchuria. Thousands died—in the last battle of the war alone, 75,000 Japanese and 90,000 Russian troops perished. In 1905, Roosevelt wrote British editor John St. Loe Strachey, "I have grown to feel an increasing horror for pointless, and of course still more unjust war." A continuation of the Russo-Japanese War, he wrote, "was of course utterly pointless and meant hideous slaughter of gallant men to no purpose aside from the waste and exhaustion of the peoples involved."[54]

Roosevelt, who wanted an "open door" in China for American products, was drawn into the conflict. Russia, backed by Germany, had closed Manchuria to goods from other countries, including the United States, while Japan, which was backed by Britain, had promised an open door. Roosevelt tilted to Japan, but he was worried, he wrote Lodge in 1905, that "Japan will drive Russia out of East Asia.[55] He thought it was "best" that Russia "be left face to face with Japan so that each may have a moderative action on the other."[56] Instead of promoting the open door, he had now become a champion of the balance of power, and cast the United States in the role of mediator among the imperial powers. He got Japan and Russia to sign a peace treaty at Portsmouth, New Hampshire, ending the war, but as part of the settlement, he acquiesced in Japan's domination of Korea and part of Manchuria. In 1907, Roosevelt would formally acknowledge Japan's role in Manchuria in the Root-Takahara Treaty.

After the Russo-Japanese War, Roosevelt also had to abandon his dream of the United States becoming "the dominant power on the Pacific Ocean," determining the fate of China through its navy headquartered in the Philippines' Subic Bay. In 1907, an administration study of America's naval power in the Pacific revealed that in case of war, the U.S. would not have the ships to defend its possessions in the Philippines against a Japanese assault. Roosevelt pulled America's defense perimeter in the Pacific back to Pearl Harbor.[57] He recognized, as historian Walter LaFeber writes, that "the nation's open door interests in China and Manchuria had to be protected by cooperative diplomatic and military efforts with allies, not by the world's second greatest fleet, which lacked the power to act unilaterally in Asia."[58] America's hopes of actively transforming the region, if not the world, would have to be postponed.*

THE PROBLEM OF CONTROL

Roosevelt had declared the war against Aguinaldo over in April 1900, but he inherited from McKinley that continuing conflict. Aguinaldo's capture led to a decline in major clashes and to a guerrilla war. On July 4, 1902, Roosevelt again proclaimed the war over, but it shifted from Luzon to the Moros in the Sulu Archipelago and to a war of Christian Americans against

---

*One of Roosevelt's most heralded initiatives was sending the "great white fleet" of sixteen battleships around the world in 1907. It was meant as a show of force to impress the Japanese. But to his dismay, Roosevelt discovered that the ships were almost forced to turn back because of the inadequacy of American ports in the Pacific. Writes historian Edward S. Miller in *War Plan Orange* (Annapolis, 1991), "American ports of the Pacific were found to lack the capacity to service the fleet under wartime conditions and procurement of fuel had bedeviled the cruise. Forty-nine colliers, mostly British, had had to be chartered. They often turned up late with inferior coal." See also Walter LaFeber, *The Clash* (New York, 1997), p. 91.

Filipino Muslims. Roosevelt instructed General Adna Chaffee, another veteran of the Indian wars, to "adopt no mistakable terms . . . the most stern measures to pacify" the rebels.[59] Chaffee responded by unleashing a campaign of death and destruction that recalled the Spanish. General J. Franklin Bell decreed that "the innocent must generally suffer with the guilty." General Jacob Smith, a veteran of Wounded Knee, sent out orders, "I want no prisoners. I wish you to kill and burn, the more you kill and burn the better it will please me."[60] Homes and whole villages were burned, innocent Filipinos were herded into concentration camps, where many died, prisoners were shot.

As reports of the massacre filtered into the press—one general warned that the U.S. actions were producing "bitter hatred"—Roosevelt defended his generals.[61] He congratulated Bell, and when, under Senate pressure, Smith was court-martialed, he recommended a light sentence.* But the continuing conflict, the opposition to occupation it sparked at home, and the rise of Japan took its toll on Roosevelt's confidence in the annexation.

In August 1907, he confessed to Secretary of War William Howard Taft that he was "uneasy" about continued American presence in the islands:

> I wish our people were prepared permanently, in a duty-loving spirit, and looking forward to a couple of generations of continuous manifestation of this spirit, to assume the control of the Philippines Islands for the good of the Filipinos. But as a matter of fact, I gravely question whether this is the case. . . . In the excitement of the Spanish war people wanted to take the islands. They had an idea they would be a valuable possession. Now they think that they are of no value, and I am bound to say that in the physical sense I don't see where they are of any value or use or where they are likely to be of any value.
>
> This leads me up to saying that I think we shall have to be prepared for giving the islands independence of a more or less complete type much sooner than I think advisable from their own standpoint, or than I would

---

*The Protestant missionary press was astonishingly supportive of the brutal war. When reports of torturing prisoners appeared, they discounted them, even arguing that it was not really torture "since the victim has it in his own power to stop the process, or prevent it" by telling his interrogators what they demanded. Lyman Abbott refused to print reports of the atrocities in *Outlook*. See Richard Welsh, *Response to Imperialism* (Chapel Hill, 1979), p. 100, and Miller, *War Plan Orange*, p. 248.

think advisable if this country were prepared to look ahead fifty years and to build the navy and erect the fortifications which in my judgment it should. The Philippines form our heel of Achilles. They are all that makes the present situation with Japan dangerous. . . . I do not believe our people will permanently accept the Philippines simply [as] an unremunerative and indeed expensive duty. I think that to have some pretty clear avowal of our intention not to permanently keep them and to give them independence would remove a temptation from Japan's way and would render our task at home easier.[62]

Roosevelt wasn't prepared to say that the conquest itself had been mistaken, or that his theory of civilizing barbarians had been simpleminded. He wasn't, above all, willing to acknowledge James's or Hobson's point that imperialism inevitably stirred a nationalist reaction that would defeat any worthy or unworthy purpose to which conquest was put. He couldn't see any resemblance between the Filipinos' rebellion and that of the American colonists in 1776. He blamed the failure of the Philippine conquest not on its instigators, including himself and Lodge, but on a public and an older mugwump political establishment that was unwilling to accept the burdens of empire. (Richard Nixon and Henry Kissinger would similarly blame opposition from the country's "Eastern establishment" for their failure to win in South Vietnam.) "It has been everything for the islands and everything for our own national character that we should have taken them and have administered them with the really lofty and disinterested efficiency that has been shown," Roosevelt wrote Taft. "But it is impossible for instance to awaken any public interest in favor of giving them tariff advantages; it is very difficult to waken any public interest in providing any adequate defense of the islands."

In a letter to Whitelaw Reid the next year, Roosevelt wrote in a broader vein about the imperialist project:

The problem of the control of thickly peopled tropical regions by self-governing northern democracies is very intricate. A legislative body most of the members of which are elected by constituencies that in the nature of things can know nothing whatever of the totally different conditions of India, or the Philippines, or Egypt, or Cuba, does not offer the best material for making a success of such government.[63]

Roosevelt never fully abandoned the imperialist cause. He continued to believe that imperialism was an unmitigated blessing for the people it colonized. In 1908, he was extolling the "enormous advantages conferred by the English occupation of the Sudan, if not on the English themselves, certainly on the natives and on humanity at large."[64] More important, he never accepted what was clear to Sumner and James—that imperialism tended to provoke a legitimate nationalist backlash. Instead, he continued to view the insurgents in the Philippines or the radical nationalists in Egypt as savages.* Yet by the end of his second term, Roosevelt had begun to acknowledge that there was a "problem." He would come to similar conclusions in the Caribbean.

THE ROOSEVELT COROLLARY

Roosevelt had to worry about European attempts to collect debts from Latin American countries. More broadly, he was concerned about protecting the Panama Canal, the construction of which began in his administration, from foreign interference. When Venezuelan dictator Cipriano Castro refused to pay Germany moneys owed from a large loan the government had made, Germany, with the support of Great Britain, France, and Italy, threatened action. In late 1902, Germany blockaded Venezuela and even landed troops. Roosevelt invoked the Monroe Doctrine, warning Germany not to try to take any Venezuelan territory, and he privately threatened military action if Germany didn't accept international arbitration of its claims. Germany finally acceded.[65]

In the Dominican Republic, Roosevelt faced a similar challenge. German and French creditors were demanding payment of their debts. At the same time, the Dominican government was facing a popular challenge from peasants unhappy with its subordination to American sugar interests. The U.S. minister to the Dominican Republic advised Roosevelt to annex the

---

*In a speech at London's Guildhall, after radical nationalists had assassinated the British-appointed prime minister, Roosevelt criticized the British for not showing sufficient firmness. "Either it is or it is not your duty to establish and keep order. If you feel that you have not the right to be in Egypt, if you do not wish to establish and to keep order there, why then by all means get out," he said. See Frederick W. Marks III, *Velvet on Iron* (Lincoln, 1981), p. 176.

country, but Roosevelt didn't want another imperialist venture. He told reporter Joseph Bishop in February 1904, "I want to do nothing but what a policeman has to do in Santo Domingo."[66] Instead, under pressure from American as well as European financial interests, he decided to seize control of the government's customs-house and to disperse the income to its creditors, while guaranteeing the country's territorial integrity.

To justify the Dominican intervention, Roosevelt invoked the "Roosevelt Corollary" to the Monroe Doctrine. It stipulated that the United States would intervene in Latin American countries to ensure and "maintain order within their boundaries" and to ensure that they "behave with a just regard toward obligations with outsiders."[67] On the surface, the measure seemed designed to enhance America's imperial presence in the region—and it did stir resentments for three decades until Franklin Roosevelt replaced it with his "good neighbor" policy—but it was actually intended to keep European powers, and Germany in particular, from using debt collection as a pretext for seizing control of a Latin American country. It was defensive rather than offensive in nature.

In Cuba, Roosevelt had backed Root's alternative of turning the country into an American protectorate rather than colony, but by Roosevelt's second term, this strategy was also beginning to backfire. The pro-American Cuban government faced a determined rebel opposition that also claimed to be pro-American, but that alarmed Americans who had a financial stake in the island. In 1906, Roosevelt sent in the troops on what he called a "peace mission." Venting his adolescent side, Roosevelt told diplomat Henry White, "Just at the moment I am so angry with that infernal little Cuban republic that I would like to wipe its people off the face of the earth."[68] But Roosevelt was circumspect in this intervention. He wrote to one correspondent, "I loathe the thought of assuming any control over the island such as we have over Puerto Rico and the Philippines."[69] Taft served as Cuba's acting governor for three years, but in 1909, departed to leave Cuba under the control of another semi-autonomous administration. By then, historian Lewis Gould concludes, "Roosevelt wanted no more expansive imperialism for the United States; he wanted only the orderly management and eventual liquidation of the tutelary duties the nation had assumed a decade earlier."[70] Roosevelt, who had championed an American imperialism at the end of the nineteenth century, would quietly abandon the cause in fact if not in name.

THE LEAGUE OF PEACE

The greatest challenge to Roosevelt's millennial illusions came from Europe. In the 1890s, Roosevelt had still dreamed of an imperial condominium among the major powers that would look after world affairs and keep the peace. But soon after he became president, the British and Germans began airing their distrust of each other to Roosevelt, and began seeking America's support for their respective side of the argument. According to Lodge, Roosevelt told him that in 1904 "England and Germany were on the brink of war—both appealed to him—England wanted our fleet sent over first to show friendship and prevent war—German emperor equally nervous and jumpy as the president said."[71] The next year, war between Germany and France seemed "imminent" to Roosevelt, when France, with Britain's support and over Germany's opposition, seized control of Morocco. [72]

While many Americans still believed that the U.S. should steer clear of any European conflicts, Roosevelt had come to recognize that wars in Europe or Asia could threaten the United States. In his inaugural address in 1905, he had said, "We have become a great nation forced by the fact of its greatness into relations with the other nations of the earth, and we must behave as beseems a people with such responsibilities."[73] At the request of the Germans, he convened a conference at Algeciras, Spain, to settle the Moroccan conflict. Under Roosevelt's supervision, the Germans and French reached an agreement, but any illusion Roosevelt might have had about peaceful cooperation among the imperialist powers was being undermined. *

In 1908, Roosevelt came to believe that Germany, where he studied as a young man, and whose civilization he had extolled, might be on the verge

---

*Alfred T. Mahan had earlier believed that the economic interdependence encouraged by imperialism would discourage war. "War has ceased to be the natural, or even normal condition of nations, and military considerations are simply accessory and subordinate to the other greater interests, economical and commercial, which they assure and so subserve," Mahan wrote in 1902. But as early as 1906, Mahan had changed his tune. In a letter to Roosevelt on July 20, Mahan wrote, "When to Germany are added the unsolved questions of the Pacific, it may be said truly that the political future is without form and void. Darkness is upon the face of the deep. We will have to walk very warily in matters affecting the future ability to employ national force." By 1912, he was warning of "the impulse to war of European states." See Jon Tetsuro Sumida, *Inventing Grand Strategy and Teaching Command* (Washington, D.C., 1997), pp. 92–93.

of starting a world war. That year, the German emperor gave an incendiary interview to the *New York Times* that Roosevelt persuaded the newspaper not to publish. In the interview, Wilhelm violently attacked Britain and the United States. Afterward, Roosevelt wrote his British friend Arthur Lee, "I have been persistently telling so many Englishmen that I thought their fears of Germany slightly absurd and did not believe that there was need of arming against Germany, I feel that perhaps it is incumbent upon me now to say that I am by no means as confident as I was in this position."[74]

Roosevelt's newfound fear of war in Europe and Asia led him to take positions that would be familiar to later American administrations but were at odds with his own stance at the end of the nineteenth century. In that burst of millennial enthusiasm, Roosevelt had imagined America playing a transformative role in creating a new-world imperial order; however, by the end of his presidency, he had reverted to more classic European balance-of-power conceptions. He now saw the United States as having to assume England's role during the nineteenth century of being the ultimate balancer and, if possible, mediator. In 1910, he told a German diplomat:

> As long as England succeeds in keeping "the balance of power" in Europe not only in principle but in reality, well and good; should she however for some reason or other fail in doing so, the United States would be obliged to step in at least temporarily, in order to restore the balance of power in Europe, never mind against which country or group of countries our effort may have to be directed. . . . In fact, we ourselves are becoming, owing to our strength and geographical situation, more and more the balance of power of the whole world.[75]

The proponents of America as the "new Israel" and of "manifest destiny" had imagined America as the seat of peaceful and prosperous millennium—as the "elected" leader, if you like, of a Lockean contractual world or of a New England town writ large. But Roosevelt now envisaged America like Hobbes's monarch, attempting to bring order to rival imperial powers who at any moment could go to war with each other. America would put in abeyance its transformative role to concentrate on maintaining the status quo, as Britain had done or tried to do through most of the nineteenth century.

Roosevelt also took another, complementary tack in attempting to prevent war among the civilized nations. In 1904, he called for a second conference at the Hague to reach international agreements to devise a "surer method than now exists of securing justice as between nations."[76] The conference finally convened in 1907 after the Russo-Japanese War. Roosevelt advocated naval arms limitations and called for strengthening the Hague Court of Arbitration, which had been set up at the first Hague conference in 1899. Roosevelt, who had insisted on the participation of Latin American nations, also introduced a resolution that no country should be allowed to use force to compel another country to pay its debts. Roosevelt's resolutions failed, but he didn't abandon the cause of international organization.

Roosevelt received the Nobel Peace Prize for his role in settling the Russo-Japanese War, and in 1910, he gave his lecture in Oslo. He reiterated his support for arbitration treaties and for the Hague tribunal, but he also introduced a new idea. "It would be a masterstroke if those great powers honestly bent on peace would form a League of Peace, not only to keep the peace among themselves, but to prevent, by force if necessary, its being broken by others."[77] Roosevelt insisted that "each nation must keep well prepared to defend itself until the establishment of some form of international police power," but he held out the possibility of some kind of higher international organization that would rule over a peaceful, prosperous world. Within less than a decade, the victors of World War I would be debating just such a proposal.

In a lecture given that same year at the University of Berlin, Roosevelt spelled out a vision of a "world movement" for civilization that would undergird this world organization. Unlike previous American millennialism, this one would focus more on a global "new Israel" in which the United States would play a large but not necessarily singular role. It would work with other countries to create a "civilization in which morality, ethical development, and a true feeling of brotherhood . . . in which a higher material development of the things of the body shall be achieved without the subordination of things of the soul; in which there shall be a genuine desire for peace and justice without loss of those virile qualities without which no love of peace or justice shall avail any race."[78]

Roosevelt was clearly moving away from the framework of 1898 toward a kind of vision that would later be embraced by Woodrow Wilson. In the years following his presidency, Roosevelt seriously modified other views of his. By 1905, he admitted his doubt that any "Anglo-Saxon race" existed. " 'Anglo-Saxon' is an absurd name unless applied to the dominant race in England between the fifth and the eleventh centuries," he wrote.[79] He repudiated the "Aryan" theorists who would form the foundation of Nazism—he described racist Madison Grant as an "addlepated ass."[80] During World War I, he declared that "race prejudice is pro-Germanism."[81]

After a visit to the West following the 1912 election, he wrote that Navajo and Hopi culture "was that of a remarkable advanced, and still advancing, semi-civilization; not savagery at all" and suggested that any plan for assimilation should "preserve and develop the very element of native culture possessed by these Indians."[82] Roosevelt embraced labor unions and became an ally of Jane Addams and women's suffrage. Just as his foreign policy views began to resemble those that would be embraced by Wilson, his domestic views, put forth in his 1912 campaign for the Progressive Party, anticipated those of his nephew Franklin Roosevelt.

But Roosevelt never finished the ideological journey that he began when he became president. After his defeat in 1912, and Wilson's victory, Roosevelt retired to Oyster Bay, New York. He despised Wilson the same way he had despised the Republican mugwumps of the 1880s who later formed the core of the anti-imperialist movement. His pronouncements with regard to Wilson and to administration foreign policy became colored by partisan dislike, and he reverted, in some respects, to the kind of opinions he had voiced before he became president.

CHAPTER FOUR

Woodrow Wilson
and the Way to Liberty

In an essay published in 1894 entitled "A Calendar of Great Americans," Princeton University political scientist Woodrow Wilson included Benjamin Franklin, Andrew Jackson, Henry Clay, Robert E. Lee, and Abraham Lincoln, but conspicuously omitted Thomas Jefferson. Explained Wilson, "Jefferson was not a thorough American because of the strain of French philosophy that permeated and weakened all his thought . . . he was a philosophical radical by nature as well as by acquirement. . . . His speculative philosophy is exotic and . . . runs like a false and artificial note through all his thought."[1] That was a harsh verdict, and also, as it would turn out, a paradoxical one, because Wilson's own record as a thinker, educator, and president would most closely resemble that of Jefferson.

Jefferson enjoyed a brilliant first term as president—highlighted by the Louisiana Purchase—but a difficult, and even disastrous, second term. His highest accomplishment was not, however, in legislation or treaties, but in his vision of America and the world. Jefferson contributed, among other things, the American secular university and the idea of an "empire for liberty," but he is best known for the Declaration of Independence and its words that "all men are created equal" and that governments derive "their just powers from the consent of the governed." Although seemingly contradicted by the practice of slavery and the limitation on the suffrage, these words helped justify the American Revolution against Britain and the expansion of American democracy over the next two centuries. Abraham Lincoln, Franklin Roosevelt, and Martin Luther King Jr. would cite the Declaration as justification for expanding civil, political, and human rights. And around the world, the Declaration had a similar effect—from the Filipino independence leader Emilio Aguinaldo in 1898 to Vietnamese communist Ho Chi Minh in 1945.

Like Jefferson, Wilson enjoyed a spectacular first term, capped by the creation of the Federal Reserve System, and a painful second term, ending in personal as well as political calamity. Like Jefferson, he was a leading intellectual and educational innovator. And while the Wilson of the 1890s liked to fancy himself a "conservative," by 1910 he had become a philosophical radical who would later try to reformulate the framework of American foreign policy. Wilson's efforts are sometimes capsulated in the phrase "making the world safe for democracy," which he included in his April 1917 address to Congress asking for a declaration of war against Germany, but his contribution was much broader than that. While Wilson, like Jefferson, didn't always act on his deepest understanding—witness, say, his imperviousness to the case of Irish independence or his meddling in Caribbean affairs—he realized that imperialism was creating a nationalist backlash that was undermining, or exposing, Western promises of democracy and higher civilization. More than any other politician he was responsible for making national self-determination an ideal to which all peoples could aspire.

Wilson also understood, as Theodore Roosevelt had begun to grasp, that the natural outcome of imperialism's struggle to divide and redivide the world was a global conflagration. Under Wilson, the United States finally intervened in World War I on the side of Great Britain and France, but during the peace talks at Versailles in 1919, while America's allies pressed for extensive reparations against Germany, Wilson advocated the gradual dismantling of imperialism through a new League of Nations. Wilson failed to get either America's allies or the Republican Congress to agree. But as Jefferson's egalitarian vision of the individual inspired future generations, so, too, would Wilson's vision of a world order based on self-determination and collective security. Franklin Roosevelt and Harry Truman would do for Wilson what Lincoln did for Jefferson—turn what initially appeared to be radical speculation into historic accomplishment.

Wilson's radical vision accorded with the American framework. He believed that the United States had a special mission in the world to spread its practice of liberty and democracy. Said Wilson in 1909, before he became president, "Every nation of the world needs to be drawn into the tutelage of America to learn how to spend money for the liberty of mankind; and in proportion as we discover the means for translating our material force into moral force shall we recover the traditions and glories of American history."[2] Wilson's vision was also deeply influenced by his Presbyterian upbringing in a family of ministers. But Wilson, like Roosevelt, sought to adapt the older millennial framework to the new realities of American power and international conflict.

Wilson believed that the United States could not simply spread its message through setting an example—by being a "city on a hill." It had to participate actively in world affairs, even in wars that began in Europe and didn't directly threaten the American continent. But after coming down from the hill, the United States couldn't single-handedly transform the world. While it could aspire to creating a world of democracies like its own, it couldn't simply impose its system on other countries. The principal role of the United States would come in leading other nations to join together in international institutions, like the League of Nations, that would promote a durable, just world order that would lead nations gradually toward democracy and would replace the fractious imperial order that had led to a devastating war. Regarding revolutions in Mexico and later in Russia, Wilson would reject intervention in favor of "watchful waiting."[3]

COVENANTS AND CONSTITUTIONS

Woodrow Wilson was born into a family of Presbyterian ministers. His father, Joseph, was raised in Ohio by Scots immigrants and trained for the ministry at the Princeton Theological Seminary. He got his first pastorate in Staunton, Virginia, in 1854, where Thomas Woodrow Wilson was born two years later. Wilson's maternal grandfather, Thomas Woodrow, and his uncle James Woodrow were also prominent Presbyterian ministers. Wilson grew up with an intimate knowledge of the Bible and of Presbyterian theology. He described his faith in Presbyterian publications and would regularly occupy the pulpit at the Princeton chapel.

Yet, while a devout Christian, Wilson was by no means what would later be called a Fundamentalist, instead accepting the findings of modern science, including Darwin's theory of evolution. When his uncle James Woodrow was forced to resign from the Columbia (South Carolina) Theological Seminary, where Wilson's father had also taught, for his support of Darwin, Wilson commented that "our dear church . . . has indeed fallen upon evil times of ignorance and folly."[4] He was also fully committed to American pluralism. As president of Princeton, he convinced the trustees, in 1906, to sever the university's connection to the Presbyterian Church and to make it an entirely nonsectarian institution, and he insisted that the Bible be subjected to scholarly inquiry. He also appointed the first Jew and first Catholic to Princeton's faculty.

Like Roosevelt, Wilson voiced the historic themes of America's civil millennialism. In his 1912 campaign for the presidency, he declared his confidence that America was "chosen, and prominently chosen, to show the way to the nations of the world how they shall walk in the paths of liberty."[5] But he endowed them with religious meaning. He saw world and American history and his own life as a struggle between good and evil. "We should perform every act as an act of which we shall some day be made to render a strict account, as an act done either in the service of God or in that of the Devil," Wilson wrote for the *North Carolina Presbyterian* in 1876.[6] He would describe himself and other Christians in Cromwellian terms as "soldiers of the Cross" and the American soldiers who fought in France in 1918 as "crusaders."[7]

Wilson didn't see any inconsistency between promoting American liberty and promoting trade. "Constitutional liberty," Wilson said in 1913, "is the soil out of which the best enterprise springs."[11] But Wilson, like Theodore Roosevelt, always put America's moral and religious mission first. America's destiny, Wilson insisted, was "not to pile up great wealth, but to serve mankind in humanity and justice."[8] He even urged American business to use their sales abroad to "convert [the world] to the principles of America."[9] One of Wilson's favorite sayings was "Business is business, which is just another way of saying that it is not Christianity."[10]

As a college president, governor of New Jersey, and president of the United States, Wilson was fully capable of compromise and conciliation, but he could also abandon political calculation to devote himself, in a quasi-religious fashion, to what he called a "cause." "Politics is a war of *causes*: a joust of principles," he declared while a law student at the University of Virginia. He made the same point in a speech ten years later in Knoxville. "One of the great influences which we call a *Cause* arises in the midst of a nation. Men of strenuous minds and high ideals come forward . . . as champions of a political or moral principle."[12] Wilson devoted himself to such a cause, defined in terms of a struggle between good and evil, at least twice in his life—during his lonely campaign to democratize Princeton, from 1908 to

1910, and during his battle for the League of Nations in 1919. He lost in both cases, but during these quasi-religious conflicts, he most clearly articulated his highest ideals.

Wilson's Presbyterianism, like Roosevelt's muscular Christianity, also contributed its own special elements to his view of America and the world. One of the key ideas of Presbyterianism is that of the covenant.[13] The term "covenant" appears in the Bible, but the Protestant idea of it was developed primarily by Presbyterians and was promulgated by the Puritans who journeyed to North America in the seventeenth century. They believed that God established a "covenant of grace" with human beings in which He forgave their sins in exchange for obedience to His laws. In this respect, the Puritan émigrés saw themselves as having made a covenant with God to create a "city on a hill" on the North American continent. "We are entered into a covenant with Him for this work," John Winthrop informed his fellow travelers.[14] As covenant theology began to be filtered through the prism of American experience, God's covenant with the Puritan émigrés turned into the idea of Americans as having a special responsibility to remake the world in their image. And the civil version of a covenant became a Constitution that embodied God's laws.

American Presbyterians like Woodrow Wilson and his father described themselves as "covenanters." As a political scientist, Wilson was fascinated with constitutions. (He himself would refer to God's law as "the divine constitution for the world.")[15] His political ideal and the title of one of his best-known works was "constitutional government."[16] And when he undertook to create a League of Nations, his first task was to write a "covenant" for the new organization. In a December 1918 visit to London just before the beginning of the Versailles peace talks, Wilson would describe his hope to

> do something like some of my very stern ancestors did, for among my ancestors are those determined persons who were known as the Covenanters. I wish we could, not only for Great Britain and the United States, but for France and Italy and the world, enter into a great league and covenant, declaring ourselves, first of all, friends of mankind and uniting ourselves together for the maintenance and the triumph of right.[17]

Wilson's contribution to American foreign policy can be expressed in religious terms. He attempted to transform the world in America's image by transposing the original Puritan covenant between God and the American settlers into a covenant for the entire world that would exchange peace and democracy for obedience to the League's laws. He would talk of creating a "conscience for the world."[18]

WITH MALICE TOWARD NONE

Wilson spent his childhood in the South, moving with his family from Staunton to Augusta, Georgia, to Columbia, South Carolina, to Wilmington, North Carolina. His first memory was "standing at my father's gateway in Augusta, Georgia, when I was four years old, and hearing some one pass and say that Mr. Lincoln was elected and there was to be war."[19] Wilson's experience growing up in the South during and after the Civil War profoundly affected him, but not in the way it affected most southerners.

The Wilsons were transplanted Yankees. Joseph Wilson's brothers, who remained in Ohio, became Union generals. Joseph Wilson accepted the secession of the South, and became a leader in the newly created southern branch of the Presbyterian Church, but he also taught a Sunday school class for Negroes. Woodrow Wilson retained an affection for the South, but not for the Confederacy. He continued to believe in segregation and Negro inferiority, but not in slavery. In a speech he gave as a law student at the University of Virginia, Wilson said, "I yield to no one precedence in love for the South. But *because* I love the South, I rejoice in the failure of the Confederacy. . . . The perpetuation of slavery would, beyond all question, have wrecked our agricultural and commercial interests, at the same time that it supplied a fruitful source of irritation abroad and agitation within."[20]

But while Wilson fully accepted the victory of the Union in the Civil War—he described the war as a "heroic remedy" for the existence of slavery—he saw the war from a much different vantage than Roosevelt and other northerners did.[21] Roosevelt, who lived in New York City during the war, saw it as a triumph of the sword over injustice. His was a memory of heroic veterans and of victory parades. He came to romanticize war itself and its benefits to an individual's and a nation's character. Wilson, who spent the war in Augusta, saw the devastation that it wrought to the people and economy of the South. Wilson was not a pacifist, but he was not sentimental about the Civil War or war itself. During World War I, Roosevelt, eager for

American intervention, would accuse Wilson of being a "Copperhead"—
one of the Democrats who during the Civil War sought an armistice with
the Confederacy—for trying to negotiate peace among the warring parties.[22]
Wilson, for his part, would charge Roosevelt with "militaristic propa-
ganda."[23]

Wilson, like Roosevelt, also saw Lincoln as a heroic figure. In his history
of the conflict, *Division and Reunion,* Wilson described Lincoln as "one of
the most singular and admirable figures in the history of modern times."[24]
But Roosevelt and Wilson saw two different people in Lincoln. Roosevelt
admired the war leader, while Wilson admired the "solemn, sweet-
tempered" Lincoln of the second inaugural who declared "with malice
toward none, with charity toward all," the Lincoln who sought reconciliation between the North and South after the war.[25] Wilson would mimic
this aspect of Lincoln in his attitude toward the peace settlement after
World War I. While France, and to a lesser extent Great Britain, would seek
vengeance against a defeated Germany and its allies, Wilson would seek out
the terms of future reconciliation.

BURKE, TURNER, AND BRIGHT

In 1875, Wilson journeyed north to attend Princeton, which at the time
was a Presbyterian college run by his father's friend James McCosh. But
Wilson did not follow his father into the ministry. At Princeton and later
at Johns Hopkins, where, in 1886, he received a Ph.D., Wilson studied history and political science. His first book, *Congressional Government,* made
his reputation as a scholar, and he continued to teach and write about government and history until he became governor of New Jersey in 1910.
There were three major influences that would also shape his view of foreign
policy: the English philosopher/politician Edmund Burke, the American
historian Frederick Jackson Turner, and the English radical John Bright.

Wilson got his view of democratic development from Burke. Like
Burke, Wilson came to see liberty as having evolved from the growth of
institutions that are themselves "established practices, habitual methods of
dealing with the circumstances of life or the business of government."[26] That
view led Burke to reject the French Revolution as an attempt to impose liberty abstractly from above, but also to support the American Revolution as

an attempt to protect the integrity of homegrown institutions against overseas rule. It led Wilson as well in two opposite directions: earlier, to oppose William Jennings Bryan's populist politics and to brand as premature attempts to grant independence to the Philippines, but later to be wary of attempts to impose liberty and democracy on other nations through conquest and colonialism. Wilson began, in other words, with the Burke who opposed the French Revolution, but ended up with the Burke who backed the American Revolution.

Wilson got his view of the American nation from Turner. Turner, whom Wilson first met at Johns Hopkins and whom he tried unsuccessfully to hire at Princeton over the trustees' objection, wrote about the influence of the frontier on American history. Wilson once wrote to another historian, "Turner and I were close friends. He talked with me a great deal about his idea. All I ever wrote on the subject came from him."[27] Wilson, like Turner, rejected the idea of American history as the projection of Anglo-Saxon civilization out of New England onto the wilderness, as put forth by historian John Burgess, one of Theodore Roosevelt's favorite teachers, and by Roosevelt himself. Wilson and Turner argued that the experience of the West had produced a unique American, one who defied a single racial designation.

Wilson carried this rejection of Anglo-American racial domination into his experience as president, and into his attempt to create a new world order. In December 1918, on the eve of the peace conference, Wilson told a British official:

> You must not speak of us who come over here as cousins, still less as brothers; we are neither. Neither must you think of us as Anglo-Saxons, for that term can no longer be rightly applied to the people of the United States. Nor must too much importance in this connection be attached to the fact that English is our common language. . . . No, there are only two things which can establish and maintain closer relations between your country and mine; they are community of ideals and of interests.[28]

Unlike his Jacksonian forbears, or the Republican imperialists, Wilson envisaged America as a fully multiethnic society. When Wilson said America was "chosen," he included eastern European immigrants as well as Anglo-Saxons in his definition of America, although, given his persistent view of blacks as inferior, he undoubtedly envisaged America as "white America."[29] Wilson, like Turner, also saw the West as a seedbed of American democracy. His was the West of the small farmer and property-owner rather than of the Indian fighter. Unlike Roosevelt or Beveridge, he would not transfer the model of the Indian wars onto America's encounters with less-developed foreign countries in Asia or Latin America.

Wilson got much of his radicalism and his view of imperialism from Bright. When he was a professor and president of Princeton, Wilson dreamed of entering and not simply writing about politics. His heroes were men of passionate conviction who devoted themselves to causes. Lincoln was probably preeminent among Americans, John Bright among the English. Like Lincoln, Bright would later serve as a political model for Wilson when he left Princeton for politics. Bright was a radical, or left-wing Whig, and pious Quaker who, along with Richard Cobden, was a leader of the Anti-Corn Law Association, which campaigned for the elimination of the tariff on imported food. The corn laws, Bright charged, subsidized Britain's landed aristocracy and impoverished workers by keeping food prices unnaturally high.

Bright, who was a cotton manufacturer, also believed that Britain, with its superior manufacturing, would benefit from pursuing free trade. Indeed, Wilson's first major accomplishment as president would be the reduction of the tariff, and free trade would figure prominently in his plans for the League of Nations. In addition, Bright was an outspoken foe of British imperialism. In 1857, with Indians revolting against the British, he advocated Indian self-rule. During the Civil War, he was, perhaps, the principal British supporter of the Union side in the Civil War. In a speech on Bright, Wilson praised him for his "passionate devotion to principle" and "complete identification with some worthy cause."[30] In 1885, he wrote his fiancée, "Burke was a *very* much greater man than Cobden or Bright; but the work of Cobden and Bright is much nearer to the measure of my powers, it seems so, than the writing of imperishable thoughts upon the greatest problems of politics which was Burke's mission."[31]

I AM A RADICAL

Wilson went through at least three different stages in the evolution of his political views. His first essays and books of the 1880s exhibited the outlines of his later progressivism. In *The State,* which appeared in 1889, when Wilson was teaching at Wesleyan, he advocated a "middle ground" between laissez-faire capitalism and socialism in which the state would regulate work hours, child labor, the "purity and quality of foods," and other areas of industrial life where corporations were unwilling to act and individuals were too weak to effect change on their own.[32] But by the beginning of the twentieth century, Wilson took a turn to the right. He identified himself as a "conservative," praised the "great trusts and combinations" as "necessary because [they are] the most convenient and efficient instrumentalities of modern business," rejected in general government regulation of business, and called for the conservative "reclamation" of the Democratic Party from the radical Bryanites.[33]

By 1909, largely under the impact of his fight with Princeton's wealthy trustees over the democratization of the campus, Wilson veered back to the left.* Wilson wrote that "the same forces were at work in the University which it had become our duty to fight throughout the nation—forces which were making war against democracy and for special privilege."[34] By the time he was elected governor of New Jersey in November 1910, he was identifying himself as a "radical" and was espousing government regulation of "the interests." In 1911, the man who had criticized Jefferson and Bryan for being radicals was writing his friend Mary Peck, "I am *not* a conservative. I am a radical."[35] In a western tour that year, he even identified himself as a "Jeffersonian."[36] And in 1912, when Wilson ran for president, he made his peace with the Bryan Democrats and the populist wing of the party.

Wilson's foreign policy views followed a similar trajectory. In the 1880s, he was sympathetic to the anti-imperialism and free-trade politics of English Liberals and southern Democrats. In 1897, he praised Cleve-

---

*At Princeton, Wilson proposed democratizing the college by eliminating the exclusive eating clubs, integrating the graduate college (which affected an Oxonian elitism and was located off the main campus) into regular college life, and admitting more public school students. He met fierce opposition from the university's wealthy alumni, leading to his resignation to run for governor of New Jersey. Wilson's plan for Princeton was at least six decades ahead of its time.

land for refusing to annex the Hawaiian Islands. In 1898, Wilson initially opposed annexing the Philippines, but in a "Meditation on the Spanish American War" the next year, he acknowledged that while he still wished "we did not have them now . . . the thing is done, cannot be undone; and our future must spring out of it. . . . We have left the continent which has hitherto been our only field of action and have gone out upon the seas, where the nations are rivals and we cannot live or act apart."[37] Wilson posed the problem starkly without answering it:

> The question is not, Shall the vital nations of Europe take possession of the territories of those which are less vital and divide the kingdoms of Africa and Asia? The question is now, Which nations shall possess the world? England Russia, Germany, France, these are the rivals in the new spoilation. . . . Of a sudden we stand in the midst of these. *What ought we do?*[38]

Over the next five years, Wilson grew increasingly supportive of the decision to take the Philippines, sounding the same themes as the imperialists. In a speech in Montclair, New Jersey, in January 1904, Wilson described the United States as showing the Filipinos "the way to liberty without plundering them or making them our tools for a selfish end." Declared Wilson, "We are a sort of a pure air glowing in world politics destroying illusions and cleaning places of morbid miasmatic gases." Like Roosevelt, he evoked the frontier spirit. "It is always well to have a frontier on which to turn loose the colts of our race. Because of our Americanism we had no patience with the anti-imperialist wailings that came out of Boston."[39]

Yet within a decade, Wilson would be making many of the same wailings against imperialism that had come from Bostonians Edward Atkinson, Harvard president Charles W. Eliot, and William James after the annexation of the Philippines. He would accept their fundamental argument that America's mission had always been to oppose rather than to promote colonialism and imperialism. Wilson would also support independence for the Philippines. This final turn in his foreign policy would come partly as a consequence of his change on domestic issues. As he became more receptive to the Bryan Democrats' arguments about corporate power, he grew more receptive to their rejection of the Taft administration's "dollar diplomacy" in Latin America and China. But Wilson would also have his own defining experience in Mexico in 1913 and 1914.

DOLLAR DIPLOMACY

In the early 1900s, Wilson believed that imperialism was consistent with America's mission—to show other peoples "the way to liberty."[40] During this period, Wilson also believed that large corporations and New York banks were instruments of social justice and efficiency. By the time he was running for president, he was attacking the "money trust" and "monopolies" that had "shut and double bolted" the door of opportunity in the country, corrupting the political system and putting small businesses and workers at their mercy.[41] And Wilson increasingly drew the conclusion that they were undermining America's foreign policy and America's historic mission in the world.

Wilson's idol John Bright had argued that Britain's landed aristocracy were using the corn laws to maintain their hold over the economy and British life. Similarly, Wilson now argued that corporate monopolies and "interests," through their lobbyists, were using the tariff to subsidize their profits and enhance their power at the expense of the rest of America. The tariff, he said in his inaugural address, "makes the Government a facile interest in the hands of private interests." Wilson also seconded the arguments against protectionism that had been made earlier by Conant and other economists.[42] "The tariff was once a bulwark; now it is a dam. For trade is reciprocal; we cannot sell unless we also buy," Wilson said in his 1912 presidential acceptance speech.[43] At this point, however, Wilson saw the tariff primarily as a domestic and international economic issue; later, he would see ending protectionism as integral to ending imperialism and an unstable balance of power.

Wilson also applied his analysis of corporate power to European and American imperialism. He denounced what had come to be called "dollar diplomacy," but which had existed for at least a century before the term was used to characterize the Taft administration's foreign policy. British Liberal theorist John Hobson had described it in his 1902 book *Imperialism*.[44] Banks, trading companies, and investment groups would make investments in Asia, Africa, or Latin America or they would loan money to regimes on these continents. If the investment were jeopardized by local insurgents, or if the government threatened to default on the loans, then the bank or trading company's home country was expected to step in. It would force compliance, and if necessary, either establish a protectorate (by taking over the country's finances and foreign policy) or annex the country as a colony. Theodore Roosevelt had followed this model in the Dominican Republic in 1905. Wilson had analyzed a version of this practice without comment in an unpublished paper in 1907:

> Since trade ignores national boundaries and the manufacturer insists on having the world as a market, the flag of his nation must follow him, and the doors of the nations which are closed against him must be battered down. Concessions obtained by financiers must be safeguarded by ministers of state, even if the sovereignty of unwilling nations be outraged in the process. Colonies must be obtained or planted, in order that no useful corner of the world may be overlooked or left unused.[45]

The difference between Roosevelt and Taft was that Roosevelt justified his dollar diplomacy on geopolitical or moral grounds, while Taft did so on economic grounds. In May 1910, Taft committed himself to "active intervention to secure for our merchandise and our capitalists opportunity for profitable investment."[46] In fact, Taft saw dollar diplomacy as an alternative to armed intervention—it meant putting relations on a commercial basis—but like Roosevelt, he found himself following the pattern that Hobson and then Wilson described, sending troops to Nicaragua and Santo Domingo when American loans were jeopardized.[47] Wilson would also eventually intervene in Caribbean countries, but he would claim, with some justification, that he was trying to solve problems that Taft and Roosevelt had created. As soon as he took office, he set official American policy in direct opposition to Taft's dollar diplomacy, and made several conspicuous efforts to keep his word.

Wilson made Bryan, who had been the leader of the anti-imperialist movement in the Senate, his secretary of state. Wilson owed Bryan a high position in his administration because of his help in the election, and the two men worked together amicably until 1915, when Bryan, an advocate of strict neutrality, quit over Wilson's decision, after the sinking of the *Lusitania,* to demand that Germany cease its submarine warfare. They agreed in their emphasis on America's moral mission and their rejection of dollar diplomacy, but they didn't reject foreign trade and government efforts to open foreign markets. On the contrary, they believed that the best way to stimulate American trade and overseas investment was to befriend other countries by forswearing imperialism. The first clear test of the administration's policy came over China.

Wilson had to appoint a new minister in China to replace William J. Calhoun, who had resigned. Wilson's first choices were John Mott of the Student Volunteer Movement for Foreign Missions and the YMCA, who was, according to Wilson, doing "the most important work in the world," and Harvard president Charles W. Eliot, one of the anti-imperialist "wailers" Wilson had attacked.[48] But both men preferred to continue what they were doing. Wilson finally turned to Paul Reinsch, one of the foremost critics of the new imperialism. Reinsch's appointment, along with that of Bryan, showed that Wilson had abandoned his earlier support for imperialism.

Even before Reinsch arrived in Beijing, Wilson made a decision on China policy that veered sharply away from the Taft administration's dollar diplomacy. The Taft administration had sponsored the participation of a few select American banks in a four-country consortium intended to establish control over China's railroads. The scheme failed when the Manchu dynasty fell to reformer and would-be warlord Yuan Shih-k'ai, but the British proposed that the consortium finance Yuan's regime, which was already being challenged by insurgents. The Taft administration went along with the scheme, which, like other loan arrangements, could easily have resulted in foreign control of China's finances. Just two weeks after taking office, Wilson, queried by J. P. Morgan bankers about American backing for the loans, abruptly canceled government support for the project. Wilson denounced the venture as a "monopoly transaction" that would threaten "the administrative independence of China itself" by encouraging "forcible interference" by the foreign governments. Participation in the loan scheme, Wilson wrote, was "obnoxious to the principles upon which the government of our people rests."[49]

Wilson also took steps to change the Taft and Roosevelt administration's policies in Latin America, which had left a residue of anti-Americanism. In October 1913, Wilson explained his Latin American policy in a speech in Mobile, Alabama. He pledged to deal with the Latin American nations on the basis of equality. "We must prove ourselves their friends and champions upon terms of equality and honor. You cannot be friends upon any other terms than upon the term of equality," he declared.[50] Wilson was laying down a principle that would later become central to his idea of postwar peace—extrapolating, as Jefferson himself had done, the equality of individuals to the equality of nations, no matter what their size or strength. Wilson reaffirmed America's earlier anti-imperial understanding of its mission. "I want to take this occasion to say that the United States will never again seek one additional foot of territory by conquest. She will devote herself to showing that she knows how to make honorable and fruitful use of the territory she has, and she must regard it as one of the duties of friendship to see that from no quarter are material interests made superior to human liberty and national opportunity."[51]

Speaking at Independence Hall in Philadelphia on July 4, 1914, Wilson reaffirmed his rejection of dollar diplomacy:

> There is no man who is more interested than I am in carrying the enterprise of American business to every quarter of the globe. . . . [But] if American enterprise in foreign countries, particularly in those foreign countries which are not strong enough to resist us, takes the shape of imposing upon and exploiting the mass of the people of that country it ought to be checked and not encouraged. I am willing to get anything for an American that money and enterprise can obtain except the suppression of the rights of other men.[52]

Wilson didn't always act on these principles. Worried about German expansionism, he took virtual control of Haiti and the Dominican Republic during World War I, but many of his and Bryan's actions were faithful to these beliefs. Wilson signed a treaty with Colombia apologizing and offering an indemnity for the seizure of the Canal Zone in 1903. Roosevelt denounced the treaty as a "crime against the United States," and Republicans prevented its ratification in the Senate.[53] Bryan tried to prevent Nicaragua and Cuba from granting special privileges to American bankers. In 1916, Wilson and his close adviser Colonel Edward House tried to set up a Pan-American Pact that would offer "mutual guarantee of political independence under republican forms of government and mutual guarantees of territorial integrity."[54] The pact was intended to foreshadow the international organization that Wilson and House wanted to create after World War I, but it could never get off the ground because of the feuds among the Latin American countries.

A PROFOUND REVOLUTION

The clearest, and most enlightening, test of Wilson's new foreign policy would come in Mexico. From 1876 to 1911, Mexico had been ruled by General Porfirio Díaz. American and British investors had fared well, but most of Mexico lived in dire poverty. Díaz retained the enthusiastic support of Roosevelt and Taft, but he was finally overthrown by nationalist Francisco Madero in early 1911. In October, Madero was elected in one of the freest elections in Mexican history. He quickly ran afoul of the American and British governments by establishing Mexico's first tax on oil production. With the tacit support of the British and Americans, former Díaz allies organized coups against Madero. The third of these, led by General Victoriano Huerta, succeeded in February 1913, a month before Wilson was inaugurated. Huerta had Madero murdered and took power, and then, on October 26, declared himself president after a rigged election.

The British backed Huerta, and State Department counselor John Bassett Moore advised Wilson to follow suit. "It might be possible to cite recent instances of much denounced despotisms with which we have been and possibly still are on very pleasant terms," Moore wrote Wilson.[55] Theodore Roosevelt also argued for American support for the Huerta government. But Wilson called on Huerta to resign. He told Congress on October 31 that Huerta's rule would bring "perhaps irrevocable ruin, political, industrial and social." He warned that the United States would do what it could to overthrow Huerta:

> We are bound by every obligation of honor and by the compulsion of sacred interests which go to the very foundations of our national life to constitute ourselves the champions of constitutional government and of the integrity and independence of free states throughout America, North and South. It is our duty to study the conditions which make constitutional government possible for our neighbor states in this hemisphere . . . and, knowing those conditions, to suffer neither our own people nor the citizens or governments of other countries . . . to violate them or to render them impossible of realization.[56]

Wilson's version of the Roosevelt Corollary entailed replacing govern-ments in the hemisphere that violated liberty. It wasn't dollar diplomacy, but it amounted to installing in Mexico a government of which the United States approved.*

Over the next five months, Wilson tried to maneuver Huerta out of power. He offered Huerta's government a loan if the general would step down. He offered to lift an arms embargo to Huerta's revolutionary oppo-nents, constitutionalists Venustiano Carranza and Pancho Villa, if they would agree to protect foreign property and lives, but they refused to cooperate with an American government that appeared to be trying to impose its will on Mexico. While fighting Huerta, they joined him in denouncing America's attempt to intervene in the country's internal affairs. Wilson appeared to understand the dilemma he faced in Mexico. If the United States tried to impose a new government on Mexico, whatever its program, the act itself would destroy whatever possibility the government had of succeeding. A frustrated Wilson told the British ambassador in Feb-ruary 1914 that what primarily ailed Mexico was its landless peasantry and that only land reform would really stem the course of revolution. Mean-while, he feared that "successful intervention would unite against the invading party all the patriotism and all the energies of which the Mexicans were capable. To put such a government into power would be to substitute for a government which people could not trust a government which they must perforce hate."[57]

But in April, Wilson lost his temper with Huerta and attempted to do just that. With the Germans prepared to land a shipment of arms for the Huerta government at Veracruz, Wilson responded to the arrest of Amer-ican soldiers in neighboring Tampico by sending an invasion force to Tampico and Veracruz. Wilson didn't expect any resistance in either place, but he encountered fierce, largely spontaneous opposition from government troops in Veracruz. Nineteen Americans were killed, and marines in Tampico had to be shifted to Veracruz to maintain the harbor. By April 22, six thousand American troops were needed to hold the port. Instead of being greeted as liberators, the American forces inspired riots and demonstrations

---

*Germany's Kaiser Wilhelm II found Wilson's foreign policy incomprehensible. "Morality is all right, but what about dividends?" he wondered.

all over the country, and united Huerta with his opponents. Carranza denounced the invasion as a violation of Mexican sovereignty. In Mexico City, schoolchildren chanted "Death to the Gringos." American businesses and shops had to close. The Mexico City newspaper *El Imparcial* declared, "The soil of the *patria* is defiled by foreign invasion! We may die, but let us kill!"[58]

At a loss, Wilson and Bryan asked Argentina, Brazil, and Chile to mediate the crisis. Negotiations dragged on through the spring and early summer, while American forces remained in Veracruz. In July, facing division within his government and the armies of Carranza and Villa, Huerta resigned and fled Mexico City, but the fighting continued between Carranza and Huerta's chosen successor, and even between Carranza and Villa. With Mexico facing chaos, Secretary of War Lindley Garrison urged Wilson to order American forces to march on Mexico City to install a government, but Wilson had finally learned his lesson from the disaster at Veracruz. He wrote back to Garrison:

> We shall have no right at any time to intervene in Mexico to determine the way in which the Mexicans are to settle their own affairs. . . . Many things may happen of which we do not approve and which could not happen in the United States, but I say very solemnly that that is no affair of ours. . . . There are in my judgment no conceivable circumstances which would make it right for us to direct by force or by threat of force the internal processes of what is profound revolution, a revolution as profound as that which occurred in France.[59]

Mexico would prove a continuing problem—so would the China of Yuan Shih-k'ai and the regimes in Central America and the Caribbean—but Wilson drew an important conclusion from his attempt to depose Huerta. Wilson continued to believe the United States had a mission to show the way to liberty, but he realized after the invasion of Veracruz that the United States could not do this simply by imposing liberty and democracy on a recalcitrant country like Mexico. To do so would not only risk inflaming anti-Americanism, it would also undermine the very purpose for which the intervention was intended. When the journalist John Reed asked Wilson in July 1914 what he would do if Yuan turned into a "dictator of Huerta's stamp," which was in the process of occurring at that very moment, Wilson replied in his best Burkean language, but it was the Burke of 1776 and not of 1789: "The power to destroy what any people have consented to is limited. It is limited to organic law, and by the interests of other people and other nations."

In his policy toward Mexico, Wilson also broke with a century-old view of the Mexicans as Indians who were incapable of self-government. The British foreign minister Sir Edward Grey had voiced his opinion to the American ambassador in London. "Mexico was really an Indian state," Grey said, "so no one could control it without Huerta's brutal methods."[60] To Wilson, the Mexicans fell under the Declaration; they were not savages or barbarians on a ladder of civilization. And this made an enormous difference to the kind of foreign policy that Wilson adopted toward Mexico and the rest of Latin America. To him, these countries were not the Wild West, filled with savages that the United States had to subdue. The residents of these lands enjoyed the same right of self-determination as the American colonists on the eve of the Revolution. Said Wilson, "The country is theirs. The government is theirs. Their liberty, if they can get it, is theirs, and so far as my influence goes while I am President, nobody shall interfere with them."[61]

CHAPTER FIVE

Woodrow Wilson and the Conscience of the World

In the first week in August 1914, while a civil war was raging in Mexico, Woodrow Wilson's wife, Ellen, died, and World War I began. In his first press conference after the outbreak of fighting, a distraught Wilson declared, "I want to have the pride of feeling that America, if nobody else, has her self-possession and stands ready with calmness of thought and steadiness of purpose to help the rest of the world."[1] Wilson tried for the next two and a half years to achieve a "peace without victory," but in April 1917, stung by the renewal of German submarine warfare against American merchant ships and by revelations about a German attempt to woo Mexico and Japan into an alliance against the United States, Wilson took the United States into war against Germany.

Wilson still harbored hopes of constructing "a peace as will satisfy the longing of the whole world for disinterested justice, embodied in settlements which are based upon something much better and much more lasting than the selfish competitive interests of powerful states."[2] As the war turned against Germany in 1918, Wilson issued his Fourteen Points for peace, including the removal of trade barriers, the impartial adjustment of colonial claims, and the creation of a "general association of nations."[3] He also advocated magnanimity toward Germany. "We do not wish to injure her or block in any way her legitimate influence or power," Wilson said. "We wish her only to accept a place of equality among the peoples of the world—the new world in which we now live—instead of a place of mastery."[4]

Germany signed an armistice in November 1918 based on the Fourteen Points, and when Wilson arrived in Europe the next month to represent the United States at the peace talks, he was greeted as a savior. Historian Margaret Macmillan writes, "Across Europe there were squares, streets, railway stations and parks bearing Wilson's name. Wall posters cried, 'We want a Wilson peace.' "⁵ In his book *The Ordeal of Woodrow Wilson,* Herbert Hoover, who had served Wilson as food administrator, wrote, "For a moment at the time of the Armistice, Mr. Wilson rose to intellectual domination of most of the civilized world."⁶

But in the negotiations over the League and over reparations from Germany, Wilson's vision of a new world order encountered stiff resistance from France, Italy, and Great Britain and its dominions. French prime minister Georges Clemenceau said in December 1918, "There is an old system which appears to be discredited today, but to which I am not afraid of saying I am still faithful."⁷ Clemenceau and other European leaders had no interest in ending colonialism; in fact, they had a lively stake in who would inherit Germany, Austria, and Turkey's former colonies, and how much Germany would pay in reparations. Wilson got the League, and a few concessions on annexations, but he had to compromise or abandon key provisions of the Fourteen Points.

Upon returning to the United States in July 1919, Wilson made an impassioned plea for the ratification of the treaty. He told the Republican-controlled Senate, "Our isolation was ended 20 years ago, and now fear of us is ended also, our counsel and association sought after and desired. There can be no question of our ceasing to be a world power. The only question is whether we can refuse the leadership that is offered us, whether we shall accept or reject the confidence of the world."⁸ But with a two-thirds majority needed, Wilson faced opposition from an unusual coalition of nationalists, isolationists, and progressives and from partisan Republicans who were determined to deny him a political victory. In late September, Wilson was crippled by a stroke during a speaking tour of the West and never fully recovered. The Senate failed to ratify the treaty.

Wilson's diplomatic efforts in 1919 were clearly flawed. He refused to admit that in dropping his insistence on the Fourteen Points, including an end to the colonial scramble, and in agreeing to massive reparations from Germany, he had, in effect, undermined any possibility that a League of Nations could create a lasting peace. But Wilson's understanding of World War I, and what would be necessary to prevent future wars, proved to be remarkably prescient. Virtually alone among the victorious leaders in Versailles, Wilson understood that the war itself was rooted not just in Prussian militarism but in a flawed international system that had encouraged and would continue to encourage war.

Wilson also understood that the United States would have to abandon both its isolationist and imperialist approaches to foreign policy. He reaffirmed the founders' opposition to conquest and colonies. For Wilson, America's mission was not to create an empire, but a global democracy of equal and independent nations. But he thought that in order to complete that mission, the United States would have to take active world leadership and work with other nations in international organizations. It would have to abandon forever Washington's and Jefferson's injunctions against "entangling alliances." Wilson wanted Americans to reaffirm the objectives of the early republic, but not the severe limits Washington and Jefferson had placed on the means to achieve them.

PEACE WITHOUT VICTORY

When war broke out in August 1914, many Europeans believed that it would soon be over. Indeed, the German general staff was counting on the kind of quick victory it had won over the French in 1870. In the United States, many Americans believed that what went on in Europe was of no consequence to them. *The Literary Digest* summed up the reaction of the American press to the conflict in Europe, "Our isolated position and freedom from entangling alliances inspire our press with the cheering assurance that we are in no peril of being drawn into the European quarrel."[9] But even in the months after the war had begun, when he was grieving his wife's loss, Wilson acutely sensed that the war would be long and disastrous and would have to involve the United States. He told his brother-in-law that

> modern conditions had brought the world into such a close neighborhood that never again would it be possible for the world at large to regard a quarrel between two nations as a particular and private quarrel, but that an attack in any quarter was an attack on the equilibrium of the world, and that the safety of the world demanded such a combination of the force of the nations as would maintain peace throughout all the world.[10]

Over the five years of war and peace negotiations, Wilson's public statements about the causes of war shifted dramatically with changes in America's role. During his attempt from August 1914 to February 1917 to achieve peace between the belligerents, he tended to blame both sides for the conflict. Once America intervened, he focused his wrath on German militarism and imperialism, but during the peace negotiations after the war, he stressed the systemic causes of the war. Yet Wilson's private statements and letters during this period show a remarkable continuity in his analysis of the war. He saw German aggression as the immediate cause of the war—and from the start privately favored an allied victory—but he also believed that the war was rooted in a fractious international system, which, if not changed, would give rise to future wars.

Wilson confessed his sympathies for the allies to his chief aide, Colonel Edward House, and to Walter Hines Page, his ambassador to Great Britain. In a conversation on August 30, 1914, House "found him as unsympathetic with the German attitude as is the balance of America."[11] Wilson believed that the German government was responsible for starting the war. By invading Belgium—a country whose neutrality the European powers had guaranteed in a treaty in 1839—Germany had turned a Balkan war in the east into a larger continental conflict that involved Great Britain. Wilson was certainly correct in this perception. What he couldn't know, and what German historians have uncovered in the last four decades, is that German leaders had been planning a continental war since at least 1912.[12] Out of this war, as Wilson feared, Germany planned to create a larger central European empire and to become Britain's equal, if not its superior, on the world stage.

Wilson also believed that the United States would be better off if the allies were to win. The British navy had helped to protect Latin America from conquests by other powers. Wilson worried that if Germany emerged from the war as the leading national power, the United States would have to be on a constant military alert to repel its incursions. Wilson also feared the triumph of Germany's authoritarian model of government and its *Machtpolitik* of "might is right." According to House, Wilson told him that "if Germany won it would change the course of our civilization and make the United States a military nation [and] it would check his policy for a better international ethical code."[13] In addition, Wilson was aware that the

United States had enjoyed the benefits of Britain's free trade policy. A triumphant Germany, Wilson feared, would attempt to carve out large exclusive trading zones for itself that would be protected by Germany's military.

But Wilson did not bring the United States into the war against Germany until April 1917—and then only as an "associate" and not as an "ally." One reason for the delay was that American public opinion was dead set against intervention. Except for Lodge and Roosevelt, who never actually advocated war until the end, most Republicans strongly opposed intervention, as did a large faction of Bryan Democrats, who in 1916 were prepared to run a candidate against Wilson if he advocated entering the war. Public opinion didn't favor war until March 1917 when the administration revealed the "Zimmerman telegram" from Germany's foreign minister promising Mexico the return of the Southwest if it fought against the United States.[14]

But more important, Wilson actually believed that the United States and the world would be better off if neither side was victorious. In November 1916, as he was preparing what would be his last attempt at securing a "peace without victory," Wilson described his reasoning in an unpublished memorandum:

> Were Germany, by a decisive victory, to bring her enemies to their knees, the partitioning of territory would at once be begun . . . and from that minute on she would have to prepare herself for another conflict which would inevitably come. . . . With the defeat of Germany, the inevitable procedure would be the annexing of her colonies, the allotting out of the territory of her allies, and an indemnity collected for the rehabilitation of Belgium, Serbia and Rumania; perhaps, too, for the reimbursement of the military expenses of the Entente. Needless to say, such an outrage to her pride would never be forgotten; it would rankle in her breast as did the rape of Alsace-Lorraine to France. Based on either of these hypotheses, an enduring peace is the empty talk of partisan dreamers.[15]

Wilson's alternative was to seek a peace that would reconcile the two warring parties to each other's existence rather than setting the stage and the terms for a future war. At Versailles, he would propose that Germany's reparations be limited to "actual damages" that it inflicted on the allies, but he would be frustrated in that effort.[16] The terms at Versailles would resemble exactly those that he described in his 1916 memorandum, and the results would be exactly as he feared.

ROOTS OF INSTABILITY

Lurking beneath Wilson's fear that victory by either side would mean an unstable peace was a deeper conviction that the international system was inherently unstable. Wilson had written in 1916:

> Have you ever heard what started the present war? If you have, I wish you would publish it, because nobody else has, so far as I can gather. Nothing in particular started it, but everything in general. There has been growing up in Europe a mutual suspicion, an interchange of conjecture about what this government and that government are going to do, an interlacing of alliances and understandings, a complex web of intrigue and spying, that presently were sure to entangle the whole of the family of mankind on that side of the water in its meshes.[17]

Wilson never spelled this view out at any length, but he made numerous references to it in his private correspondence and memoranda and in the last speeches he gave defending the League of Nations. He looked at the system from different angles and vantages rather than on the basis of a single unified analysis:

Balance of power. Europe's diplomacy had been based upon a balance-of-power philosophy, but what Europeans saw as a "balance," Wilson saw as "organized rivalries," and an invitation to instability and war, as the countries vied with one another for commercial and military supremacy.[18] The rivalries extended back centuries, but those that had led to World War I began after the Franco-Prussian War, when Germany, in victory, claimed Alsace-Lorraine from France. That led to France's drive for overseas empire, and to the Entente with Britain and Russia against Germany. It led to Germany's alliance with Austria, its growing resentment of France's imperial success in Africa, and to the crises over Morocco in 1906 and 1911. One reason for Germany's final decision to go to war in 1914 was its fear of encirclement from the Entente.

Rivalry over colonies: The balance of power was rendered even less stable by rivalries over colonies in Africa, Asia, and the Middle East. The kaiser and other German officials resented the fact that even though Germany's economic and military might rivaled that of Britain and surpassed that of France, Germany trailed both countries in colonial possessions. The kaiser's program was to obtain for Germany a "place in the sun" by making it a "world state" to rival Britain.[19] Such ambitions could not be attributed simply to Wilhelm II's personal eccentricity. They were integral to the pyramidical structure of world imperialism in which national strength and greatness were measured by colonial possessions. French imperialist Paul Leroy-Beaulieu had declared that "the nation which has the most colonies is the preeminent people; if it isn't today, it will be tomorrow."[20] Wilson put the problem simply in a conversation in 1916 with Ambassador Walter Hines Page. According to Page, Wilson "described the war as a result of many causes—some of long origin. He spoke of England's having the earth, of Germany's wanting it."[21]

Commercial rivalry: The rivalry over colonies was fed by commercial rivalries. Wilson's analysis of commercial imperialism was similar to that of Hobson and Reinsch.[22] Nations sought colonies for commercial advantage, and when they acquired them, closed them off to their rivals. That exacerbated the struggle for colonies, and led eventually to war. In October 1918, Wilson wrote that "the experiences of the past . . . have taught us that the attempts by one nation to punish another by exclusive and discriminatory trade agreements have been a prolific breeder of that kind of antagonism which oftentimes results in war."[23] In St. Louis on September 5, 1919, Wilson said, "The real reason that the war that we have just finished took place was that Germany was afraid her commercial rivals were going to get the better of her, and the reason why some nations went into the war against Germany was that they thought Germany would get the commercial advantage of them. The seed of the jealousy, the seed of deep-seated hatred was hot, successful commercial and industrial rivalry. . . . This war, in its inception, was a commercial and industrial war. It was not a political war."[24]

What Wilson didn't say, and probably would not have acknowledged, is that American high tariffs had probably contributed both to the scramble for colonies and to Germany's decision to go to war. In 1884, French premier Jules Ferry had blamed American tariffs for his own country's rush to colonies. It had occurred, he said, because next door Germany is setting up trade barriers; because across the ocean the United States of America have become protectionists, and extreme protectionists at that; because not only are these great markets . . . shrinking, becoming more and more difficult of access, but these great states are beginning to pour into our own markets products not seen there before.[25]

Germany was equally concerned with American high tariffs. According to industrialist and politician Walther Rathenau, the kaiser wanted to unify the European continent as a defensive measure against America's high tariffs. "His plan" was for "a United States of Europe against America," Rathenau reported Wilhelm saying.[26]

Might is right: The drive for national power and for colonies was met with cries of injustice from the colonized and conquered, and from some citizens of the imperial nations, but the governments of those nations often viewed the overall struggle for power in the world as being outside the realm of justice and right or wrong. On the eve of the peace negotiations, Clemenceau told British prime minister Lloyd George's companion Frances Stevenson over lunch, "I have come to the conclusion that *force* is right. Why is this chicken here? Because it was not strong enough to resist those who wanted to kill it. And a very good thing too."[27] When European powers assembled their alliances, and coerced small countries in Europe into joining them, they were following age-old practices that had ensured national survival. They believed they were entirely justified, because justification was irrelevant.*

Wilson blamed the rush to war on this amoral balance-of-power philosophy and the perverse social Darwinism that was used to justify it. In St. Louis in 1919, he explained that Europe's politics had been based on "the

---

*The philosophy of "might is right" has bedeviled philosophers since the dialogue between Socrates and Thrasymachus in Plato's *Republic*. There are at least three interpretations of what it means. First, it can be taken to mean (as Wilson did) that justice is simply irrelevant to international relations—the equivalent of "all is fair in love and war." Second, it can be taken to mean what Clemenceau (in line with Thrasymachus) implies above—that what is right or just is whatever result emerges from a struggle for power. Third, it can be taken to mean that the powerful determine what is right by imposing their own justification on the less powerful— through something like what Marx called an "ideology." Thus, Americans justified the Indian wars and Europeans their imperial conquest through an elaborate philosophy of the stages of civilization. Wilson's argument, as it would emerge in the peace talks, was that international relations should be governed by a moral code, but that it should be a moral code that reflects the equal rights of nations regardless of power.

contention that the strong had all the rights and that all that the weak could enjoy was what the strong permitted them to enjoy; that no nation had any right that could not be asserted by the exercise of force, and that the real politics of Europe consisted in determining how many of the weak elements in the European combination of families and of nations should be under the influence and control of one set of nations and how many of those elements should be under the influence and control of another set of nations."[28]

Democracy and autocracy: Wilson suggested that the struggle over colonies finally erupted into war because some of the countries involved were autocracies and not democracies. Autocracies like czarist Russia or Germany (in which the kaiser had unchallenged responsibility for foreign policy) didn't have to subject their decisions to public vote and to their public's fear of war. Wilson told the *Washington Post* in 1916, "I am convinced that only governments initiate such wars as the present, and that they are never brought on by peoples, and that, therefore, democracy is the best preventive of such jealousies and suspicions and secret intrigues as produce wars among nations where small groups control rather than the great body of public opinion." He reiterated the point in his speech the next April asking for a declaration of war. "A steadfast concert for peace can never be maintained except by a partnership of democratic nations. No autocratic government could be trusted to keep faith within it or observe its covenants."[29]

Wilson the political scientist might have produced a systematic account of these causes of war. President Wilson, for whom words were acts of diplomacy, never did. He pressed the point about Germany's lack of democracy in the course of blaming that country for the war, but he stressed commercial and national rivalry and the absence of international morality in explaining the underlying causes of the war. The real connection between them lay not so much in Wilson's explanation of causes but in his vision of a solution. Wilson saw the victorious nations as having to choose between the continuation of imperialism and the movement toward global democracy. He made this point in his speech before the Senate in July 1919:

> For my own part I am as intolerant of imperialistic designs on the part of other nations as I was of such designs on the parts of Germany. The choice is between two ideals; on the one hand, the ideal of democracy, which represents the rights of free peoples everywhere to govern themselves, and, on the other hand, the ideal of imperialism, which seeks to dominate for force

and unjust power, an ideal which is by no means dead and which is earnestly held in many quarters still.[30]

Democracy, in this sense, was not just an electoral exercise, but the antithesis of imperialism. It meant national self-determination, liberal capitalism, and equality among nations.

By adopting a more complex understanding of the causes of the war, Wilson resisted the temptation to which America's millennial framework had made its statesmen prey: portraying conflict as Armageddon and the enemy nation as the personification of evil. Wilson railed against "Prussian militarism," but he also tried to turn Americans' attention to the imperial rivalries, and the structure of imperialism, that underlay the war. Military victory over the kaiser and his armies would not be enough; to create an enduring peace, a new "world order" would have to be created that would discourage the scramble for colonies. Unfortunately, however, many Americans, including members of Wilson's own administration, did not share this understanding. Instead, they had turned the war into a crusade against the Hun, and secondarily against German-Americans and antiwar activists, and when the war was over, against Bolsheviks and immigrants.

THE FOURTEEN POINTS

During the war, Wilson, with the aid of the House, set out to define his vision of a solution to war and imperialism. In September 1917, House organized a group of geographers, journalists, and historians—called "The Inquiry"—to draw up war aims and peace terms for Wilson. In January, on the basis of its recommendations, Wilson presented his Fourteen Points to Congress, which he further elaborated on in subsequent speeches over the coming year and incorporated into a "covenant" for a League of Nations that he drafted. By the time he arrived in Paris in January 1919, however, he had gone beyond the initial fourteen points and beyond some of the Inquiry's more cautious recommendations. Journalist Walter Lippmann, the secretary of the Inquiry, recounted they had "repeatedly but with little success, tried to slow the President down on self-determination."[31] Taken together, Wilson's recommendations represented the rudiments of a world order that was dramatically different from the one that existed.

In the Fourteen Points, Wilson had called merely for giving native populations "equal weight" with "the government whose title is to be determined" in settling colonial claims, but in a speech to Congress the next month he called for the principle of self-determination—a concept that had been invoked by the Russian revolutionaries in April 1917. The idea was susceptible to different meanings—it could apply to peoples under colonial rule or to nationalities within a proposed nation—but Wilson made clear he was directing it at the colonial situation as well as at the nationalities of central Europe. He told Congress: "Peoples are not to be handed about from one sovereignty to another by an international conference or an understanding between rivals and antagonists. National aspirations must be respected; peoples may now be dominated and governed only by their own consent."[32]

Wilson believed that all peoples were capable of self-government. "When properly directed, there is no people not fitted for government," Wilson said upon his arrival in Paris.[33] In this sense, he believed that colonialism could eventually be eliminated. But while Wilson was radical in his ends, he could be realistic in the means by which he pursued them. He acknowledged that not all peoples were ready for self-government, and in the first drafts of the covenant, he introduced a strategy for bringing them to that point. The League would appoint trustees who would be mandated—they would have "mandates"—to oversee the colonies and ready them for self-government. These trustees would not be chosen from the imperial powers, but from smaller states like Sweden.[34] Later, Wilson specifically proposed that the Middle Eastern countries that had formerly been part of the Ottoman Empire be allowed to choose their own trustees.[35] He didn't call for the dissolution of the British or French empire—that would have made *any* agreement in Paris impossible. But his support for self-determination was widely interpreted around the world as opposition to colonialism in all its forms.

Among the nations that had already achieved self-government, Wilson sought to replace the balance of power with a "community" or a "concert" of power. Within a balance of power, Wilson argued, the strong preyed upon the weak. In a community of power, the same moral principles would prevail that existed among individuals within a democratic nation like the United States. Said Wilson, "We are at the beginning of an age in which it will be insisted that the same standards of conduct and of responsibility for wrong done shall be observed among nations and their governments that are observed among the individual citizens of civilized states."[36]

Equality among nations did not mean that all nations would be equal in economic or military power; it meant that each would enjoy freedom from external aggression. In his January 1917 address advocating a "peace without victory," Wilson had proposed that

> the nations should with one accord adopt the doctrine of President Monroe as the doctrine of the world: that no nation should seek to extend its policy over any other nation of people, but that every people should be left free to determine its own polity, its own way of development, unhindered, unthreatened, unafraid, the little along with the great and powerful.[37]

Wilson's new world order also had an economic dimension. In a memo to his secretary of state in 1916, Wilson had described the elimination of protectionist trading blocs as essential to the creation of an enduring peace. Wilson favored, he wrote, "a mutual guarantee against such economic warfare as would in effect constitute an effort to throttle the industrial life of a nation or shut it off from equal opportunities of trade with the rest of the world."[38] In his Fourteen Points, Wilson had called for "the removal, so far as possible, of all economic barriers and the establishment of an equality of trade conditions among all the nations consenting to the peace and associating themselves for its maintenance." This provision, historian Carl Parrini wrote, was directed "at America's co-belligerents, not its enemies."[39]

THE POISON OF BOLSHEVISM

Wilson is most often remembered for saying that "the world must be made safe for democracy."[40] As historian Arthur Link pointed out, Wilson did not mean that "the war was one for democracy. . . . He never deluded himself into thinking that the United States and the Allies were fighting for the same objectives."[41] But Wilson believed that in the long run, the world would have to choose between the ideal of imperialism and the ideal of democracy, and he made no secret of which he preferred. He believed in the improvement of mankind by means of a "reformed and socially responsible democratic capitalism."[42] Broadly speaking, he believed in the worldwide spread of the kind of progressive capitalism that he and Theodore Roosevelt had championed in the United States and that Lloyd George had promoted in Great Britain. The question was how to bring it about.

Wilson thought that through mandates, countries could be nudged closer to self-government, but his experience in Mexico had convinced him that the United States could not simply impose its system on other countries. In the draft of an address in 1916, he wrote, "It does not lie with the American people to dictate to another people what their government shall be or what use shall be made of their resources, what laws or rules they have, or what person they should encourage or favor."[43] He would apply this same principle to the Russian Revolution of 1917.

The revolution began in February 1917, and reached its climax in October with the seizure of power by Lenin's Bolshevik party. Wilson despised Bolshevism, describing it in his talk aboard the *George Washington* as a "poison."[44] Russia, he said later, had "come out of one tyranny to get into a worse."[45] But he resisted entreaties of the French and English to send an armed force to overthrow the Bolsheviks. When British envoy William Wiseman asked him why he was not participating in the allied talks on Russian intervention, Wilson replied, "My policy regarding Russia is very similar to my Mexican policy. I believe in letting them work out their own salvation, even though they wallow in anarchy for a while."[46]

When France's Marshall Foch submitted his intervention plan to the peace talk's Council of Four in March 1919, Wilson responded, "In my opinion, trying to stop a revolutionary movement by troops in the field is like using a broom to hold back a great ocean."[47] Wilson finally agreed to send troops to Siberia to aid Czech soldiers who were trying to make their way to the Pacific Ocean, and to block the Japanese from seizing territory, but Americans remained neutral in the revolutionary war. As Wilson recognized, the British and French stood no chance whatsoever of overthrowing the Bolsheviks in Russia. What the two nations stood a good chance of doing was setting in motion a train of fear, resentment, and misunderstanding that would last into the 1930s and contribute to the failure of Britain and France to secure the Soviet Union's support against the greater Nazi threat.

Wilson and Lloyd George, who were committed to social reform at home, also insisted that the Bolshevik philosophy was directed at genuine social and economic injustices, which, if not corrected in the wake of the war, would lead to continued spread of the "poison." Wilson told the Inquiry aboard the *George Washington,* "The only way I can explain susceptibility of the people of Europe to the poison of Bolshevism is that their governments have been run for the wrong purposes, and I am convinced that if this peace is not made on the highest principles of justice, it will be swept away by the peoples of the world in less than a generation."[48] According to his personal physician, who accompanied him to the peace talks, Wilson condemned the Bolsheviks' "campaign of murder, confiscation, and complete disregard for law" but insisted that "some of their doctrines have been developed entirely through the pressures of the capitalists, who have disregarded the rights of the workers everywhere."[49]

THE LEAGUE OF NATIONS

While Wilson didn't believe the United States could single-handedly transform the world into a global democracy, he believed that by means of the League of Nations, the United States could help to create a new world of freely trading independent nations. The League would "establish the independence and protect the integrity of the weak peoples of the world."[50] Wilson was initially vague about how the League could do this, but by May of 1919, he had settled on the idea of the small council of Great Powers within the League—similar to what would later be the United Nations Security Council—that could use the power of sanctions to enforce the provisions of the League's covenant. In a secret plenary session in May 1919, Wilson acknowledged that "the Great Powers, by virtue of their military and economic strength, must necessarily bear the chief burden of maintaining the peace of the world."[51]

But would the Great Powers work cooperatively toward this end? Why wouldn't the same conflicts reemerge? As he arrived in Europe in December 1918 and in Paris the next month, Wilson believed that as a result of the war, the nations would abandon the older *Machtpolitik* for a new ethic of democracy and equal rights. In Great Britain, on the eve of the peace conference, Wilson said that what the world is now seeking to do is to return to the paths of duty, to turn away from the savagery of interest to the dignity of the performance of right. And I believe that as this war had drawn the nations temporarily together in a combination of physical force, we shall now be drawn together in a combination of moral force that will be irresistible . . . it is the conscience of the world that we are trying to place upon the throne that others would usurp.[52]

Wilson's concept of the "conscience of the world," like his idea of the covenant, had its roots in Presbyterian, and more broadly Protestant, theology. In lectures on international law at Princeton, Wilson had argued that Christian belief in the brotherhood of man laid the basis for a "universal conscience of mankind." [53] His optimism that this consciousness was emerging was probably inspired by his own popularity in Europe. And it would also be partly vindicated by the very fact that French, British, and Italian and large parts of American opinion were willing to contemplate some kind of collective security through an international organization. But Wilson's faith in a league, working through the conscience of the world, lacked foundation in 1919.

Wilson correctly saw that for the great powers to create an enduring peace, they would have to dismantle the structure of imperialism, including their own colonial possessions. But Britain, France, Italy, and Japan were clearly unwilling to do this—they wanted, if anything, to expand their empires at the expense of Germany and Austria-Hungary. And the United States was not strong enough, nor, as Wilson would discover, determined and united enough in its purpose, to force them to do so. There was no basis yet for united action through an international organization, and the mere existence of a League of Nations would not force the issue. Wilson would confront, but not necessarily accept or absorb, these unhappy truths in the bitter and protracted negotiations that followed.

A NEW HOLY ALLIANCE

When Wilson came to Paris, he was confident that he could have his way with his fellow victors. He had written House, "England and France have not the same views with regard to peace that we have by any means. When the war is over, we can force them to our way of thinking, because by that time they will among other things be financially in our hands."[54] But in 1919, England and France still had their empires intact and could look forward to enlarging them at Germany's and Turkey's expense; and the American military, while vastly stronger than it had been before the war, did not tower over that of its co-belligerents. Moreover, America was still seen as the new kid on the block. Before 1890, only Great Britain had seen fit to station an ambassador in Washington.

In the immediate aftermath of the war, Wilson probably suffered from the same illusions of omnipotence that McKinley and the Republicans had experienced after the "splendid little war" against Spain. Anything seemed possible. But as it turned out, almost nothing was. With Britain's support, Wilson won on some important issues—he was able to keep France from annexing the German Saar region or from turning the German Rhineland into an independent state and was able to prevent Italy from gobbling up Croatian Fiume—but he lost, and lost badly, on the key issues he had brought with him from America.

There was nothing about trade barriers, free trade, or the open door in the League covenant. If anything, America's fellow victors, and later America itself, were moving in the opposite direction. Even more telling, there was nothing about self-determination in the final League document. Not simply the words, but the concept itself was excised from the final draft. The system of mandates remained, but only in name. The victorious powers themselves held the mandates. When Wilson asked Australian prime minister Billy Hughes whether he planned to treat formerly German New Guinea as an annexed colony, Hughes replied irreverently, "That's about the size of it, Mr. President."[55] Margaret Macmillan writes of the mandates, "The mandatory powers sent in annual reports to the League but otherwise went their own way."[56]

Wilson suffered his worst defeat on the Japanese acquisition of Shandong, the prized Chinese peninsula that Germany had occupied before World War I and that Japan seized soon after the war had begun. During the war, Japan had coerced the Chinese government into signing a treaty granting it control of Shandong, and at the peace talks, Japan threatened to walk out if its agreement with the Chinese was not honored. Wilson, fearful that a walkout by Japan, coming on the heels of Italy's angry departure over Fiume, would discredit the League and the final peace treaty, assented to their continued control of Shandong. Wilson told his physician, Admiral Cary Grayson, "It is the best that could be accomplished out of a dirty past."[57] But Wilson's abdication on Shandong opened him to charges of hypocrisy from the Italians and to the betrayal of principle from progressives in the United States.

Wilson gave in to the Allies on trade and self-determination, because he thought he had gotten them to agree to a core provision committing the League to "respect and preserve as against external aggressions the territorial integrity and existing political independence of all members of the league." Wilson himself read this Article Ten of the League covenant as striking "at the taproot of war" in opposition to "the very things that have always been sought in imperialistic wars."[58] And it was backed by compulsory sanctions if, in disregard of the League's arbitration process, a country went to war. But progressive critics read it as committing the United States to protecting the imperialist status quo from disruption. How, for instance, would the possibility of American aid to Ireland's anticolonial movement be understood? *The Dial,* a popular progressive magazine, editorialized that Article Ten seemed "in effect to validate existing empires." Writing in *The Nation,* Hobson called the League itself a "new Holy Alliance" of the five great powers. The noted political economist Thorstein Veblen called it "an instrument of Realpolitik, created in the image of nineteenth-century imperialism."[59]

At the peace talks, Wilson had thought he could get what he wanted. Then, when he failed, he rationalized these defeats by imagining that once the League began to function, its very existence, and the presence of American leadership, would inspire nations to remedy defects in the initial covenant. After one setback on self-determination, he told House, "At least, House, we are saving the Covenant, and that instrument will work wonders, bring the blessing of peace, and then when the war psychosis has abated, it will not be difficult to settle all the disputes that baffle us now."[60] He told William Howard Taft that he was not worried about nations seceding from the League, predicting a time "when men would be just as eager partisans of the sovereignty of mankind as they were now of their own national sovereignty."[61]

What he brought back to the States in July 1919 was a treaty and the plan for an organization that was at best a shadow of his own early intentions. Perhaps, if the United States had been willing to put its economic and military power behind Article Ten, and to insist that it be interpreted as Wilson intended, the League might have impeded, if not halted, the col-lapse of the peace in the 1930s. But Wilson faced a different, but no less adamant, opposition to his principles when he returned home. If Europe was not ready for Wilson's concept of collective security, neither were the Republicans who controlled the United States Senate.

ROOSEVELT AND LODGE

Theodore Roosevelt did not live to see the final text of the League's covenant. He died in January 1919 just as the peace talks were beginning. Roosevelt had turned against Wilson's presidency when Wilson failed to back Huerta in Mexico and when he offered Colombia an indemnity for the United States having seized the Panama Canal zone. But at the beginning of the war, Roosevelt had taken the same kind of neutral stance as Wilson. He wrote immediately after the German invasion of Belgium, "We have not the smallest responsibility for what has befallen her."[62] He questioned the usefulness of a balance of power and called for a new international organ-ization. But by late autumn 1914, he began to turn against the adminis-tration, and by the next year was vigorously denouncing it.

Some of Roosevelt's criticisms were both predictable and justifiable. He attacked the administration for neglecting the country's ability to go to war if it was forced to do so. Roosevelt wrote in 1915, "Surely one does not have to read history very much or ponder over philosophy a great deal in order to realize the truth that the one certain way to invite disaster is to be opulent, offensive, and unarmed."[63] Wilson, who was hamstrung by paci-fists in his own party, didn't begin to accelerate military spending until 1916. But Roosevelt also harshly rejected Wilson's strategy for "peace without victory." He had come to see the war as a simple contest between good and evil. When Wilson, having led the country into war, offered his Fourteen Points a year later, Roosevelt was contemptuous of him for his failure to "stand by France, England, and our other allies."[64] Wrote Roosevelt, "Let us dictate peace by the hammering guns and not chat about peace with the accompaniment of the clicking of typewriters."[65]

After the Armistice, Roosevelt proposed that the United States continue its wartime alliance with Britain and France in lieu of a League of Nations. He said the United States should "avoid the position of an international

Meddlesome Matty."[66] He rejected Wilson's internationalism for the nationalism of the League opponents. He attacked "professional internationalists" as "a sorry crew" who appeal to "weaklings, illusionists, materialists, lukewarm Americans, and faddists of all types that vitiate sound nationalism." "I am insisting upon Nationalism against Internationalism," he wrote Beveridge.[67] He wanted a powerful America, in alliance with Britain, to defend righteousness against the forces of evil and disorder. His was a vision of America's mission, but it was focused primarily on Armageddon, not on the thousand years that would follow.

Republican senator Henry Cabot Lodge went even farther than Roosevelt in opposing Wilson, even making common cause with Republican treaty opponents who would later become isolationists. Citing Article Ten, he accused Wilson of substituting "an international state for pure Americanism" and for wanting to "move away from George Washington to . . . the sinister figure of Trotsky, the champion of internationalism."[68] Both Lodge and Roosevelt succumbed to partisanship and to raw hatred of Wilson, and Lodge's behavior as chairman of the Senate Foreign Relations Committee would resemble that of the conservative Republicans of the late 1990s who put partisan concerns above any semblance of national interest. When the hearings on the League's treaty began in July 1919, Lodge demonstrated his contempt for the treaty by spending the first two weeks reading all 246 pages of it aloud to the Senate. He filled the witness list with the treaty's harshest critics, and put forth 46 Republican amendments, which would have eliminated American obligations toward the League.

But Lodge and the other men who, in the 1890s, had advocated for the United States to join the worldwide scramble for colonies did not oppose the treaty on behalf of an American imperialism. Roosevelt, Lodge, and Beveridge now referred to themselves as "nationalists." Beveridge called for "a pure and exclusive nationalism versus mongrel and promiscuous internationalism."[69] And in opposing the treaty, Lodge happily joined forces with senators like Wisconsin's Robert La Follette who opposed it because it failed to live up to the anti-imperialist spirit of Wilson's Fourteen Points. Indeed, the amendments that Lodge backed would include those directed at Japanese and British imperialism.

THE IDEAL OF DEMOCRACY

Facing a determined opposition, Wilson set out in September 1919 on a speaking tour designed to rally support for the league. Wilson spoke extemporaneously without a microphone to crowds that sometimes numbered in the thousands. He often had to shout. He was also afflicted by sleeplessness and by severe headaches that were a prelude to his collapse at the end of the month. Wilson was a great orator who, like Jefferson, Lincoln, and Roosevelt, wrote his own speeches. His addresses during his first term as president or during the war itself were models of eloquence and articulation, but in his defense of the treaty to the Senate and during these last, difficult speeches, Wilson ventured onto the mountain heights where Jonathan Edwards, Jefferson, and Lincoln (at the very end of his life) had also journeyed. He tried to spell out a vision of the American mission and of the millennium.

Wilson saw America's unique role as being a "mediator" that would establish the basis for universal peace and prosperity. He attributed this role not to America's Anglo-Saxon or Protestant heritage, but to its being a nation of immigrants that included the blood of all nations. Said Wilson, "This nation was created to be the mediator of people, because it draws its blood from every civilized stock in the world and is ready by sympathy and understanding to understand the peoples of the world."[70] As mediator, the United States was ready to lead the world toward the "ideal of democracy" and away from the "ideal of imperialism." Wilson spelled out this ideal of democracy, and its origin in the founding of the United States, in Billings, Montana, on September 11. The fundamental idea of the League, Wilson said,

> had its birth and has had its growth in this country, that the countries of the world belong to the people who live in them, and that they have a right to determine their own destiny, and their own form of government and their own policy, and that no body of statesmen, sitting anywhere, no matter whether they represent the overwhelming physical force of the world or not, has the right to assign any great people to a sovereignty under which it does not care to live.[71]

Wilson's vision of the world was the United States writ large. The nations of the world would eventually form a federal system under the League of Nations, or its successor, in which nations, like individuals, would enjoy the benefits of equal rights regardless of their size and strength. They would be bound together by a written "covenant" expressing the "conscience of the world."

Wilson's deepest appeal was moral. It reflected his conviction that "America is the only national idealistic force in the world, and idealism is going to save the world. Selfishness will embroil it."[72] But Wilson also made his case for a new global democracy on grounds of interest and selfishness. He said in St. Paul, "If you say, 'Why should we rehabilitate the world?' I will not suggest any altruistic motive; but if you want to trade you have got to have somebody to trade with . . . if the business of the world lags, your industries lag and your prosperity lags."[73] In another speech in St. Louis, Wilson assured his audience that within a peaceful world without economic barriers between nations, America's native ingenuity and productivity would ensure its prosperity: "Now, let us mix the selfish with the unselfish. . . . If we are partners, let me predict we will be the senior partner. The financial leadership will be ours. The industrial primacy will be ours. The commercial advantage will be ours. The other countries of the world are looking to us for leadership and direction."[74]

Wilson posed the alternatives in terms of what America would look like under the ideal of democracy and the ideal of imperialism. Under the ideal of democracy, it would enjoy peace and prosperity, but under the ideal of imperialism, it would be burdened by the constant threat of war. If the United States were to abandon the League and the efforts to bind other nations together in a commitment to peace, Wilson warned,

> it means that we shall arm as Germany was armed, that we shall submit our young men to the kind of constant military service that the young men of Germany were subjected to. It means that we shall pay not lighter but heavier taxes. It means that we shall trade in a world in which we are suspected and watched and disliked, instead of in a world which is now ready to trust us, ready to follow our leadership, ready to receive our traders, along with our political representatives, as friends, as men who are welcome, as men who bring goods and ideas for which the world is ready and for which the world has been waiting.[75]

Wilson's speeches during this last journey were met with sustained applause. And while scientific opinion polls did not yet exist, historians estimate that about a half to two thirds of Americans backed Wilson and the League at that point. The decision to ratify the treaty, however, rested in the Republican-controlled Senate, where Lodge as Senate Majority Leader and head of the Foreign Relations Committee could tilt the debate against it. In his first term, Wilson might have been able to subdue or out-flank his opponents as he did on the tariff. But as the treaty came up for discussion, Wilson lay crippled by a stroke in his bed.[76] He could neither outmaneuver nor negotiate with Lodge.

The League provided an easy target for its Republican opponents. Lodge converted the forty-six amendments into fourteen reservations to the treaty. Some of these were reasonable—for instance, reserving the right of Congress to decide upon the commitment of the United States to war—but others were not—such as one exempting the United States from the obli-gation to pay its dues to the league. When Wilson refused to compromise with Lodge, Senate Democrats, joined by a few Republicans, were able to defeat the reservations. But the treaty's backers didn't have the two-thirds vote to pass the treaty without reservations, and Wilson was not willing to make any compromises with its critics. This was a political failure, but Wil-son's intransigence was also based in his understanding of the treaty. If the League were to work, the United States had to play a leading role. Writes his-torian Frank Ninkovich, "For Wilson, American membership without American *leadership* was of little value."[77] What the reservations did was con-sign the United States to the sidelines of international politics.

Wilson survived until 1924—long enough to see the new Republican administration elected in 1920 abandon much of his foreign policy, includ-ing the pledge to grant independence to the Philippines. When he died, his friend Frederick Jackson Turner said, "Fate has dealt hardly with him, but Time, the great restorer, and, let us believe, History, will do him jus-tice."[78] That would certainly be the case. While Wilson's attempt to refor-mulate America's foreign policy would fail to win the assent of his own country or of Europeans in 1919 and 1920, it would be revived during World War II and the Cold War. And to the extent that Americans would follow Wilson's approach—addressing the structural causes of war, includ-ing colonialism and protectionism—they would enjoy remarkable success over the remainder of the century.

Even by 1921, when Wilson left the presidency, he had already revolutionized American foreign policy. Roosevelt had quietly abandoned the project of imperial expansion that he had advocated as a young assistant secretary of the navy, but Wilson had made explicit what was merely implicit in Roosevelt's actions. Americans would differ over the next decades as to how zealously they should attempt to dismantle other nations' empires, but no president for the remainder of the twentieth century would advocate the growth of an American empire. Wilson had finally laid that alternative to rest. Wilson also redefined the American millennium. Prior to Wilson, American presidents including McKinley and Roosevelt and American intellectuals like Mahan, Strong, and Fiske had defined the American objective in terms of race and religion. It was to create a "Christian civilization" dominated by Anglo-Saxons. With Wilson, America became understood as a multiethnic nation, the American ideal became defined as democracy, and America's goal abroad became creating a world of democracies.

CHAPTER SIX

Franklin Roosevelt
and the Four Freedoms

In 1919, a young assistant secretary of the navy wangled his way to Paris at the beginning of the peace talks. When he was called back to Washington that February, he traveled on the *George Washington* with Woodrow Wilson, who, carrying a draft of the Covenant of the proposed League of Nations, was coming home for a brief visit. Franklin Roosevelt, a nephew of Theodore Roosevelt, saw himself following in his uncle's footsteps, but he was a Democrat, and a member of the Wilson administration. During the trip aboard the *George Washington,* Wilson had lunch with Roosevelt and his wife, Eleanor, and invited Roosevelt to his cabin to explain the Covenant of the League. "The United States must go in or it will break the heart of the world, for she is the only nation that all feel is disinterested and all trust," Wilson told Roosevelt.[1]

Roosevelt was dazzled, and when he disembarked in New York, counted himself a champion of the new League. In 1920, when he was nominated as Ohio governor James Cox's vice presidential running mate, he focused his campaign on attacking Republicans for blocking its ratification. "Modern civilization," he would declare in his acceptance speech at the Democratic convention, "has become so complex and the lives of civilized men so interwoven with the lives of other men in other countries as to make it impossible to be in this world and not of it."[2]

In his campaign, however, Roosevelt discovered that while the voters liked him, they had lost their early enthusiasm for Wilson's League. Wrote Roosevelt's advance man during the campaign, "The bitterness toward Wilson is evident everywhere and deeply rooted."[3] Cox and his running mate were routed by the ticket headed by Ohio Republican senator Warren Harding, who campaigned on a promise of a "return to normalcy." And over the next twelve years, Harding and his Republican successors would repudiate much of Wilson's foreign policy. The Republicans would reaffirm the policy of narrow nationalism and high tariffs that Republicans had advocated earlier.

Franklin Roosevelt would become president in 1932 in the wake of the Great Depression, and would enjoy a Democratic Congress over his four terms, but in the face of widespread public indifference to the rest of the world, he would have to suppress or muffle his Wilsonian internationalism. Even after Germany had begun to swallow up Europe and Japan and much of Asia, many Americans believed that they would not be affected. Only after the Japanese bombed Pearl Harbor in December 1941, and Germany declared war on the United States, did the country fully awaken to the threat it faced. At that point, Roosevelt, who had been quietly preparing the country for war since 1939, embraced publicly many of the principles that he had learned when he served in the Wilson administration. He would revive Wilson's internationalism, including his attempt to dismantle imperialism through new international institutions.

THE ISOLATIONISTS

During the 1920s, Americans recoiled from the memory of World War I and from Wilson's policies in Paris. While the Republicans in office implicitly endorsed Wilson's opposition to an American imperialism, they made no effort to dismantle the international structure of imperialism. They were willing to negotiate specific arms reductions and modifications in Germany's reparation payments, but they resisted any association with the League of Nations. The Harding administration even refused to answer mail from the League's office in Geneva. America's principal focus was economic. Declared Herbert Hoover, who, before becoming president, served as secretary of commerce, "The dominant fact of this last century has been economic development. And it continues today as the force which dominates the whole spiritual, social and political life of our country and the world."[4] One of the best-selling books of the 1920s was Bruce Barton's novel *The Man Nobody Knows,* about Jesus' returning to earth as a businessman. Its implicit message was that Americans and the world would seek their salvation through economic success.

Wilson had argued that discriminatory trade policies had helped stimulate the scramble for colonies, but in 1922, the Republican Congress passed the Fordney-McCumber Tariff, repealing Wilson's 1913 reductions; and in 1930, the Republicans passed the infamous Smoot-Hawley Treaty that hiked duties on nine hundred products. Smoot-Hawley is often blamed for deepening the depression of the 1930s. But its more important effect may have been on the struggle for imperial supremacy. By closing off the world's largest market, Smoot-Hawley encouraged other countries to create imperial trading blocs. The British cited Smoot-Hawley to justify erecting tariff walls around their colonies and dominions in a 1932 agreement in Ottawa. The Germans could cite it in 1936 to justify creating economic self-sufficiency through expansion in central Europe; and the Japanese to justify their Greater East Asia Co-Prosperity Sphere.

During the 1920s, the Republican administrations did not completely abandon the attempt to achieve a lasting peace, but they adopted the methods of William Jennings Bryan rather than Wilson. Bryan had advocated that countries sign arbitration treaties with each other promising not to go to war without prior negotiation and mediation. Bryan believed the power of conscience could render the strength of arms irrelevant. Wilson had tolerated and sometimes applauded Bryan's compulsive treaty-making, but during and after World War I, he rejected antiwar initiatives that could not be backed up by the threat of force. He warned an antiwar group in 1916 that "a nation which, by the standards of other nations, however mistaken those standards may be, is regarded as helpless, is apt in general counsel to be regarded as negligible."[5] But the Republican administrations of the 1920s took their lead from Bryan. In 1928, American secretary of state Frank Kellogg and French foreign minister Aristide Briand began soliciting the signatures on a pact outlawing war as an instrument of national policy. Sixty-five nations, including Germany, signed the Kellogg-Briand Pact. "Public opinion will suffice to check violence," declared Hoover.[6]

But public opinion proved impotent in the face of the continuing struggle for world supremacy. The terms of the Paris peace had not only failed to dismantle the structure of imperialism, but had inspired a new, even more disastrous, contest for territory. In the 1930s, Hitler's Germany sought to recoup its losses at Versailles, while Italy and Japan sought to build on their gains. Declared Italian dictator Benito Mussolini, "The tendency toward imperialism is one of the elementary trends of human nature, an expression of the will to power."[7] Three years after the Kellogg-Briand Pact, Japan, one of the signatories, seized Manchuria from China. In 1935, Italy went to war with Ethiopia. In 1936, Germany moved into the Rhineland. And the next year, Japan invaded China. Aboard the *George Washington,* Wilson had warned the members of the Inquiry, "I am convinced that if this peace is not made on the highest principles of justice, it will be swept away by the peoples of the world in less than a generation . . . there will follow more than mere conflict but cataclysm."[8] That is exactly what would happen.

Yet Wilson's perspective was lost through much of the 1930s as well as the 1920s. He had argued in 1914 that "an attack in any quarter was an attack on the equilibrium of the world," but even as German tanks rolled across Poland, a majority of Americans continued to discount the prospect of war. There were exceptions, but many Americans turned in the mid- and late 1930s from a narrow nationalism to what is properly called "isolationism." They drew back from any political and military entanglements. They wanted nothing to do with the rest of the world, and particularly Europe, and didn't appear to care what happened to it. In 1935, the Senate passed 79 to 2 a Neutrality Act forbidding the shipment of arms or loans to belligerents in the case of war. When Roosevelt suggested that same year, which was probably the height of his political popularity and power, that the United States join the World Court at the Hague, he was peremptorily turned down. "To Hell with Europe and with the rest of those nations," Minnesota Republican senator Thomas D. Schall responded.[9]

The Americans of the 1930s were like the Fundamentalists who organized churches at the beginning of the century in reaction to Darwin and the Protestant Social Gospel. The Fundamentalists were premillennialists who sought salvation not by creating a Kingdom of God on Earth but by withdrawing from mankind to achieve piety on their own in preparation for the Second Coming. The isolationists were the secular equivalent; they withdrew from the rest of the world to seek salvation in the midst of the conflagration around them.

AMERICAN CENTURY

Many of Roosevelt's top foreign policy appointees, including Secretary of State Cordell Hull, Undersecretary of State Sumner Welles, and Secretary of the Treasury Henry Morgenthau, were ardent Wilsonians. But during his first five years in office, Roosevelt, distracted by the Great Depression and constrained by popular opinion, failed to challenge the public's support for isolationism. In 1936, he declared, "We are not isolationists except in so far as we seek to isolate ourselves completely from war."[10] It was only after the Japanese invasion of China that Roosevelt began a campaign to win public support for intervention.

In October 1937, Roosevelt called for a "quarantine of aggressor nations." Echoing Wilson's warnings about indivisibility of conflict in the modern world, Roosevelt warned that even though "we are determined to keep out of war, yet we cannot insure ourselves against the disastrous effects of war and the dangers of involvement."[11] Roosevelt's speech caused outcries of "warmonger." Finally, with the election of 1940 behind him and with the Battle of Britain in full swing, Roosevelt came out unequivocally for aiding the allies against Germany, Italy, and Japan. In a December 29, 1940, Fireside Chat, Roosevelt called for America to become "an arsenal for democracy" by sending military aid to Britain against the "unholy alliance" of the axis nations.[12] He framed the war in Europe and Asia as "democracy's fight against world conquest."[13]

A week later, he invoked America's special role in the world in justifying intervention. "Since the beginning of our American history, we have been engaged in . . . a perpetual peaceful revolution," Roosevelt declared. "The world order which we seek is the cooperation of free countries, working together in a friendly civilized society." Roosevelt described a world founded upon "four essential human freedoms . . . freedom of speech . . . freedom of every person to worship God in his own way . . . freedom from want [and] freedom from fear." It was the New Deal ideal projected onto the world. Roosevelt added, "That is no vision of a distant millennium," but it was an updated vision of the civil millennialism that underlay American foreign policy.

Roosevelt was an inspired orator, but at the time, the most dramatic and memorable statement of America's mission in the world came from *Time-Life* founder Henry Luce. In an essay entitled "The American Century" published in *Life* in February 1941, Luce called on America to assume active world leadership.[14] "In the field of national policy," Luce wrote, "the fundamental trouble with America has been, and is, that whereas their nation became in the 20th century the most powerful and the most vital nation in the world, nevertheless Americans were unable to accommodate themselves spiritually and practically to that fact. Hence they have failed to play their part as a world power—a failure which has had disastrous consequences for themselves and for all mankind."[15]

Luce, the son of Protestant missionaries in China, framed the task of leadership in frankly evangelical terms. "We have some things in this country which are infinitely precious and especially American—a love of freedom, a feeling for the equality of opportunity, a tradition of self-reliance and independence and also of co-operation," Luce wrote. "It now becomes our time to be the powerhouse from which the ideas spread throughout the world and do their mysterious work of lifting the life of mankind from the level of beasts to what the Psalmist called a little lower than the angels."[16] Luce's essay was widely quoted during the war, and his conception of the American Century was used repeatedly to describe America's mission and its importance in the world.

THE LIBERATION OF PEOPLES

Roosevelt defined the war as a struggle between good and evil—"between those who believe in mankind and those who do not"—but like Wilson, he did not allow this vision of Armageddon to cloud his understanding of the underlying causes of war and of what was necessary to prevent future wars.[17] Roosevelt and the Wilsonians who dominated his foreign policy team certainly believed that Hitler, Mussolini, and Japan's Hideki Tojo were responsible for starting World War II, but they also believed that the imperial structure of the international political economy had made war inevitable. "The colonial system means war," Roosevelt said in Casablanca in 1942 after a disturbing stopover in the British colony of Gambia before his meeting with British prime minister Winston Churchill.[18] At the meeting, Roosevelt railed against European imperialism. Afterward, he told his son Elliott, "Don't think for a moment, Elliott, that Americans would be dying in the Pacific tonight, if it hadn't been for the shortsighted greed of the French and the British and the Dutch."[19]

Sumner Welles, who had grown up with Roosevelt and often echoed his sentiments, saw the scramble for colonies creating a contest between "have" and "have not" states. "With few exceptions there has been exploitation by European powers with very little if any advantage to the peoples concerned. The control by those powers made possible the argument that some powers control all the sources of the world and that other powers are have-nots."[20] In the State Department, Welles led a planning group, including several veterans of Wilson's Inquiry, to devise a strategy for ending imperialism after the war. Said Welles, "If this war is in fact a war for the liberation of peoples it must assure the sovereign equality of peoples throughout the world, as well as in the world of the Americas. Our victory must bring in its train the liberation of all peoples. Discrimination between peoples because of their race, creed or color must be abolished. The age of imperialism is over."[21]

To eliminate imperialism, Roosevelt and Welles favored a plan to create a system of colonial trusteeships that they saw as "an extension of the mandate principle" that Wilson had advocated in Paris.[22] They wanted all the colonies placed under trustees who would be responsible to a new international organization, the United Nations. Explained Welles, "The liberation of peoples should be the main principle. Many of these peoples cannot undertake self-government at this time. This is where trusteeship comes in. The UN should endeavor to develop the ability of these peoples to govern themselves as soon as possible."[23] Welles proposed that the United Nations appoint "a citizen of some disinterested country—perhaps a Swede or a Swiss" to administer a country like Korea until it was ready for self-government.[24] It was Wilson's plan right down to the Swedish administrator.

The U.N. itself would be modeled on the League of Nations, with a Security Council dominated by the Great Powers and a General Assembly of all member states. The most important, and fateful, difference was that each of the four, and later five, permanent Great Powers on the Security Council would be granted a veto over decisions. Like Wilson, Roosevelt rested his hopes for its success on agreement among the Great Powers. In 1943, reporter Forrest Davis, granted extensive interviews with the president, recounted Roosevelt's views on the new organization. Wrote Davis, "The President holds that a genuine association of interest on the part of the great powers must precede the transformation of the United Nations' military alliance into a political society of nations."[25] In Roosevelt's mind, like Wilson's, the U.N. would eventually transform the balance of power into a community of power.*

Like Wilson, Roosevelt also saw protectionist trading and currency blocs as a cause of imperial conquest and rivalry and therefore of war. Roosevelt said in 1936, "Without a more liberal international trade, war is a natural sequence."[26] Hull made the same point in a 1938 speech: "I know that without expansion of international trade, based upon fair dealing and equal treatment for all, there can be no stability and security either within or among nations," Hull declared. "I know that the withdrawal by a nation from orderly trade relations with the rest of the world inevitably leads to regimentation of all phases of national life, to the suppression of human rights, and all too frequently, to preparations for war and a provocative attitude toward other nations."[27]

During the war, the State and Treasury Departments began devising plans for international organizations linked to the U.N. that would guarantee an open trading system and a stable international currency. At the State Department, Undersecretary of State Will Clayton planned an International Trade Organization (ITO). Said Clayton, "It is quite impossible to obtain collective security throughout the world if economic warfare as it was waged throughout the world in the inter-war period is to continue."[28] At Treasury, Secretary Morgenthau put his chief economic adviser, Harry Dexter White, in charge of developing institutions that would oversee currency convertibility and industrial reconstruction. Said White, "Just as the failure to develop, League of Nations has made possible two devastating wars within one generation, so the absence of a high degree of economic collaboration among the leading nations will, during the coming decade, inevitably result in economic warfare that will be but the prelude and instigator of military warfare on an even vaster scale."[29]

---

*In interviews with Forrest Davis, Roosevelt implicitly contrasted his views of the U.N. with Wilson's views of the League, and historians have praised him for injecting "realism" into Wilson's approach. But there is little difference between the two men's conceptions. Wilson recognized that the Great Powers would dominate decision-making through the League's council. And he and Roosevelt both tragically overestimated the degree of unanimity that would prevail among the Great Powers and therefore the effectiveness of the organizations themselves.

THE FOLLY OF EMPIRE

BRETTON WOODS

In 1942, Morgenthau and White introduced a plan for what was originally called a United Nations Stabilization Fund and a Bank for Reconstruction of the United and Associated Nations. After negotiations, primarily between White and British economist John Maynard Keynes, forty-three nations, meeting in Bretton Woods, New Hampshire, agreed, in July 1944, to establish two institutions, the International Monetary Fund (IMF) and the International Bank for Recovery and Development (IBRD, later simply called the "World Bank"). Their purpose, the plan originally stated, was "to prevent disruption of foreign exchanges and the collapse of monetary and credit systems; to assure the restoration of foreign trade; and to supply the huge volume of capital that will be needed virtually throughout the world for reconstruction, relief and for economic recovery."[30] But their broader purpose was to create the economic conditions for an enduring peace. By putting debt relief and development assistance in the hands of international institutions, the plan removed a principal means by which imperial powers had won control over the finances of Asian, African, and Latin American nations. Historian Carl Parrini writes that during the heyday of Western imperialism

> governments and bankers of the industrial countries used currency loans to developing countries as levers to obtain monopolistic investment outlets. The IMF neutralized this by giving U.S. and European governments mutual vetoes over one another's ability to do this. In similar fashion the IBRD was supposed to provide that [contracts for] infrastructure in the developing world would be parceled out on the basis of the Open Door of competitive bidding.[31]

In the Senate, Republican nationalists threatened to defeat the Bretton Woods Agreement. Ohio senator Robert Taft described the treaty as "pouring money down a rat hole" and complained that "no international body should have any jurisdiction over the domestic policies of the United States."[32] During Senate hearings, White responded to Taft's charges:

And if you say that we are not in control in the sense that we should be in a position to ram down the throats of every other country whatever the opinion of the United States should be, I say that is not in the Fund Agreement, and I say that the representatives of this country at Bretton Woods would be the first to insist that it should not be. After all, the Fund Agreement provides for an international institution, not machinery to impose our views on others.[33]

White's candid explanation of the treaty was perfectly consistent with Wilson's approach: the Roosevelt administration was seeking to fulfill its mission in the world through working cooperatively with other nations. But according to Richard Gardner, who wrote a definitive history of Bretton Woods, White's candor enflamed the Republican opposition. White and the administration had better luck when they argued that the treaty would help American business and when they explained how it would prevent wars. Said White: "I think history will look back and indict those who fail to vote the approval of the Bretton Woods proposals in the same way that we now look back and indict certain groups in 1921 who prevented our adherence to an international organization designed for the purpose of preventing wars."[34]

That argument won over a large group of undecided Republicans, and the treaty passed, 52 to 31, in July 1945. The IMF and World Bank began operation the next year. Over the next fifty years, the IMF would change the way it stabilized the world's currencies, and the World Bank would vastly expand its loans and broaden its scope. Yet both institutions have substantially the same purpose as before. Not normally considered part of foreign policy or part of Wilson's legacy, they are clear testimony to how the ideas of 1919 finally became realized after World War II. Both institutions have had their failures, but the world would have been less prosperous, and in some cases poorer and more dangerous, without them.

FREE TRADE

In 1943, the State Department began working on a plan for the International Trade Organization (ITO), based on the assumption, a department memo stated, that "a great expansion in volume of international trade after the war will be essential to the attainment of full and effective employment in the United States and elsewhere, to the preservation of private enterprise, and to the success of an international security system to prevent future wars."[35] The United States, the memo argued, was "the only nation capable of taking the initiative in promoting a worldwide movement toward the relaxation of trade barriers." In Wilsonian style, the U.S. would take the initiative in setting up a multilateral organization that would assume responsibility for removing trade and investment barriers and ending the kind of discriminatory trade agreements that had been a spur toward empire and war.

In 1948, with Harry Truman having succeeded Franklin Roosevelt, Clayton and his economic adviser Clair Wilcox brought back from international negotiations in Havana a treaty establishing the ITO. But with the Republicans now in control of the Senate and Taft the majority leader, the treaty faced stiff opposition. To make matters worse, business lobbies, who looked at the treaty narrowly from the standpoint of whether their individual members might be hurt by tariff reductions, joined the opposition. With business behind them, the Republicans bottled up the treaty in committee and kept it from ever coming to a vote. Without American support, the ITO was stillborn. Clair Wilcox lamented, "Too many are reluctant to admit that our foreign relations, whether political or economic, are indivisible."[36]

But Hull, Clayton, and Wilcox would eventually have the last laugh. In the fall of 1947, Clayton had brought together eighteen other countries in Geneva to agree to joint tariff reductions, with the United States dropping its tariffs to 1913 levels. This agreement, dubbed the General Agreement on Tariffs and Trade (GATT), was supposed to be incorporated into the ITO, but when the ITO died for lack of American support, GATT took on a life of its own. More countries joined the agreements, and the countries themselves, meeting in successive "rounds," slashed tariffs still further. GATT fulfilled an important part of the original function of the ITO. It was, like the IMF and World Bank, a triumph of the Wilsonian approach.

Roosevelt's fondest hopes were reserved for the new United Nations, which was supposed to incorporate the IMF, World Bank, and ITO. It was to be a "universal organization" that would replace the spheres of influence and empires that "have been tried for centuries—and have always failed."[37] It was supposed to deter potential aggressors from war and to oversee the dismantling of the older imperial system. Roosevelt died before the U.N.'s first meeting in San Francisco in June, but Truman had no trouble in winning Senate approval for the new organization. Even Republican isolationists, put on the defensive by charges that they had helped cause World War II by derailing the League of Nations, voted for the new organization.

The U.N. would enjoy considerable success over the next decades, but it would not turn out to be the universal organization Roosevelt had hoped for. Nor would it replace the older balance of power by a new all-embracing community of power. Instead, it would find itself subsumed, and sometimes consumed, by the Cold War that would break out between the United States and the Soviet Union. Wilsonian principles would endure during the Cold War, but not in the form that Roosevelt, or for that matter Wilson, had anticipated.

CHAPTER SEVEN

Cold War Liberalism
from Truman to Reagan

In the winter of 1919, Woodrow Wilson worried that conflict among the victors of World War I, and between them and the vanquished, would derail the League of Nations. He didn't worry so much about the Republicans in Congress, nor about the new Soviet Union. He saw the Soviet Union as Mexico writ large—a nation that was in the throes of a profound revolution and a nation that, if restrained in its external ambitions, might eventually become a member of the League's community. During World War II, Franklin Roosevelt, impressed by the Soviet contribution to the war and by Stalin's amiability at Teheran and Yalta, became convinced that the Soviet Union would become a member in good standing of the new United Nations.

Roosevelt assumed that the Big Five in the Security Council—the United States, Great Britain, France, the Soviet Union, and China—would be able to reach agreement on critical questions in the same way that the Big Three had been able to do during World War II. And he saw, if anything, the prospect of growing agreement rather than conflict with the Soviet Union. According to Sumner Welles, Roosevelt adhered to the widely held belief that the United States and the Soviet Union were actually becoming similar—the United States more collectivist and the Soviet Union more democratic. Wrote Welles, "He regarded this trend as making it more likely that no fundamental conflict between the two countries need ever become inevitable, providing Soviet communism had permanently abandoned its doctrine of world revolution."[1]

But soon after Roosevelt died and the war ended, the two nations' paths diverged. With Germany and Japan defeated, sharp differences over the fate of Germany and eastern Europe began to divide the United States and Britain from the Soviet Union. By 1950, the United States and Soviet Union, armed with nuclear weapons, were staring at each across a divided Europe, and backing different sides in the Korean War. The Cold War had begun, and it would undermine Roosevelt's dreams of a united world organization. Roosevelt's successors would not abandon Wilson's approach to foreign policy, but they would have to adapt it to a divided world.

THE SOVIET CHALLENGE

After 1945, the United States faced two different challenges that appeared to be integrally related: containing the expansion of the Soviet Union and coming to grips with the continuing struggle in Asia, Africa, and Latin America against the vestiges of American and European colonialism. The United States and its allies would succeed admirably in meeting the Soviet challenge in Western Europe. But the United States would fail abysmally to understand the movements against imperialism in places like Vietnam, Guatemala, Cuba, and Egypt. Part of the problem lay in how the United States understood the Soviet threat, and part lay in how it understood the anti-imperialist movements that often identified with, or at least were supported by, the Soviet Union.

The Soviet Union was heir to an imperial *and* a millennial tradition.[2] The czars saw Russia not only as the seat of a large continental empire, but also as the "third Rome" of Christianity after Rome and Constantinople. The two ambitions overlapped with, and supplemented, each other, but were not identical in their reach. The Soviet Union's ambitions were very similar. As Marxists and advocates of national self-determination, the Bolsheviks repudiated Russia's imperial past, but in their behavior, they increasingly embraced its objectives. They granted cultural but not political autonomy to non-Russian nationalities in the Soviet Union, and later, in the Nazi-Soviet pact of 1940 and after World War II, Stalin sought to regain and expand upon the older Russian empire. Stalin's foreign minister Vyacheslav Molotov, who negotiated the Nazi-Soviet pact, would later write, "My task as minister of foreign affairs was to expand the borders of our fatherland."[3]

At the same time, Lenin, Stalin, and Nikita Khrushchev were committed Marxists who believed the Soviet revolution was the beginning of a new stage in world history that would lead to the worldwide victory of communism. The Soviet Union would become the "third Rome" of international communism. But the Soviet leaders did not conceive of world communism as a system of Soviet protectorates or colonies. The dream of world communism was not strictly the same as that of empire, although the two reinforced each other. Soviet territorial ambitions were limited; Soviet ideological ambitions were unlimited.

That was certainly the case after World War II. As a revolutionary Marxist, Stalin looked forward to the victory of world communism, but as the custodian of the Soviet empire, he was cautious in his foreign policy. He did not seek to provoke war with capitalist nations. After two wars, he was worried about a rearmed Germany, but at the time of Yalta in 1945, he does not seem to have envisaged a closed, Soviet-dominated system in eastern Europe, but a sphere of influence similar to the American sphere of influence in Latin America. He expected that the United States would withdraw from Europe after World War II as it had withdrawn after World War I and that the Soviet Union would enjoy military superiority on the European continent.

Stalin's outlook changed with the American explosion of the atomic bomb (which negated the Soviet advantage on the ground and made American withdrawal less meaningful) and with the American commitment to the Marshall Plan (which meant a revived Germany). Stalin became convinced that he had to create a buffer between the Soviet Union and the West. In Eastern Europe, he turned a sphere of influence into an empire as a means of obtaining military security. Stalin's former foreign minister Maxim Litvinov told a CBS correspondent in 1946 that the Soviet Union had adopted "the outmoded concept of security in terms of territory—the more you've got, the safer you are." A disillusioned Litvinov predicted that "the best [that] can be hoped for is a prolonged armed truce."[4]

The Soviet threat was not clearly understood. In an essay whose title gave the Cold War its name, columnist Walter Lippmann argued that the "Soviet Union is the successor of the Russian Empire and . . . Stalin is not only the heir of Marx and Lenin but also of Peter the Great, and the Czars of all the Russians," but some American officials, and much of the public, as well as the Soviets themselves, saw Cold War as being primarily a clash of millennial powers.[5] Americans saw the struggle as an Armageddon between the forces of good and evil. The Truman administration, eager to win support for the Marshall Plan and NATO, reinforced this view. "The earth is deeply divided between free and captive people," Truman declared. "And much as we trust in God, while He is rejected by so many in the world, we must trust in ourselves."[6] Truman summed up the challenge in a speech in Boston in October 1948: "Yesterday, the free peoples of the world were threatened by the black menace of fascism. The American people helped to save them. Today, the free peoples of the world are threatened by the red menace of communism. And again, the American people are helping to save them."[7]

As might be expected, this view of the clash lent itself to domestic repression of suspected communists, on the one hand, and, on the other hand, to impassioned pleas, especially on the political right, for the United States to use its nuclear weapons in a unilateral, preemptive strike against the Soviet Union.[8] It also encouraged a view of the communist movement as an undifferentiated monolith led by Moscow, when it was, in fact, a collection of competing and sometimes hostile movements and nations whose understanding of communism reflected their particular national circumstances. It blinded Americans to the difference between the challenges it faced in Europe from an expansionist Soviet Union and in Asia, Africa, and Latin America from a militant, and sometimes openly communist, but also deeply nationalist, anti-imperialism.

U.N. STALEMATE

The first casualty of the Cold War was the unanimity that Roosevelt had expected, and hoped for, at the United Nations. The Security Council, which was designed to be a forum in which the great powers would meet to resolve conflicts between lesser powers, became an arena of conflict between the great powers themselves. The Security Council and U.N. could function when the powers were not at odds—for instance, in establishing the partition of Palestine or encouraging Indonesian independence against the Dutch—but they were unable to deter major conflicts when, as often happened, the U.S. and Soviet Union found themselves backing opposing sides.

Matters were made worse by the American reaction to the Chinese Revolution. Roosevelt had insisted that China be one of the permanent members of the Security Council because he wanted a counterweight to Japan in Asia and because he thought Chiang Kai-shek's China would be a dependable ally of the United States on the council. When the Chinese communists defeated Chiang's armies in 1949 and took control of the country, they demanded China's seat on the Security Council. A year earlier, George Kennan and other State Department officials had argued for detaching the United States from Chiang, but the Republican-inspired outcry over "Who lost China?" strengthened the hand of those officials who saw Chinese communism as simply an arm of Soviet communism. Instead of recognizing the new government in Beijing, the United States insisted that Chiang's government, which had fled to Taiwan, continue to occupy China's seat on the council. This decision by the United States exacerbated the Cold War and undermined the legitimacy of the Security Council.

Roosevelt's plan to have the U.N. use a system of trusteeship to oversee the end of imperialism also fell victim not only to British and French intransigence but to the Cold War. Over objections from his War Department, which wanted to use Japan's islands in the Pacific as military bases, Roosevelt had insisted that the U.N. retain trusteeship over all "non-self-governing territories." But in January 1945 at Yalta, Roosevelt's secretary of state Edward Stettinius (who had replaced the ailing Hull) capitulated to Churchill when the British prime minister exploded at the suggestion that Britain's colonies be put under trusteeship.* He agreed that only former League of Nation mandates and colonies seized from the Axis powers during the war be placed under U.N. trusteeship. That severely limited the scope of the U.N.'s trusteeship system.

After Roosevelt's death, the Truman administration retreated even further. On the eve of the San Francisco conference, representatives from the Big Five quarreled over what the organization should demand of its members that still held colonies. The Soviet Union and China proposed that members of the U.N. commit themselves not only to "promote the well-being of the inhabitants" of their colonies, but that they also prepare them for eventual independence. The British and French vociferously objected to any mention of independence. A year earlier Roosevelt would have taken the

---

*Churchill had already resisted Roosevelt's arguments about colonialism during meetings off the coast of Newfoundland and at Casablanca and Teheran. When Wendell Willkie, visiting Britain in 1942 as Roosevelt's emissary, recommended independence for the British possessions, Churchill had responded publicly, "I have not become the King's First Minister in order to preside over the liquidation of the British empire."

Soviet side, but the Truman administration, already warily eyeing the Soviets, took the side of the British and French. They voted down the Russian and Chinese wording and engineered a compromise in which U.N. members committed themselves merely to developing "self-government."⁹

The U.S. didn't entirely abdicate its former position. By committing members with colonial possessions to reporting to the U.N. on the well-being of their inhabitants, the declaration opened the door to Security Council and General Assembly scrutiny of the colonial conflicts that would arise over the next four decades. But it removed from the U.N. and the Security Council any initiative in dismantling imperialism. The destruction of the older French, British, Italian, Dutch, and Portuguese empires, which Roosevelt had wanted to leave to the United Nations, became swept up in the Cold War.

CONTAINMENT AND NATO

The Truman administration and its successors fared far better in containing Soviet expansion in Europe. While it couldn't use the U.N. for this purpose, it adopted a strategy that reflected Wilson's general approach. It sought to save Europe and the world from communism not by acting on its own but by banding together with other countries that shared the same objective. It also didn't attempt to vanquish its adversaries at one stroke, but to create the conditions under which they might eventually turn away from communism toward a liberal reform capitalism. The American strategy of containment was a militant version of Wilson's "watchful waiting."

The key institution in this Cold War strategy was NATO, the North Atlantic Treaty Organization, which the United States, Canada, and ten European nations established in 1949. At first glance, NATO was a conventional alliance like the Entente of the early twentieth century. But it went well beyond a commitment to common defense. It established close military ties, including an integrated command structure, among the member countries and their armies, and it undermined the military, Prussian-style nationalism that had contributed to past wars. NATO was, in many respects, the kind of institution that Wilson had wanted the League, and Roosevelt had wanted the United Nations, to become. It was based, unlike the U.N. Security Council, on a "genuine association of interests."

NATO also rested on the common economic and political ties that the Marshall Plan had nourished. This included a commitment by the United States to helping liberal and social democratic movements in Europe that could promote a reform capitalism. Wrote Daniel Bell: "In the 1950s, the CIA, as a matter of government policy, decided to support and sustain a host of liberal and socialist international organizations, at a time when such organizations could not find the means to be self-sustaining, in order to strengthen opposition to Communist domination of certain milieus."[10] The policy, dubbed "Cold War liberalism," was the heir of Roosevelt's Four Freedoms and contributed to Europe's revival after World War II and Soviet communism's ultimate defeat.

The U.S. and NATO were remarkably successful in containing the Soviet Union in Europe. After NATO's founding, the Soviet empire failed to grow in Europe, and would be faced by periodic revolts and upheavals that would cause Soviet intervention. Communist parties in Western Europe also failed to gain ground.

THE THIRD WORLD

Where the United States had difficulty was in applying the lessons of 1919 to what came to be called the "third world." Many of the wars, revolutions, and uprisings that took place after World War II were directed against foreign colonial powers like the French in Algeria and Indochina or against regimes like those in Egypt, Iraq, and Cuba that were identified closely with or under the informal control of former colonial powers. As heirs of Wilson and Franklin Roosevelt, the liberal Democrats and Republicans who directed American foreign policy in the first decades after the war would have been expected to support these uprisings. But they were pulled in the opposite direction by their opposition to Soviet imperialism and by their identifying of these uprisings with their Soviet supporters.

Most of these movements were products of an indigenous nationalism that mimicked nineteenth-century European nationalism, but took root in response to the spread of Western imperialism. Third world nationalism was the child of first and second world imperialism. After World War I, many of these movements, facing opposition from the West, turned to the Soviet Union for support, and even identified themselves as "communist" or "socialist." But while their victory might have led to a government that called itself "communist," this government would not necessarily take its orders from Moscow or Beijing in the way that the governments in Rangoon or Manila had once taken their cues from colonial overseers. Indeed, many of these movements distrusted their Soviet and Chinese backers, and would later break with them. And if they remained allied to them, it was often because they were driven to do so by American hostility.

Most of America's allies distinguished these movements from the Soviet Union's international aspirations. Britain recognized China after the Civil War. French president Charles de Gaulle, after France's disastrous experiences in Algeria and Vietnam, recognized China and advised the United States to do likewise and not try to hold on to Vietnam as France had done. But Americans were blinded by their millennial vision—by their view of the Cold War as Armageddon in which there was no middle ground between good and evil. The result was a major setback for American foreign policy that probably prolonged the Cold War and cost several million lives.

America's opposition to these nationalist movements also created rampant hostility to the United States in Latin America, the Mideast, and Asia. Even if the United States wasn't trying to colonize countries, it was perpetuating a kind of foreign domination, and it became the last protector of international imperialism. Dwight Eisenhower, who was president from 1953 to 1961, recognized the problem. He fretted in 1954 that because of American support for the French in Indochina, "We should be everywhere accused of imperialistic ambitions."[11] After American setbacks in Egypt and Lebanon, Eisenhower advised his secretary of state, John Foster Dulles, to stop interpreting Arab nationalism as communism. Said Eisenhower, "Since we are about to get thrown out of the area, we might as well believe in Arab nationalism."[12] Indeed, the two clearest examples of how American foreign policy went awry during the Cold War were in Vietnam and in the Mideast.

THE VIETNAM WAR

In 1919, Ho Chi Minh, working in Paris as a kitchen hand at the Ritz, sent a petition to Woodrow Wilson for Vietnam's independence from France. Wilson never saw the petition, and the cause of Vietnam was ignored in

Versailles. But over the next two decades, Ho, working with other Vietnamese expatriates and the Indochinese Communist Party he founded, organized an independence movement to oust the French and the Japanese. In September 1945, after the Japanese left, Ho proclaimed Vietnam's independence at a ceremony attended by U.S. Army officers in which the "Star-Spangled Banner" was played and a declaration of independence modeled upon the American declaration was read. Vo Nguyen Giap, who would later lead Vietnam's armies, spoke warmly of Vietnam's "particularly intimate relations" with the United States.[13]

The Vietnamese communists might not have known it, but they had reason to speak warmly of their relationship with the United States. Roosevelt had been hostile toward the French occupation of Vietnam. "The case of Indochina is perfectly clear. France has milked it for 100 years. The people of Indochina are entitled to something better than that," Roosevelt had told the Pacific War Council in 1944.[14] But when the French moved back into Vietnam in late 1945 and established a puppet government, the United States backed them. In May 1947, Secretary of State George Marshall, overriding his own staff, sent a telegram to officials in Paris calling for "a continued close association between newly-autonomous peoples and powers which have long been responsible [for] their welfare."[15] When Ho's Viet Minh began an armed revolt, the United States sent military aid to the French.

In 1954, the Vietnamese defeated the French at Dienbienphu, and at a conference at Geneva, which the United States attended, the French and Vietnamese agreed to a temporary partition of Vietnam between the North, controlled by the Viet Minh, and the South controlled by pro-French South Vietnamese forces. France would leave and nationwide elections would be held in 1956 to unify Vietnam. But when France abandoned Vietnam, the United States, claiming that a communist Vietnam would have a "domino effect" on Southeast Asia, moved into the South and helped install a new government led by Ngo Dinh Diem, a Catholic in a predominately Buddhist country. When the time for elections came, the United States, fearful of a victory by Ho Chi Minh, backed Diem's refusal to participate. Eisenhower's secretary of state John Foster Dulles later explained, "I said that I thought that the United States should not stand passively by and see the extension of communism by any means into Southeast Asia."[16] Soon afterward, local insurgents, backed by Ho in the North, began the conflict that within a decade would escalate into a full-scale war involving more than half a million American troops.

During the Kennedy administration, a few officials—among them George Ball—expressed skepticism about the American commitment to Diem and the South, but they were ignored. Instead, Kennedy followed the advice of people like General Maxwell Taylor, who insisted that minimal American forces could turn the tide. South Vietnam, he told Kennedy, "is not an excessively difficult or unpleasant place to operate."[17] Other officials argued that the United States had no choice. On his return from a visit in May 1961, Vice President Lyndon Johnson declared that "the battle against Communism must be joined in Southeast Asia . . . or the United States, inevitably, must surrender the Pacific and take up our defenses on our own shore."[18]

As opposition to the war grew, government officials insisted that the United States was fighting for the freedom and independence of the Vietnamese. Hubert Humphrey, who was Lyndon Johnson's vice president, said, "We are not the French. . . . We are not colonialists. We have no empire to save. We are not fighting against a whole people. We are fighting for the freedom of that people."[19] Certainly, on one level, Humphrey was right. The U.S. didn't plan to colonize Vietnam the way the French had. But by taking over for the French in Vietnam, and propping up a succession of pro-American regimes, the United States, as Eisenhower had feared, put itself squarely on the side of imperialism and colonialism. It was practicing an informal kind of imperialism. It also failed to take heed of what Wilson had learned in Mexico in 1914: that the United States, acting alone, could not transform countries overnight into models of democracy and freedom. America's Diem had turned into a corrupt autocrat, and in 1963, he was overthrown and replaced by a succession of military dictators who had no more claim to the title of freedom-loving democrat than Ho's communists.

The final victory of the North Vietnamese in 1975—coming after about fifty thousand Americans and at least a million, and perhaps two million, Vietnamese had died—did not lead to a rash of communist takeovers in Southeast Asia. No dominoes fell. Nor did it create a larger unified world communist movement. By 1979, Vietnam and China, which had been age-old enemies, would be at war again. And Vietnam would gradually move into the community of nations, abandoning the rigid model of communist development and even introducing very rudimentary forms of democracy.

It was exactly as Wilson would have predicted, but American foreign policy during the Cold War was so blinded by the threat of Soviet communism that it misjudged the challenge of anti-imperialism and nationalism in Asia, Africa, and Latin America.

THE GREAT SATAN

Of all the world's regions, the age of empire cast the longest shadow in the Mideast. The conflicts spawned by imperialism precipitated almost continual wars from 1919 into the twenty-first century. Many of the key nations had their boundaries and national identities created by France and Great Britain after World War I out of the breakup of the Ottoman Empire. That led to continued clashes over boundaries and over the rights of nationalities and religious groups within the artificially created nations. Oil was also critical. With the Persian Gulf alone containing about 60 percent of the world's oil reserves, the great powers continued to take a lively interest in who ruled the different countries and what their economic policies were.

From 1798, when Napoleon Bonaparte conquered Egypt, until World War II, the British and French were the main imperial powers in the Mideast, but after World War II, the United States displaced them in the region. While the United States didn't attempt to colonize states in the region, it was driven by fear of Soviet incursion and interest in the area's oil to adopt the strategy of indirect or informal control that the British had used after World War I. That strategy did not spare the Americans the hatred and resentment that many in the region had formerly felt toward the British. The United States was still seen as an imperial power, and became the chief target of Arab and Iranian nationalism, and later of radical Islam.

The British developed their strategy for indirect rule in Egypt, Iraq, and Iran primarily in response to nationalist rebellion against outright British domination. After World War I, the British and French divided up the region that now includes Lebanon, Syria, Iraq, Jordan, and Israel into new states. The British created Iraq, which they also called Mesopotamia, out of three former Ottoman provinces. The British representative in Iraq, Arnold Wilson, initially planned to rule Iraq as a formal colony. When the Iraqi Sunnis and Shiites revolted, Wilson blamed the rebellion on outside agitators. "There was no real desire in Mesopotamia for an Arab government. . . . The Arabs would appreciate British rule," Wilson assured the British cabinet in London.[20] But after the British had suffered two thousand casualties, Winston Churchill, the colonial secretary, decided to substitute indirect rule. In 1920, the British installed Faisal, who had been deposed as king of Syria by the French and who had never set foot in Iraq, on the Iraqi throne. The British sought to retain their influence through him and later through their control of the Iraqi Petroleum Company.

In Iran, where oil had been discovered in 1908, the British ousted Reza Shah Pahlavi in 1941, out of fear that he would tilt to the Nazis, and installed his son, the more pliable Mohammad Reza Pahlavi. After the war, the British maintained a hold on the Shah and control of the Anglo-Iranian oil company, which paid much more in taxes to the British government on its Iranian oil income than it paid in royalties to Iran's government.[21] In 1951, facing a revolt from Iranian nationalists, the Shah was forced to appoint their leader, Mohammad Mosaddeq, as prime minister. Ignoring the Shah, Mosaddeq called on the British to grant Iran the same terms as American oil companies had granted the Saudis. When the British refused, Mosaddeq nationalized their holdings.

The United States had also become active in Iran after World War II because of its oil and its proximity to the Soviet Union. Fearful that Mosaddeq would turn to the Soviet Union, the Eisenhower administration ordered the Central Intelligence Agency to work with army officers to overthrow him. The coup took place in August 1953. The Shah's power was restored, and a new petroleum deal gave American companies the largest single share of Iranian production. As Britain withdrew from the region, the United States funded the growth of the Shah's police and military. The Shah was seen as holding the American proxy in the Persian Gulf—as the protector of America's interests.

The United States also pressured the Shah to undertake social and economic reforms. But the Shah's secular "white revolution," combined with his brutal repression of dissent, united Iran's liberal middle class and its Shiite clerics, led by the Ayatollah Khomeini, in opposition to his rule. At the center of this rebellion was the charge, dating from 1953, that the Shah was America's puppet. The Shah, Khomeini charged, "enacted his so-called reforms in order to create markets for America and to increase our dependence on America."[22] As the rebellion became a full-fledged revolution, the

Carter administration tried to dissociate the United States from the Shah, but the damage had been done decades before.

America's attempt to maintain informal control in the manner of the British failed miserably. As a result of its efforts in Iran, as well as in Iraq in 1963, where it helped Saddam Hussein and other militants depose a left-wing regime demanding a greater share of Western oil profits, the United States would end up as what Khomeini called the "great Satan" of the Middle East. It would inherit not only the power of British imperialism, but also the hatred and resentment that many in the region felt toward it. Iran itself would become a center of anti-American protest and terror during the next decades.

By backing the Shah in 1953 or aiding the overthrow of Iraq's left-wing Colonel Karim Kassem in 1963, the United States had probably delayed the oil nationalizations that finally occurred in the 1970s. That may have meant millions to the oil companies, but the enmity that the United States earned in the process cost it money and lives. It may have deterred the Soviet Union in the region, but there was never significant evidence that the Soviet Union wanted to colonize the Mideast, or that the region's governments wanted to become Soviet satellites. The U.S. policy in the Mideast represented another instance where the Cold War clouded America's commitment to dismantling imperialism.

THE MILLENNIAL HARBINGER

The Cold War would begin winding down during the last two years of Ronald Reagan's administration—a fine irony since Reagan had devoted his first five years in office to raising the temperature of the Cold War with the Soviet Union, reviving the heated, quasi-religious rhetoric of the early Cold War days, and to expanding the American offensive against anti-imperialist movements in Central America, Africa, and the Mideast. Yet in his last years in office, Reagan, like Woodrow Wilson, would transcend the seeming limits of his own rhetoric and his religious background. Reagan would uncover the possibility of peace and of an end to the Cold War.

Reagan was brought up in the Disciples of Christ, an evangelical sect whose founder, Alexander Campbell, published in the 1830s a periodical called *The Millennial Harbinger*. Campbell was a postmillennialist, but by

Reagan's time, the sect had moved closer to premillennialism. When Reagan became governor of California in 1966, he also came under the sway of premillennial theologians like Billy Graham and Hal Lindsey, who predicted the world's end rather than the Kingdom of God on Earth. Their influence, however, was countered by Reagan's memory of Franklin Roosevelt, the great rhetorical love of Reagan's life, from whom he borrowed his political cadence and postmillennial optimism, incorporating Roosevelt's phrases like "rendezvous with destiny" in his earliest speeches.

As a result, Reagan was torn between premillennial and postmillennial visions. His rhetorical language (which his speechwriters adapted) was filled with references to America as the "city on a hill" that enjoyed the blessings of a "Divine Providence." At the same time, he envisaged nuclear war as Armageddon and the Soviet Union as the "evil empire" or the "focus of evil in the modern world."

In his first term, Reagan was held captive by his premillennial fears of Armageddon. He hiked military spending to meet what turned out to be an illusion of Soviet military superiority. "Today in virtually every measure of military power, the Soviet Union enjoys a decided advantage," Reagan declared in November 1982.[23] While declaring his willingness to negotiate arms control with the Soviet Union, he proposed a "Star Wars" program to protect the United States from incoming missiles—a program that is still not remotely feasible two decades later and that conjured up destabilizing fears of an American first strike. Reagan would later claim that his military buildup was a clever tactic to bankrupt the Soviet Union, but it's not clear that Reagan's intelligence officials were fully aware of Soviet economic problems. While Reagan occasionally voiced doubts about Soviet strength, the bulk of his statements exaggerated Soviet capabilities.

TERROR IN THE MIDEAST

Reagan also saw the older imperial conflicts that predated the Cold War through the prism of U.S.-Soviet rivalry. In Nicaragua, which the United States had periodically occupied during the early part of the century, Reagan sought to overthrow the Sandinistas, who had in 1979 forced the brutal pro-American dictator Anastasio Somoza out of office. Reagan saw them as an arm of Soviet communism. His Central Intelligence Agency recruited and trained a right-wing guerrilla force, the Contras, led by former members of Somoza's National Guard, to defeat the Sandinistas.

In the Mideast, Reagan ran squarely into another thorny legacy of the age of empire, the conflict between Israel and Palestinians. This conflict dated at least from World War I and Britain's commitment prior to and during the peace talks to establish a "home" for Jews in Palestine. Zionist leader Chaim Weizmann had sold Israel to the British partly as an "Asiatic Belgium" that would be an outpost for their imperial ambitions in the Mideast, while the Arabs saw the Jews who began emigrating and raising the new blue-and-white flag of Israel as colonial agents of Western imperialism.[24]

After World War II, the Truman administration had recognized the new State of Israel. In the wake of centuries of European anti-Semitism culminating in the Holocaust, that was certainly the right thing to do, but it created a situation in which two peoples had legitimate claim to the same land. The Truman administration sought but failed to solve the problem of 750,000 Palestinian refugees. By 1964, when the Palestinian Liberation Organization (PLO) was founded, the problem of refugees had become a problem of Palestinian self-determination.

After the Six-Day War in 1967, the Israelis occupied the West Bank and Gaza on which Palestinians lived. The Israeli occupations created the basis for an enduring conflict, but also for a resolution of conflict through exchanging land for peace—a Palestinian homeland on the West Bank and Gaza for Palestinian and Arab state recognition of Israel's right to exist. The Johnson, Nixon, and Carter administrations attempted to broker this kind of agreement, but they were frustrated by Palestinian hostility to Israel's very existence and by the insistence of Israel's right-wing Likud Party, which took power in 1977 from the Labour Party, that the occupied lands were part of historic Israel and could not be ceded to the Palestinians. To make a fact of this fancy, the Likud Party expanded Jewish settlements in the West Bank.

With the Soviet Union gaining influence over Israel's neighbors, and with Iran no longer an ally, Reagan and Secretary of State Alexander Haig began to envision Israel as the outpost of American anticommunism in the Mideast. In 1981, Reagan signed an Israeli-American memorandum calling for a "mutual security relationship . . . to deter all threats from the Soviet Union."[25] Reagan rejected the Carter administration's support for Palestinian autonomy in the West Bank and Gaza. The West Bank, Reagan declared, should not belong to the Palestinians, but "should be open to all people—

Arab and Israeli alike."[26] To Reagan, the Palestinians and their Arab allies were instruments of Soviet communism.

In 1982, Reagan and Haig failed to stop Israeli defense minister Ariel Sharon from undertaking an invasion of Lebanon aimed at destroying the Palestinian Liberation Organization. As a result, the United States became inextricably tied to Israel's attempt to deny self-determination to the Palestinians. Reagan saw the danger, and George Shultz, who replaced Haig as secretary of state, advocated sending American marines to Lebanon to facilitate the safe passage of the PLO out of Beirut and of Israel out of Lebanon. But it was already too late. The marines became embroiled in the Lebanese civil war and in the conflict between the new Islamic militants and the Israeli occupation force. They were fired upon, and they fired back.

On April 18, 1983, a delivery van carrying 400 pounds of explosives slammed into the American embassy in Beirut, killing sixty-three people, and wounding a hundred others. Then, on October 23, 1983, a truck loaded with explosives and driven by members of Islamic Jihad rammed into the marine barracks in Beirut, killing 241 Americans.

The embassy and truck bombing were as significant as the September 11, 2001, attack. They represented the first use of suicide terror tactics against the United States by Arab nationalists, and their success—the United States would pull out of Lebanon by the next spring—inspired the use of such tactics over the succeeding decades against the militarily superior United States and Israel. The invasion of Lebanon, the continuing Israeli occupation of the West Bank and Gaza, and American intervention helped to spawn the radical Islamic movements. Islamic Jihad and Hezbollah, both of which were funded by Iran, achieved prominence during the 1980s and were soon succeeded by Hamas and other Islamic organizations. American supporters of Israeli's Likud Party would later try to pigeonhole these organizations as creatures of Islam, but they grew out of the continuing attempt by Arab and Iranian nationalists to rid the region of the vestiges of the age of empire.

COLD WAR'S END

In his last two years in office, Reagan abruptly changed course. One reason was an involuntary shakeup within his administration. The Iran-Contra scandal of 1986, which grew out of the administration's policies in Central

America and the Mideast, forced out of the administration some hardline conservatives, including White House officials John Poindexter and Oliver North. CIA director William Casey would die of a brain tumor. Other officials, including Secretary of Defense Caspar Weinberger and Assistant Secretary Richard Perle, also left. These officials had often reinforced Reagan's worst instincts.

Meanwhile, a new Soviet leader, Mikhail Gorbachev, assumed office in 1984. Gorbachev, as it turned out, was committed to a policy of political reform, arms reduction, and withdrawal from the war in Afghanistan. Administration hardliners in the Pentagon had attempted to sabotage Reagan's first meeting with Gorbachev by issuing a tendentious report on Soviet nuclear treaty violations that the Joint Chiefs of Staff subsequently repudiated.[27] But to Reagan's credit, he recognized at this December 1985 Geneva meeting that he would be able to negotiate with the new Soviet leader. Like Theodore Roosevelt and Wilson, Reagan, faced with a new reality, was able to transcend his own most deeply held convictions. In 1987, he signed an arms control agreement with Gorbachev to eliminate Soviet and American intermediate-range nuclear missiles. Reagan's former conservative allies denounced the treaty—*National Review* called it "nuclear suicide"—but Reagan understood that it signaled the end of the Cold War. Asked whether the Soviet Union was still an "evil empire," Reagan explained that the United States and Soviet Union now had "an entirely different relationship."[28]

Reagan and his secretary of state, George Shultz, also began winding down the administration's attempt to overthrow the Sandinistas in Nicaragua. In August 1987, he and Shultz agreed to a plan for a negotiated settlement. In protest, conservatives sported buttons that said "Support the Contras, Impeach Reagan," but Reagan no longer saw Central America as a front in the Cold War. In his memoir, dictated immediately after he left office, Reagan even displayed some misgivings about his unquestioning support for Israel. Wrote Reagan, "Without Israel agreeing to 'land for peace,' I don't think there will ever be peace in the Middle East."[29]

No president since Franklin Roosevelt had seen the circumstances of world politics change so dramatically during his terms in office. When Reagan was inaugurated in January 1981, the Cold War seemed to have reached dangerous heights, but by the time he left office eight years later, it was coming to an end—and without the Armageddon Reagan had feared and sought earnestly to avoid.

CHAPTER EIGHT

Bush, Clinton, and the Triumph
of Wilsonianism

George H. W. Bush succeeded Ronald Reagan in 1988 with as impressive a foreign policy résumé as any president in the twentieth century. He had been U.S. ambassador to the United Nations, envoy to China, and director of the Central Intelligence Agency, before serving eight active years as vice president. Yet perhaps because of his extensive experience, he had developed a hardened skepticism about change. He initially refused to recognize that the Cold War was ending. He brushed aside Gorbachev's offers for further arms reductions, and he continued to champion the Contras in Nicaragua. But when the Berlin Wall fell in November 1989, and the Soviet hold over Eastern Europe crumbled almost overnight, Bush realized that the terrain of diplomacy had been irrevocably altered. In November 1990, Bush announced, "The Cold War is over."[1]

The Cold War's end would throw into question those institutions and policies that had been developed to meet the challenge of the Soviet Union. Was NATO necessary anymore? Should the United States even worry about what happens in the former Yugoslavia? Should it still support the United Nations and the International Monetary Fund? But it would also remove a large obstacle to the full realization of the foreign policy that Wilson and Roosevelt had developed. It would create the possibility of a genuine "association of interest" among the advanced industrial nations. Bush and his successor, Bill Clinton, were the first presidents to operate on this new terrain, and after initially stumbling, both men established important landmarks in foreign policy.

LINGERING CONFLICTS

Some political scientists and historians have described Bush and Clinton's world as "postimperial," but it is probably best understood as being in transition between the age of empire and a new world in which the contest for colonies was no longer a factor.[2] The age of empire began in 1871 after the Franco-Prussian War, and continued through World War I, the ugly interwar period of imperial rivalry, and World War II. Indeed, it is probably most accurate to see the two world wars as part of a thirty years' war. Roosevelt expected World War II to bring an end to imperialism, but it lingered and even expanded.

Britain, France, Holland, and Portugal refused to give up their own possessions without a fight. The British granted India independence in 1947; the Dutch were forced out of Indonesia in 1949; France lost wars in Vietnam in 1954 and Algeria in 1962; the British had to abandon the Suez Canal in 1956 but didn't leave Kuwait until 1969; the Portuguese were finally forced out of Africa by liberation movements in the mid-1970s; and in the Caribbean and Central America, regimes closely identified with the American imperial past were overthrown. But most important, the Soviet Union, having adopted the imperial agenda of czarist Russia, secured and held onto a large swath of nations and nationalities to its west, south, and east until the whole edifice collapsed from 1989 to 1992.

The disintegration of the Soviet empire eliminated one crucial component of the age of empire—the conflict among great powers for domination of the world. That aspect of imperialism no longer existed. The United States was the one remaining superpower, but it had ceased to follow a strategy of expansion through annexation during Theodore Roosevelt's second term, and Wilson had reinforced the opposition to an American imperialism during his presidency. It had attempted to exercise informal control of countries in Asia and Latin America during the Cold War, but the fall of Soviet communism removed the most important reason for doing so. Europe had moved even farther away from its imperial past. European nations, mindful of their own disastrous history, had subordinated their own national ambitions in forming the European Economic Community, which would become the European Union.[3] The EU was a genuine postimperial institution. Like NATO, it was a limited, but real, application of Wilson's ideal of collective security.

The underlying structure of capitalism had also changed. Before World War II, many countries assumed that the only way they could enjoy rapid and stable economic growth was by establishing a closed trading and investment system, but the economic record after World War II suggested that many countries could benefit from a managed international trading and currency system that discouraged the creation of these closed systems. Japan had become the world's second largest economy without the benefit of a co-prosperity sphere, while the closed Soviet economy, which had been the model of development for many Asian and African countries, had lost ground to the capitalist West in spite of its monopoly of Eastern European markets and its own wealth of raw materials. The IMF, World Bank, and GATT had reinforced this relatively open system. And in 1994, most of the world's nations became members of a new World Trade Organization (WTO), which looked very much like the old International Trade Organization that congressional Republicans had killed in 1948.

But even with the disappearance of the Soviet empire in Eastern Europe, the age of empire lingered. It could be found in a few continuing anti-colonial struggles—for instance, in Russian Chechnya. It could be found in regions like the Balkans, where the removal of imperial control had led to the emergence of suppressed national conflicts. It could be found in South Asia, the Korean peninsula, Israel, and along the Taiwan Straits, where imperial domination had created artificial boundaries or created or exacerbated conflicts between nationalities that had never been resolved. And it could be found in regions where the great powers still maintained informal control—or where, at a minimum, governments owed their existence or longevity to the backing of great powers rather than to popular support. This was particularly the case in the Middle East.

Wilson and Franklin Roosevelt had expected that through international organizations, the great powers could manage, and eventually resolve, exactly these kinds of conflicts, but after World War II, the Cold War had made this kind of cooperation impossible except in isolated cases. The disintegration of the Soviet Union, and the end of imperial rivalry, removed this barrier. It didn't make cooperation inevitable—there were still issues that make cooperation between, say, the United States and France or Russia and China very difficult—but it made it possible in a way it had never been before. The Bush administration would skillfully exploit this potential in its response to Iraq's invasion of Kuwait.

THE GULF WAR

On August 1, 1990, Iraq invaded Kuwait, and a week later annexed it. Its invasion of Kuwait was another by-product of the age of empire. Iraq, along with Syria, Lebanon, Jordan, and Palestine, had been carved out of the Ottoman Empire by Britain and France after World War I. It did not exist as a country before that, and the boundaries and sometimes the sovereignty of all these countries have remained issues ever since. Iraq had been contesting its boundary with Kuwait, a British colony to its south, since the 1930s, and with the discovery of oil in the Rumaila fields spanning the boundary between the two countries, the dispute became more heated. On the eve of its invasion, Iraq was demanding more of Rumaila and several off-shore islands, as well as the forgiveness of $30 billion that Iraq still owed Kuwait for loans during its war with Iran. When the Kuwaitis balked, Iraqi president Saddam Hussein invaded Kuwait.

Upon learning of the invasion, Bush immediately called the U.S. ambassador to the U.N., Thomas Pickering, and asked him to convene an emergency meeting of the Security Council. Bush recalled afterward, "I was keenly aware that this would be the first post–Cold War test of the Security Council in crisis. I knew what happened in the 1930s when a weak and leaderless League of Nations had failed to stand up to the Japanese, Italian and German aggression. . . . The U.N. had been set up to correct the failings of the League, but the Cold War caused stalemate on the Security Council. Now, however, our improving relations with Moscow and our satisfactory ones with China offered the possibility that we could get their cooperation in forging international unity to oppose Iraq."[4] Within a week, Bush had secured a 14 to 0 vote demanding Iraq's unconditional withdrawal from Kuwait and placing an embargo on Iraq's trade.

In November, as Saddam Hussein continued to defy U.N. demands, the administration won a Security Council vote to go to war if Iraq didn't withdraw by January 15. And when the war to liberate Kuwait began, the United

States was joined by thirty-three other countries, including Saudi Arabia, Syria, the United Kingdom, France, and the United Arab Emirates, who together provided a quarter of the troops. Brian Urquhart, former U.N. undersecretary general, called the Persian Gulf War "the first exercise in the unanimous collective security that we've been talking about since the days of Woodrow Wilson."[5]

Bush's argument for forcing Iraq out of Kuwait stemmed in part from the Persian Gulf's importance to the world oil supply. If Iraq were to control Kuwait, it would gain control of about a quarter of the world's reserves; if it were to advance upon Saudi Arabia, it would have control of over half. That could give Iraq inordinate power over the world's economy. "An Iraq permitted to swallow Kuwait would have the economic and military power, as well as the arrogance, to intimidate and coerce its neighbors—neighbors who control the lion's share of the world's remaining oil reserves," Bush said in a televised address to Congress in September 1990.[6]

Bush, who had served in World War II, also "saw a direct analogy between what was occurring in Kuwait and what the Nazis had done, especially in Poland."[7] This argument had special appeal to the small nations in the United Nations who saw the purpose of the organization as defending them against aggression from larger, more powerful states. And it was a reaffirmation of Jefferson's and Wilson's attempts to expand the Declaration's principle of equality from individuals to nations. Some critics, including the antiwar and environmental group Greenpeace, charged that Bush's *real* motives were to secure Kuwait's oil rather than to defend its freedom. "No blood for oil," Greenpeace proclaimed on its placards. But Bush's motives in challenging Iraq represented a happy marriage of ideal and interest.

As the administration assembled its coalition, it began to see its own actions as setting an important precedent. Bush and his national security adviser, Brent Scowcroft, talked of establishing a "new world order"—a term Bush unveiled in his September speech and then used repeatedly over the next year to describe the administration's objectives. As Bush explained to Congress, it referred both to a multilateral process of decision making— "a world in which nations recognize the shared responsibility for freedom and justice"—and to a system of international lawfulness—"a world where the rule of law supplants the rule of the jungle."[8]

In April, after the United States had ousted Iraq from Kuwait, Bush tried to spell out this concept of a new world order. Bush, who was reluctant to engage in what he called "the vision thing," nonetheless placed this idea squarely in America's millennial tradition:

> The New World Order really is a tool for addressing a new world of possibilities. This order gains its mission and shape not just from shared interests, but from shared ideals. And the ideals that have spawned new freedoms throughout the world have received their boldest and clearest expression in our great country, the United States.[9]

STABILITY AND FREEDOM

The coalition drove Saddam Hussein's forces out of Kuwait in a hundred days, and on February 27, Bush declared, "Iraq's army is defeated and Kuwait is liberated." Bush had frequently compared Saddam Hussein to Hitler, inviting criticism when he pulled back coalition forces without trying to depose the Iraqi dictator. But Bush's stance showed that he, unlike his critics, understood the historical context in which America was acting.

In the Mideast, the age of empire was not yet over. If the United States was perceived to be going to war in order to establish control over an Arab state, it would provoke a nationalist backlash throughout the region. By acting through the U.N. and winning the support of Iraq's Arab neighbors, the United States had avoided the charge of trying to revive Western imperialist control. Wrote Bush afterward:

> I firmly believed that we should not march on Baghdad. Our stated mission, as codified in the UN resolutions, was a simple one—end the aggression, knock Iraq's forces out of Kuwait, and restore Kuwait's leaders. To occupy Iraq would instantly shatter our coalition, turning the whole Arab world against us, and make a broken tyrant into a latter day Arab hero. It would have taken us way beyond the imprimatur of international law bestowed by the resolutions of the Security Council. . . . It could plunge that part of the world into even greater instability and destroy the credibility we were working so hard to reestablish.[10]

Bush also showed that he understood what Wilson had learned in Mexico about the pitfalls of America trying alone to remake another country in its image. Bush wrote: "We would have been forced to occupy Baghdad and, in effect, rule Iraq. . . . Under those circumstances, there was no viable 'exit strategy' we could see. . . . Had we gone the invasion route, the United States could conceivably still be an occupying power in a bitterly hostile land."[11]

But Bush also stopped short at the war's end of crippling Iraq's army. The administration even allowed Saddam's regime to keep and fly its armed helicopter gunships. And when Iraqi Shia and Kurds rose up against the regime—in response partly to American urgings during the war that were broadcast throughout Iraq—the administration didn't intervene on their side. As a result, Saddam was able to use his remaining forces, including his helicopter gunships, to brutally suppress the uprising. The reason Bush and Scowcroft later gave suggested that what they meant by a "new world order" didn't really include "the idea that all people everywhere must be free."

The administration wanted Saddam to be overthrown, but by his fellow Ba'ath Party generals and officials rather than by a fractious popular uprising. Bush and Scowcroft believed that the United States needed Iraq to balance the power of Iran in the region, and it would be better to have an Iraq under Saddam that balanced Iran than a revolutionary and chaotic Iraq that could fall prey to Iranian pressure.[12] Bush admitted that destroying Iraq's army would have had benefits, but "the trick there was to damage his offensive capability without weakening Iraq to the point that a vacuum was created, and destroying the balance between Iraq and Iran, further destabilizing the region for years."[13]

Bush's prescription turned out to be shortsighted, leading to a decade of strife without reestablishing Iraq as a balance against Iran. It also didn't square with America's millennial framework, which since Wilson has been based on creating a democratic world. Bush and Scowcroft's decision to keep Iraq in the hands of the Ba'ath Party, if not Saddam himself, had fallen prey to the European realism of former secretary of state Henry Kissinger, under whom both men had served. This kind of realism, most closely associated with former German chancellor Otto von Bismarck, defined world order in terms of stability rather than justice. It was not concerned with self-determination, human rights, or democracy. Bush and Scowcroft would later take this same approach toward Gorbachev's Soviet Union, opposing self-determination for the non-Russian republics out of fear for stability.

In the government departments of universities, European realism has always had its defenders, but it is alien to the American political tradition. By the time he left office, Kissinger was despised both by the left for his sponsorship of the brutal Christmas bombing of Hanoi in 1972—an act without any military rationale—and by conservatives and Cold War liberals for his indifference to Soviet human rights activists. By the time Bush left office, he, too, would suffer similar rejection from both the left and the right. Bush had taken a huge step forward in recognizing the post–Cold War, postimperial world in which America was now operating, and in affirming the rights of small nations to be free from subjugation by large ones, but in adopting Kissinger's realism, he had obscured, if not undermined, this considerable achievement.

ENLARGING DEMOCRACY

Bush's successor, Bill Clinton, came to office with little experience or interest in foreign policy. Writes former aide Sidney Blumenthal, "He had entered the office naively believing that the world could be held at bay; or that he could subcontract international affairs to his foreign policy team while he himself dealt with domestic policy."[14] He was similar to the presidents of the 1920s. They wanted to put World War I behind them; Clinton and many of the people who voted for him and for third-party candidate Ross Perot wanted to put the Cold War behind them. They suffered from "Cold War leadership fatigue."[15]

To the extent Clinton came to office with an approach to foreign policy, he, like Herbert Hoover, saw it primarily as an extension of domestic economic policy. "We have put our economic competitiveness at the heart of our foreign policy," his 1994 budget message declared.[16] His vision of the future was framed in dollars and cents. Clinton described the World Trade Organization—an effort that dated from the Roosevelt administration's attempt to construct an enduring peace—as "a golden opportunity to add $1,700 to the average family's income in this country."[17] His vice president, Al Gore, touted it as "the biggest tax cut in history—a record $774 billion reduction in tariffs."[18] These statements, of course, were crafted for public appeal, but they also reflected Clinton's initial mind-set as he took office.

Throughout his presidency, Clinton continued to put economics at the center of his foreign policy, but in response to repeated challenges from abroad, he developed a broader view of America's role in the world. It drew together strands of Wilsonian policy—the commitment to global democracy and to removing trade barriers—with his own concern with domestic prosperity. Clinton called the policy by the ungainly term "democratic engagement and enlargement."

Clinton based his foreign policy on one of Wilson's pet ideas. Like Wilson, Clinton argued that by promoting democracy, the United States would be promoting peace, because democratic nations do not go to war against each other. "The habits of democracy are the habits of peace," Clinton declared in a September 1993 speech at the United Nations. "Democracy is rooted in compromise, not conquest. It rewards tolerance, not hatred. Democracies rarely wage war on one another."[19] Unfortunately, this idea probably had more validity in 1919 than in 1993. Wilson had based his argument on the fact that if the citizens who might die in battle got to vote on whether to go to war, nations would be less likely to fight each other. But the kind of high-technology weaponry unveiled in the Gulf War, and later used in the Balkans and the war against Iraq, made it possible for democracies to wage war in certain circumstances without substantial risk to their populations, or even to their soldiers. What seemed to prevent war was not democracy by itself, but the integration of democracies with one another. Clinton would implicitly recognize this point in dealing with the question of what to do about NATO.

Instead of abandoning NATO, or reducing America's commitment, as many Democrats and Republicans suggested, Clinton endorsed the organization's enlargement as a means of expanding democracy. Clinton grasped that NATO was not simply a military alliance, but an "association of interest." NATO didn't create democracies, it created an important condition for them. In Europe, the military had traditionally been a source of reactionary nationalism and authoritarianism, but by joining NATO, nations like Spain, Greece, and Turkey had to submit their own military to Atlantic supervision. In 1994, Clinton took the initiative in promoting NATO's expansion into Eastern Europe. He also urged the European Union to expand eastward and southward. To join the EU, countries like Hungary and Poland would have to become stable democracies. And once they were in the EU and NATO, their national aspirations would be subsumed beneath the larger multinational commitments of these organizations. Clinton wanted "a peaceful, undivided and democratic Europe."[20]

Clinton also believed in a theory of economics and democracy that went back to nineteenth-century British liberalism. He contended that by removing trade and investment barriers, nations would move toward free-market capitalism; as they did so, they would move toward democracy. They would benefit, and so would the United States, which would discover new markets and outlets for investment. Clinton outlined this logic in a strategy paper that he delivered to Congress in February 1996:

> We believe that our goals of enhancing our security, bolstering our economic prosperity and promoting democracy are mutually supportive. Secure nations are more likely to support free trade and maintain democratic structures. Free market nations with growing economies and strong and open trade ties are more likely to feel secure and to work toward freedom. And democratic states are less likely to threaten our interests and more likely to cooperate with the United States to meet security threats and promote free trade and sustainable development. These goals are supported by ensuring America remains engaged in the world and by enlarging the community of secure, free market and democratic nations.[21]

In Clinton's presidency, the highlights of this approach were the passage of the North American Free Trade Agreement (NAFTA) and the WTO, NATO expansion, and the cultivation of China and Russia as trade and investment partners.* China was particularly important. Clinton boasted that his administration had "actively engaged China on trade issues through extension of its Most Favored Nation status and vigorous pursuit of China's adherence to the rules-based regime of the World Trade Organization."[22]

---

*NAFTA was a more ambiguous application of Wilson's approach. The Bush administration originally conceived the treaty partly as a means of stabilizing and improving the Mexican economy, which would have the effect, it hoped, of curbing political unrest and preventing large-scale immigration to the north, but the terms of the treaty were largely dictated by American corporations looking for cheap labor and by banks and financial institutions looking to take advantage of the privatization of the Mexican economy. The Clinton administration sold it disingenuously to the public as a boon to American jobs. In its final form, it bordered on regional protectionism rather than "free trade." And its political and economic benefits to Mexico are yet to be proven.

Most of what Clinton actually did to enlarge "the community of secure, free market and democratic nations" was entirely consistent with Wilson and Franklin Roosevelt's approach to foreign policy. Wilson and Roosevelt certainly would have backed the membership of China in an organization like the WTO. But the logic of Clinton's policy remained unproven. Removing trade and investment barriers had been at the heart of dismantling the older imperialism. But it didn't seem to have encouraged democracy in Russia or China. It may not have even furthered prosperity in Mexico and in the less-developed nations of Africa and Latin America. Clinton himself would realize the limitations of these simple equations between free trade and democracy before his presidency was over.

NETWORK OF ALLIANCES

Clinton initially hoped that he could use the United Nations to deal with war and disorder and with what he called "rogue states"—a highly misleading concept that detached countries like Iran, Iraq, Libya, and North Korea from their history. His U.N. ambassador, Madeleine Albright, who would later become secretary of state, promoted what she called "assertive multilateralism." [23] But Clinton lost his enthusiasm for a strategy centered on the U.N. after eighteen American soldiers, part of a U.N. peacekeeping force, were killed in Somalia. George Bush had initiated the effort to help relief supplies get through to starving Somalis during a civil war, but under Clinton, the U.N. had gotten entangled in the civil war itself. Afterward, Clinton refused to commit the United States to a U.N. intervention in Rwanda.

Clinton also vacillated about intervening in the Balkans, where the dissolution of Yugoslavia—a nation created in 1919 out of the ruins of the Ottoman and Austro-Hungarian empires—had led to wars of secession between the Serbs and the Bosnian Muslims, Croats, and Kosovar Albanians. When French president Jacques Chirac visited Washington in June 1995, he complained afterward that the post of leader of the free world was "vacant"—a fine irony in view of French foreign minister Hubert Védrine's later characterization of the United States as a "hyperpuissance." [24]

In the summer of 1995, Clinton, spurred by the widely publicized massacre of Bosnian Muslims at Srebrenica, finally took action in the

Balkans. Clinton called for large-scale NATO air strikes against the Bosnian Serbs. With the Serbs in Belgrade under retreat from the Croatian armed forces, Clinton and Assistant Secretary of State Richard Holbrooke were able to bring the warring parties together for peace talks in Dayton, Ohio, which resulted in an agreement in October ending the war. Clinton volunteered twenty thousand American troops to help police the agreement. Four years later, Clinton would also win support from NATO for air strikes to stop the Serbs from massacring Kosovar Albanians.

Clinton's interventions in the Balkans were consistent with his program of enlarging democracy. Anthony Lake, who was Clinton's national security adviser during his first term, later described the interventions as "essential to the pursuit of our vision of an undivided Europe."[25] It was particularly important to NATO's growth and survival. NATO had splintered under the disagreements over the Balkans. But after Bosnia, it revived. France, which had withdrawn from NATO's military committee during the Vietnam War, sent its defense minister back after Bosnia. And the nations of Eastern Europe became eager to join the organization.

Clinton learned from these interventions that while the United States needed to act multilaterally in conflicts that had occurred outside its own hemisphere, it had to take a leading role. The American president had to occupy the post of leader of the free world. Clinton also learned to rely not just on the United Nations, but on a variety of international organizations. In a speech in San Francisco commemorating the U.N. in 1999, Clinton said that the United States had "built a network of security alliances to preserve the peace, and a global financial system to preserve prosperity."[26] Wilson had been obsessed with the idea of a single international organization. So, too, had Roosevelt and Truman. The IMF, World Bank, and ITO were conceived of as part of the U.N. But what Clinton finally put into words was that the United States, and the rest of the world, had to rely on a number of different international organizations. NATO, far from being obsolete, had proven to be integral to that network.

THE THIRD WAY

Clinton also attempted to develop a new international network, dedicated to what he and British prime minister Tony Blair called "the Third

Way." The term itself has a long history, but Clinton originally used it to refer to a domestic politics that transcended both laissez-faire conservatism and New Deal liberalism, just as Blair used it to refer to politics that transcended old Labour's socialism and Margaret Thatcher's laissez-faire conservatism. In a series of conferences that took place in Clinton's last two years in office, the two men attempted to develop an international version of the Third Way that could initially unite politicians from North America and Europe, but could also be expanded to include politicians from democratic capitalist countries in Latin America, Africa, and Asia.

Clinton called the Third Way in international politics "putting a human face on the global economy."[27] In June 1999, he said, "Globalization is not a proposal or a policy choice, it is a fact. But how we respond to it will make all the difference. We cannot dam up the tides of economic change any more than King Canute could still the waters. Nor can we tell our people to sink or swim on their own. We must find a third way—a new and democratic way—to maximize market potential and social justice."[28] The Third Way in international politics transcended the market economics of business and of conservatives and the protectionism of labor and the left. It promoted international trade agreements, but they would include some kind of environmental and labor safeguards so that trade would not entail a "race to the bottom." Said Clinton at a Third Way meeting in Florence, Italy, in November 1999:

Ordinary people all over the world are not so sure about the globalization of the economy. They're not so sure they're going to benefit from trade. They want to see if there can be a human face on the global economy, if we can raise labor standards for ordinary people, if we can continue to improve the quality of life, including the quality of the environment.[29]

The Third Way also incorporated global environmental standards. The Bush administration had agreed in 1992 to purely nonbinding limits on the emission of greenhouse gases, which scientists believed were causing the planet to heat up, with unforeseen but perhaps disastrous consequences at the end of the twenty-first century. But Clinton and Gore agreed with other developed countries to reduce emissions from American factories and automobiles over the next thirteen years, and in December 1997, Vice President Gore signed the Kyoto Protocol on global warming.[30]

Clinton's Third Way was in line with Wilson's attempt to spread a "reformed and socially responsible democratic capitalism" and with Roosevelt's commitment to extending the "four freedoms" throughout the world. It was an attempt to flesh out, and adapt to new international circumstances and challenges, America's original millennial vision. At the meetings, the last of which was held in Berlin in June 2000, the discussion ranged from educational reform and global warming to the "digital divide" and debt relief for poor countries. The participants, who came from thirteen different countries, including Argentina, Chile, and South Africa, issued a joint communiqué calling for a "new international social compact" that "recognizes interdependence, mutual effort, and mutual responsibility for common goals."[31]

At the close of the Berlin talks, Clinton tried to sum up the experience of the last years:

> The Cold War ended, the global economy arose. There was a general consensus that the economy could run off half-cocked without a role for government in the greater relations among nations. People like us began to get elected. We began to realize some common ground across the divides we represent. So we started these meetings. I thought we could help each other do well. More of us could be elected and the world could take another direction.[32]

But Clinton would have to leave office, and several of the key participants in Berlin would fail to win reelection. The world would be headed in a different direction, but not one consistent with the promise of the Third Way. Clinton, like Wilson, would see his attempt to update America's millennial mission repudiated by a successor.

THE DISCOVERY OF AL-QAEDA

Clinton's last year in office was consumed by the Israeli-Palestinian conflict and by the threat from Islamic terrorist organizations. Both were legacies of the age of empire. The Israeli-Palestinian conflict dated from World War I, if not before, and the Islamic terrorist organizations, which had emerged in the 1970s and were responsible for the bombing of the marine barracks in

Beirut in 1983, were offshoots of Arab nationalism and anti-imperialism. Organizations like Islamic Jihad arose out of the failure of secular nationalism to achieve the destruction of Israel and successful and independent economic and social development. They took their inspiration, and in some cases their funding, from the Iranian revolution. They adopted the agenda of Arab nationalism, but added their own Islamic Fundamentalist wrinkle.

Clinton had only been in office for a month when an Islamic terrorist cell, headquartered in Jersey City, tried to blow up the World Trade Center. The effort killed six, and injured up to a thousand people. In a letter to the *New York Times* afterward, the group responsible for the bombing demanded that the United States "stop all military, economical and political aid to Israel . . . [and] not . . . interfere with any of the Middle East countries' interior affairs."[33] In 1996, terrorists destroyed the Khobar Towers in Saudi Arabia, where American airmen were housed. Two years later, explosions at the American embassies in Kenya and Tanzania killed over three hundred, and in October 2000 a small boat loaded with explosives rammed the U.S.S. *Cole* off of Aden, killing nineteen.

Iranians were responsible for the Khobar Towers explosion, but the other bombings were the work of al-Qaeda, a shadowy terrorist network that had been founded in 1989 by Osama bin Laden, the son of a wealthy Saudi family. Bin Laden's organization got its start in Afghanistan and some of its cadre fought in Bosnia against the Serbs, but its real target was Israel, the United States, and the Arab regimes that it saw as dependent on the United States. Bin Laden had been exiled from Saudi Arabia because of his protest against the stationing of American troops there after the Persian Gulf War. In 1998, bin Laden announced "The World Islamic Front for Jihad Against Jews and the Crusaders." His objective was the same as that of secular Arab nationalists: to drive the United States—"the crusaders"—and Israel out of the Mideast.[34]

By the late 1990s, Clinton saw international terrorism as the principal problem he faced. At the Third Way meeting in Florence, Clinton said: "I believe that the biggest problems to our security in the twenty-first century and to this whole modern form of governance will probably come not from rogue states or people with competing views of the worlds in governments but from the enemies of the nation-state, from terrorists and drug runners and organized criminals."[35]

Clinton would enjoy some success—stopping attempts to blow up American airliners over the Pacific in 1993 and thwarting the Millennium plot, which would have included bombing Los Angeles International Airport and a Radisson Hotel in Amman, Jordan—but as Clinton left office, Osama bin Laden's network of terrorists, headquartered in Afghanistan but with cells all over the world, remained intact and was preparing to strike again.[36]

In July 2000, Clinton also made a last effort to resolve the differences between the Israelis and the Palestinians. During his first year in office, Israel and the Palestinians had signed a secret agreement at Oslo that laid out a series of negotiating steps toward a two-state solution to the century-old conflict. With Clinton's encouragement, the peace talks had progressed under Israeli prime minister Yitzhak Rabin and PLO chairman Yasir Arafat, in spite of the first suicide bombings from the Islamic organization Hamas and the diehard opposition of the Likud Party. But Rabin was assassinated by a right-wing Israeli, and in 1996, the Likud Party's Benjamin Netanyahu won the prime minister's office and stalled the negotiations. In 1999, however, the Labour Party's Ehud Barak defeated Netanyahu and got Clinton to convene talks at Camp David in July 2000 between him and Arafat.

Clinton clearly saw the connection between the Israeli-Palestinian conflict and Islamic terrorism. He recognized that terrorism *within* Israel had been designed to wreck the peace process. But he also believed that if the Israelis and the Palestinians could come to terms that would end the occupation, that would remove a major source of support in the Mideast for groups like al-Qaeda. Richard Clarke, who was in charge of counter-terrorism for Clinton's National Security Council, described the White House thinking: "If we could achieve a Middle East peace much of the popular support for al Qaeda and much of the hatred for America would evaporate overnight."[37] But even though Barak made significant concessions, Arafat was not ready to reach a final agreement. By that fall, the Second Intifada, provoked by Likud Party leader Ariel Sharon's demonstration at the Al-Aqsa mosque, had begun. The age of empire was over in Europe, but it lingered painfully in the Mideast, as Clinton's successor, George W. Bush, would soon discover.

CHAPTER NINE

George W. Bush Sees Evil

Like Bill Clinton, George W. Bush entered the presidency without any experience in foreign policy. He also didn't seem to know or care much. During the campaign, Bush confused Slovenia and Slovakia and couldn't identify the president of Pakistan or the prime minister of India. Some of his statements suggested a darker view of the world than that of his father or Clinton, and a more skeptical and constricted concept of overseas military intervention, but any suggestion of a clear difference seemed to be contradicted by his appointment of Colin Powell as secretary of state. Powell, a Scowcroft disciple, had served under the first Bush and Clinton. Yet by the end of George W. Bush's third year in office, he had taken America down a completely different road not only from his immediate predecessors, but from Wilson and Franklin Roosevelt.

The most obvious difference was in Bush's approach to international organization. In his first year, he repudiated the Clinton administration's support for the Kyoto Protocol (refusing even to renegotiate the terms of the treaty), the nuclear test-ban treaty, a new protocol to the biological weapons treaty, a pact to control the illicit trade in small arms, and the International Criminal Court. He expressed skepticism about the International Monetary Fund and World Bank and, in his second year, defied the World Trade Organization by slapping a tariff on foreign steel. The administration had a rationale for each of these actions, but taken together, they cast doubt on Bush's support for a fundamental principle of Wilsonian internationalism: that to create a peaceful, prosperous, and safe world, the United States would have to commit itself not simply to ad hoc coalitions but to enduring international organizations and treaties.

The significance of these decisions paled, however, before Bush's decision to invade and occupy Iraq in March 2003. The United Nations was created specifically to prevent a stronger nation from attacking and conquering a weaker one without provocation, as Germany had done in the world wars, but Bush and the United States did exactly that. Bush claimed to be averting a future threat to the United States (as Germany in World War I had claimed to be averting a threat from Russia's military buildup), but instead of addressing this threat directly by eliminating Iraq's military facilities and weaponry, the United States invaded and occupied the country.

Bush insisted that America was "not an imperial power" but "a liberating power."[1] Yet what the United States tried to do when it invaded Iraq—installing a government of its own liking and opening Iraq's economy, and particularly its oil fields, to American investors—was very similar to what the British Colonial Office had done in the region's oil states before World War II. It also recalled America's strategy of informal control in the Caribbean and Central America, going back to 1900. If the similarity with old-time colonialism was not apparent to the American electorate, it was very clear to the people of Europe and the Mideast. Bush, whether in name or not, was reviving the imperial policies that Wilson and Franklin Roosevelt had repudiated.

The Bush administration would claim that its invasion of Iraq was in direct response to the terrorist attacks in New York and Washington on September 11, 2001, and to the specter of weapons of mass destruction getting in the hands of a "rogue state." But there were conservative Republicans, including members of the Bush administration, who were advocating unilateralism, a new American imperialism, and the ouster of Iraq's Saddam Hussein well before September 11. They provided the "seed of thought," in Mahan's words, which suddenly blossomed under the impact of September 11 and the war in Afghanistan in the same way as the ideas of the Roosevelt-Lodge imperialists had blossomed under the impact of the explosion on the *Maine* and the Spanish-American War.

NATIONALISTS AND NEOCONS

The 1990s were a time of boom rather than bust, but other than that they were similar to the 1890s—they were a time of religious fervor, industrial transformation, and newfound uncertainty about America's role in the world. The administrations of George H. W. Bush and Clinton used the end of the Cold War to redeem the promise of Wilson's and FDR's foreign policy, but they did so amid growing opposition, particularly within the Republican Party. The opposition initially took the form of a revival of isolationism. The key figure was columnist Pat Buchanan, who ran for president as a Republican in 1992 and 1996 and as a third-party candidate in 2000.

Buchanan, who had served in the Nixon and Reagan White Houses, founded an America First Committee, named after the 1940 organization that had opposed America's entry into World War II. He favored leaving the United Nations, pulling American troops out of Europe and Asia, and slapping tariffs on Japanese imports. He opposed the Gulf War, and accused George H. W. Bush of diverting American resources and risking American lives in unnecessary foreign adventures while the economy was being battered by Japanese imports. In an article entitled "Now That Red Is Dead, Come Home America," Buchanan wrote, "The incivility and brutality of our cities, the fading away of the Reagan Boom, the rise of ethnic hatred, are concentrating the minds of Americans on their own society. What doth it profit a nation if it gain the whole world, and lose its own soul?"[2]

Some of Buchanan's views were echoed by presidential candidate H. Ross Perot in 1992 and 1996, but most congressional Republicans were not full-fledged isolationists. They were the descendants of the Republicans of the 1920s—nationalists who applied a strict test of national interest to foreign policy. If the United States was not directly and immediately threatened or if it didn't benefit, they saw no need for it to act. They opposed the interventions in Haiti, Bosnia, and Kosovo. "We should . . . bring our troops home and let the people in Europe deal with a European problem," Indiana Republican congressman Dan Burton declared.[3] Said Florida representative Porter Goss of the intervention in Kosovo, "The people in my district . . . want to know how this fits into our national interest, and they want to know the costs."[4] They disliked the U.N., opposed "nation-building," rejected money for peacekeeping forces but favored a strong defense, including national missile defense, and opposed trade protectionism.

Some of them, like House Majority Leader Dick Armey from Texas, were provincials who seemed indifferent to the outside world. Armey bragged that he had only been to Europe once and didn't plan to return. Other nationalists, like former secretaries of defense Dick Cheney and Donald Rumsfeld, agreed with Armey about nation-building, peacekeeping, and paying too much attention to the U.N. and other international institutions, but they were well versed in international affairs and had an expansive view of

America's national interest. These latter nationalists would play a leading role in George W. Bush's administration.[5]

In the mid-1990s, neoconservative Republicans entered the fray in opposition to both the Clinton administration and to the Republican nationalists and neoisolationists. These neoconservatives were the second and third generations of the intellectuals who had moved from left to right at the end of the 1960s. William Kristol was the son of Irving Kristol, the co-editor of *The Public Interest,* and John Podhoretz, the son of *Commentary* editor Norman Podhoretz. Former Reagan administration official Richard Perle and former Reagan and Bush administration official Paul Wolfowitz, who would join the new Bush administration, were protégés of first-generation arms theorist Albert Wohlstetter. Third generationer Douglas Feith, who would serve under Wolfowitz in George W. Bush's Pentagon, was a protégé of Perle; and I. Lewis "Scooter" Libby, who would be Vice President Dick Cheney's chief of staff, had studied under Wolfowitz at Yale.

The second- and third-generation neoconservatives like William Kristol or Wolfowitz took a different view of foreign policy than first-generation neoconservatives like Jeane Kirkpatrick or Irving Kristol. Many of the latter, after being different variants of socialists—Irving Kristol and Wohlstetter were both Trotskyists—became nationalists who were strongly anticommunist but wary of global democracy as a goal of American foreign policy. Some of them supported dictatorships in Chile or Honduras as long as the governments were anticommunist. They were almost invariably critical of Carter's human rights advocacy. As ex-leftists, they were anti-utopian and skeptical of anything that called itself "radical" or "revolutionary." By contrast, many in the second and third generation saw themselves as radical democrats in their foreign policy. As is often the case, the members of the new generation adapted to their purposes the abandoned views of the previous generation. In this case, the neoconservatives of the 1990s tried to adapt the revolutionary internationalism of their ideological, or real, fathers and grandfathers to Republican conservatism.

The neoconservatives were clustered around Bill Kristol's magazine, *The Weekly Standard,* which was funded by Australian conservative media baron Rupert Murdoch, and around the American Enterprise Institute, which housed Perle, Iran-Contra figure Michael Ledeen, conspiracy theorist Laurie Mylroie, and future Cheney aide David Wurmser. Like the intellectuals and officials who attended Henry Adams's dinners at Lafayette Square in the 1890s, the neoconservatives were also part of a broader network of writers, editors, academics, and activists that gave them access to the *Wall Street Journal*'s editorial page, Murdoch's Fox News, *The New Republic,* the *Washington Post* editorial page, and a host of friendly conservative publications including the *National Interest, Policy Review, Commentary,* and *National Review,* as well as conservative talk radio. They also created organizations. In 1997, Kristol founded the Project for a New American Century, which would play a key role in lobbying for an invasion of Iraq.

The neoconservatives rejected what Kristol called "the utopian multilateralism of Woodrow Wilson and Bill Clinton" in favor of "the muscular patriotism of Teddy Roosevelt and Ronald Reagan."[6] They wanted to create a Pax Americana in the twenty-first century modeled on the "Pax Britannica" of the nineteenth century.[7] Thomas Donnelly, the deputy executive director of the Project for the New American Century, and Max Boot, an editorial page writer for the *Wall Street Journal,* called openly for a new American imperialism, but others like Kristol and Robert Kagan, a former State Department official, used terms like "benevolent hegemon."[8] Explained Donnelly about his fellow neoconservatives' use of the term "imperial power," "There's not all that many people who will talk about it openly. It's discomforting to a lot of Americans. So they use code phrases like 'America is the sole superpower.' "[9]

The neoconservatives often referred back to Reagan's foreign policy, but their real lodestar was Theodore Roosevelt. Wrote Kagan in 1999, "The central transitional figure in introducing the idea of responsibility into American foreign policy was not Woodrow Wilson but Theodore Roosevelt."[10] Kristol and David Brooks, a writer at the *Weekly Standard,* proposed a "national greatness" conservatism derived from Roosevelt.[11] On the eve of the 2000 election, Kristol and Kagan wrote, "The real debate in the coming year will be: What brand of internationalism? This is the debate between the internationalism of Theodore Roosevelt and that of Woodrow Wilson."[12] Marshall Wittman, who would run a Kristol organization called the Conservative Reform Project, even set up a Web page called the "Bull Moose."

It was invariably the Roosevelt of the late 1890s and his first term as president that the neoconservatives would cite. In *The Savage Wars of Peace,* Boot would praise Roosevelt for believing that American "ideals . . . could be exported only by military force" and would claim that Wilson, who took the country into World War I, "almost inverted" Roosevelt's aphorism "Speak softly and carry a big stick."[13] In searching for words to praise George W. Bush's speech before Congress after September 11, 2001, David Brooks would compare its "strenuous tone" to "Theodore Roosevelt's famous 1899 speech, 'The Strenuous Life.' "[14] The neoconservatives didn't cite Roosevelt's doubts about American expansionism, his Oslo address, or his support for international law and organization. And probably because few of them had fought in battle, they rarely alluded to Roosevelt's call to personal bravery and sacrifice in war.

The neoconservatives of the mid-1990s were as critical of the Republican nationalists and neoisolationists as they were of the liberal Wilsonians. "Conservatives are adrift," Kristol and Kagan announced in *Foreign Affairs* in 1996.[15] *The Weekly Standard* and other second-generation neoconservatives backed the Clinton administration's intervention in Bosnia and Kosovo and accused congressional Republicans of going back to 1930s isolationism. "In the current crisis," Kagan wrote, "candidates and legislators alike have flirted with another Republican tradition, the isolationism of William Borah, Robert Taft and Patrick Buchanan."[16] *New Republic* senior editor Lawrence F. Kaplan, who worked on *The National Interest* and co-authored a book on Iraq with Kristol, says, "These guys forged their ideas in battles with the right as much as with the left."[17]

There was an irony in the neoconservatives' break with the Republican nationalists and neoisolationists. While Kristol and Kagan continued to deride Wilson's internationalism, they were also products of Wilsonianism.[18] They saw the goal of American foreign policy as global democracy, not, as Theodore Roosevelt most often saw it, as "Christian civilization." Declared Michael Ledeen in 2000, "The only truly realistic American foreign policy is an ideological one that seeks to advance the democratic revolution wherever and whenever possible."[19] Warned Kristol and Kagan:

> The United States achieved its present position of strength not by practicing a foreign policy of live and let live, nor by passively waiting for threats to arise, but by actively promoting American principles of governance abroad— democracy, free markets, respect for liberty. Without a broader, more enlightened understanding of America's interests, conservatism will too easily degenerate into the pinched nationalism of Buchanan's "America First," where the appeal to narrow self-interest masks a deeper form of self-loathing.[20]

Yet while adopting Wilson's end of global democracy, the neoconservatives insisted upon employing McKinley's and Theodore Roosevelt's means to achieve it. They believed in transforming the world in America's image, but sought to do so through the unimpeded use of American power rather than through international cooperation and organization. They were as hostile to the United Nations as the nationalists.

Many of the neoconservatives were Jewish, and they were often portrayed by Buchanan and other critics as being driven by their concern for Israel. Indeed, some neoconservatives—among them Perle, Feith, Wurmser, Wolfowitz, and Elliott Abrams—were preoccupied with Israel's fate, and had been hostile to Palestinian self-determination, but that was not what defined neoconservative politics.* The neoconservatives of the 1990s were producing a version of America's civil millennialism—a millennialism that goes back to dissenting Protestantism. They reveled in American exceptionalism, and they defined America's exceptional role as creating a world in its image. Kagan wrote, "The benevolent hegemony exercised by the United States is good for a vast portion of the world's population."[21] Or as Donnelly put it, "American imperialism can bring with it new hopes of liberty, security, and prosperity."[22]

The neoconservatives were a "network," not a disciplined party. Although they sometimes acted as if they were a Leninist "cadre"—converging suddenly and in a myriad of seemingly unrelated venues on a heretical idea and its author—they also disagreed among themselves. Charles Krauthammer, a *Weekly Standard* contributing editor and *Washington Post* columnist, opposed the intervention in the Balkans. In the 2000 Republican presidential primaries, Kristol and Marshall Wittman backed Arizona senator John McCain, while Wolfowitz and Perle advised George W. Bush. Similar disagreements had divided the imperialists of the 1890s. But just as Roosevelt, Lodge, Adams, and the other imperialists closed ranks during the Spanish-

---

*In the Reagan administration, Wolfowitz had tried to stymie administration overtures toward the Palestinian Liberation Organization (see James Mann, *Rise of the Vulcans* [New York, 2004] p. 113). In 1996, Perle would chair an eight-person commission for an Israeli think tank, the Institute for Advanced Strategic and Political Studies, calling for a "clean break" with the Israeli Labour Party's conciliatory policies toward the Palestinians and for the ouster of Saddam Hussein, including the encouragement of an Israeli plan to restore the Hashemite monarchy in Iraq. Members of the commission would include Douglas Feith and David Wurmser. See *A Clean Break: A New Strategy for Securing the Realm* (IASPS, 1996).

American War, and became a powerful lobby for a new foreign policy, the neoconservatives in Washington would close ranks during Bush's first year in office. When, after September 11, they joined forces with the nationalists, they completely dominated the foreign policy of the Bush administration.

EVIL REMAINS

During the 2000 campaign, Bush came across as a narrow nationalist. What he most disliked about Clinton's foreign policy, it seemed, was its attempt to enlarge the democratic community. "We should not send our troops to stop ethnic cleansing and genocide in nations outside our strategic interest," Bush said in a television interview in January 2000.[23] In one of the debates with Vice President Al Gore during the campaign, the following revealing exchange occurred:

> *Gore*: The world's coming together ... they're looking to us. I think that in the aftermath of the Cold War, it's time for us ... to step up to the plate, to provide the leadership: leadership on the environment, leadership to make sure the world economy keeps moving in the right direction.
>
> *Bush*: I'm not so sure the role of the United States is to go around the world and say, "This is the way it's got to be. We can help." ... I think one way for us to end up being viewed as the ugly American is for us to go around the world saying, "We do it this way, so should you."[24]

Bush was, perhaps, creating artificial distinctions. Gore wasn't saying, after all, that the United States should *impose* its way of life on recalcitrant nations, but what Bush said did suggest a discomfort with the Wilsonian commitment to global democracy that united liberal Democrats and neo-conservative Republicans.

During the campaign, Bush also revealed a dark, pessimistic view of the world that came, perhaps, from his religious awakening in the mid-1980s. Bush's religious beliefs seem to have grown out of a sense of personal redemption from sin—in his case, alcoholism—but during this period, he also fell under the influence of premillennial evangelists Billy Graham and his son Franklin Graham. Theirs was a vision of good arrayed against an ever-present evil.[25] Bush's vision of the world was similar. During the campaign he described "a world of terror and missiles and madmen" and warned that "the [evil] Empire has passed, but evil remains."[26]

This Hobbesian view provided him with a rationale for a national missile defense but not for an aggressive war against terror or madmen. Like Jefferson, who in his first inaugural address thanked Providence for separating the United States "from the exterminating havoc of one quarter of the globe," he used this image of a foreign evil to justify disengagement and withdrawal. During the campaign, Bush displayed the same wary but also disinterested attitude toward the world—the same mixture of nationalism and provincialism—as Armey, Senator Kay Bailey Hutchinson, and other Texas politicians. Bush's sense of evil would survive and even sharpen during his presidency, but after September 11, he would lose his detachment.

During the campaign, Bush surrounded himself with both nationalists and neoconservatives, but he was drawn to the nationalists. Condoleezza Rice became his chief campaign adviser and Cheney his running mate. He would make Rice his national security adviser, and would accept Cheney's recommendation that Rumsfeld, another nationalist, be secretary of defense. The neoconservatives got second- and third-level jobs in the Pentagon and on the National Security Council and vice president's staff. Paul Wolfowitz, who was nominated as deputy secretary of defense, was the highest-ranking neoconservative, occupying a position in the Bush administration comparable to that which Theodore Roosevelt occupied in the McKinley administration. Perle turned down the number three position at the Pentagon, but he was made chairman of the Defense Policy Board, which he used as a bully pulpit for his views and those of other neoconservatives like former CIA director James Woolsey. Powell, a Wilsonian internationalist, got secretary of state, but from the beginning he lacked the access to and influence over Bush that Rice, Rumsfeld, and Cheney enjoyed.

During his first nine months in office, Bush would sometimes side with Powell, but only when Cheney, Rumsfeld, and Rice concurred. When a Chinese jet collided with an American spy plane over the South China Sea in April, and the plane and its crew were forced to land on a Chinese island, Bush took Powell's and the nationalists' advice and offered China a muted, but real, apology in exchange for the crew's return. The neoconservatives were livid. Kristol and Kagan called the apology a "profound national humiliation."[27] But Bush sided with the nationalists and neocon-servatives against Powell in abandoning the negotiations between the Israelis and the Palestinians and in repudiating international treaties. By the eve of September 11, 2001, journalists had already noted Cheney's extraordinary influence and Powell's absence of clout.

THE TIGER ROARED

On September 11, Osama bin Laden's Afghan-based organization, al-Qaeda, carried out devastating suicide attacks against Washington and New York using hijacked airliners. The attack took Bush by surprise. He had paid little attention to al-Qaeda before September 11. He had made no effort either to destroy the organization and its leader or to address the issues that underlay the Islamists' appeal in the Mideast. The attacks changed his attitude toward foreign policy. He "saw evil" in the attacks, he told the nation that evening, but he no longer took the evidence of evil in the world as a reason for withdrawal.[28] Bush now saw his role as eradicating rather than ignoring evil. Wrote policy experts Ivo H. Daalder and James M. Lindsay, "The Bush philosophy turned John Quincy Adams on his head and argued that the United States should aggressively go abroad searching for monsters to destroy."[29]

In waging what he called a "war on terror," Bush appeared for the first time to be comfortable in the presidency. He adopted a tough guy, no-nonsense frontier style. What had seemed like shallowness now appeared to be decisiveness. He revived the rhetoric of the Indian wars and the war in the Philippines to characterize the struggle against al-Qaeda. He described members of al-Qaeda as "barbaric criminals" and framed the contest as one between civilization and barbarism: "We're fighting against men without conscience, but full of ambition—to remake the world in their own brutal images. For all these reasons we're fighting to win—and win we will. There is a great divide in our time—not between religions or cultures, but between civilization and barbarism."[30]

In the three months after September 11, the nationalists, international-ists, and neoconservatives worked together brilliantly. They gathered international support to attack al-Qaeda's headquarters and base of support in Afghanistan. When the Afghanistan's Taliban government refused to turn over bin Laden, American forces backed the anti-Taliban Northern Alliance's efforts to oust the government. In late October, the prospects for victory looked dim. "We said it would be long, we said it would be difficult," Rumsfeld warned.[31] But by the first week in December, Kabul and Kandahar had fallen, and the Taliban had fled into the caves in the mountains and across the Pakistani border. In a speech aboard the U.S.S. *Enterprise,* Bush heralded the victory:

> Just as we were 60 years ago, in a time of war, this nation will be patient, we'll be determined, and we will be relentless in the pursuit of freedom. This is becoming clear to al-Qaeda terrorists and the Taliban. Not long ago, that regime controlled most of Afghanistan. Today, they control not much more than a few caves. Not long ago, al-Qaeda's leader dismissed America as a paper tiger. That was before the tiger roared.[32]

In the wake of the surprisingly easy victory in Afghanistan, Bush, Cheney, and the Pentagon experienced the same rush of national power and the same illusion of omnipotence that the McKinley administration had experienced after the "splendid little war" against Spain. In 1899, the McKinley administration put aside qualms about overseas expansion and annexed the Philippines. In 2002, the Bush administration set aside obvious objections to invading and occupying a large, populous Middle Eastern nation and decided to invade Iraq. And like McKinley's decision a century before, the president's decision confirmed a course of action that influential, but hitherto marginal or dissenting, intellectuals and policy-makers had been recommending for years.

THE CASE FOR WAR

Both the nationalists and neoconservatives had begun to call for Saddam's ouster in the late 1990s after the U.N. inspectors left Iraq. In 1998, Rumsfeld joined Wolfowitz and other neoconservatives in signing the Project for the New American Century's open letter to Clinton calling for Saddam's ouster. Rumsfeld advocated removing Saddam at one of the first meetings of Bush's National Security Council, and Wolfowitz made a pitch for attacking Iraq at a meeting at Camp David right after September 11. But, as might be expected, the nationalists and neoconservatives came to the same conclusion from somewhat different perspectives.

Cheney, Rumsfeld, and the nationalists were genuinely concerned about preventing nations hostile to the United States from acquiring nuclear weapons. They saw an invasion of Iraq as a warning shot that would deter other "rogue states" from trying to acquire nuclear weapons. But Iraq was of special importance because of the threat that Saddam's regime posed to the Persian Gulf oil fields. Said one administration official of the plan to invade Iraq, "If the Gulf produced kumquats, would we be doing this."[33] In a strategy paper that Cheney had produced in his last year as secretary of defense for Bush's father, he had set out as one of America's goals "to preclude any hostile power from dominating a region critical to our interests."[34] The Mideast was one of those regions. "In the Middle East and Southwest Asia, our overall objective is to remain the predominant outside power in the region and preserve U.S. and Western access to the region's oil," a classified draft of the strategy had said.[35] Cheney and Rumsfeld were still thinking along these lines.

The nationalists did not want to invade Iraq in order to enrich a specific American oil company like Chevron, on whose board Condoleezza Rice had sat. Indeed, many of the oil companies were leery of an invasion. Rather, the nationalists wanted to ensure a dependable, low-cost supply of oil to the United States and other oil-consuming nations and to prevent a hostile power from being able to hold the world hostage by controlling access to the region's oil. A secret National Security Council memorandum in February 2001 proposed that the NSC "meld" its work with Cheney's energy task force. "The review of operational policies towards rogue states," the report said, should take into account "actions regarding the capture of new and existing oil and gas fields."[36] The energy report, which Cheney released in July 2001, warned that "Middle East oil producers will remain central to world oil security." The report predicted that by 2020, Saudi Arabia, Iraq, and their neighbors would supply "between 54 and 67 percent of the world's oil."[37]

Iraq was expected eventually to rival Saudi Arabia as the region's top oil producer. If Iraq were also to acquire nuclear weapons, its power over the region and the world economy would expand exponentially. It would "dominate a region critical" to American interests. So the nationalists wanted to remove Saddam at the first opportunity. At the first National

Security Council meeting in the new Bush administration, when the subject of Iraq was broached, Rumsfeld had said, "Imagine what the region would look like without Saddam and with a regime that's aligned with U.S. interests. It would change everything in the region and beyond it."[38]

The nationalists saw two elements to that strategy. One was putting in power, through appointment or elections, a ruler or a party that was strongly pro-American. The other was opening Iraq's oil industry to private, and particularly American, investment, which would give the United States a hold over Iraq's future and vast oil reserves, as well as enriching American companies.[39] "The best way to reduce vulnerability," Cheney's report argued, was "to open up areas of their energy sectors to foreign investment."[40] At one of the first National Security Council meetings, Rumsfeld's Defense Intelligence Agency distributed maps showing Iraq's existing and potential oil fields, along with a list of foreign suitors for them.[41] To put both elements of this strategy into effect, the nationalists, as well as the neoconservatives, were counting on the pro-American Iraqi exile Ahmed Chalabi. Chalabi, whom they were grooming to replace Saddam, had already pledged that "American companies will have a big shot at Iraqi oil."[42]

The nationalists also reasoned that if Iraq were to open its oil industry to private companies, OPEC would no longer be able to set prices by limiting the supply of oil. That would help keep world prices down, and it would also deprive the Saudi regime of the kind of leverage over the United States, Europe, and Japan it exercised during the 1973 oil boycott. On the eve of the war, one administration official said, "Iraq has an enormous amount of oil. It has been isolated for a long time. They are certainly capable of producing two or three million more barrels, and put that together with increased Russian production, and you have the beginning of the end of OPEC."[43] Predicted a Washington consultant who worked closely with the administration before the war, "I think that OPEC's days are numbered."[44]

The nationalists also wanted a pro-American Iraq as insurance against the Saudis turning against the United States and as a wedge against Syria and Iran. The United States needed a country in the Persian Gulf that could defend American interests the way the Shah's Iran had once done. A new Iraq, they hoped, could play that role. Karen Kwiatkowski, who served in the Pentagon's Near East South Asia directorate, listed the Pentagon's objectives as "more bases from which to flex US muscle with Syria and Iran, and better position for the inevitable fall of the regional ruling Sheikdoms."[45] While Rumsfeld would later deny that he was planning American bases in Iraq, he would tell a private meeting in January 2003 that plans for such bases were under way. [46]

The neoconservatives shared the nationalists' concern about Iraq dominating the Gulf's oil fields. In 1979, well before Saddam had acquired a reputation as a tyrant, Wolfowitz had supervised a Pentagon study of what would happen if Iraq gained control of Gulf oil fields, either directly through invasion or through intimidation. "Wolfowitz's earliest interest in Iraq," journalist James Mann writes, "arose from concerns about oil, geopolitics and the balance of power in the Persian Gulf, not from concerns about Saddam Hussein's behavior."[47] Some of the neoconservatives also remembered that the Saudis had used the oil boycott against Israel in 1973 and wanted to use Iraqi oil to counter the Saudi dominance over oil supplies.

Some neoconservatives like Feith and Perle, as well as nationalists like Rumsfeld, saw the overthrow of Saddam Hussein as essential to Israel's security. The neoconservatives, *Financial Times* columnist John Dizard wrote, "saw the invasion of Iraq as the precondition for a reorganization of the Middle East that would solve Israel's strategy problems, without the need for an accommodation with either the Palestinians or the existing Arab states."[48] Chalabi had promised the neoconservatives that if he came to power, he would recognize Israel and even rebuild the oil pipeline between Mosul and Haifa.[49]

The big difference with the nationalists, however, was over "nation-building." Unlike the nationalists, the neoconservatives attached great importance to creating a "democratic" Iraq—by nation-building, if necessary. They believed that a democratic Iraq would provide a model that would discredit the autocracies in the Gulf, Syria, and Egypt and marginalize Palestinian radicals and militants. Wolfowitz told the *New York Times* in September 2002:

> I don't think it's unreasonable to think that Iraq, properly managed—and it's going to take a lot of attention, and the stakes are enormous, much higher than Afghanistan—that it really could turn out to be, I hesitate to say it, the first Arab democracy. . . . And I think if it's significant for Iraq, it's going to cast a very large shadow, starting with Syria and Iran, but across the whole Arab world.[50]

The neoconservative network amplified these arguments. Neoconservative Daniel Pipes, whom Bush would appoint to the U.S. Institute for Peace, predicted that "a famous American victory in Iraq and the successful rehabilitation of that country will bring liberals out of the woodwork and generally move the region toward democracy."[51] Max Singer, a co-founder of the conservative Hudson Institute, predicted that if the United States were to create a democratic Iraq, "there will be an earthquake throughout the region" that could topple the Saudi government.[52]

THE DISSENTERS

Powell and the internationalists in the State Department favored attempting to contain Saddam through U.N. inspections and sanctions. Powell had always been skeptical about "regime change" in Iraq. "We don't just want to replace one bad guy with another bad guy," Powell had said at an early NSC debate on Iraq.[53] After the war in Afghanistan, Powell wanted the administration to focus on resolving the conflict between Israel and the Palestinians. Like Clinton and his officials, Powell believed that this conflict, and the U.S. identification with Israel, was fueling anti-Americanism in the Mideast and contributing to the popularity of al-Qaeda. He argued that by unilaterally attacking Iraq, the U.S. would only further inflame anti-Americanism.

Powell himself didn't make this case publicly, but Brent Scowcroft, who conferred frequently with Powell, did so on his behalf.[54] In a column in the *Wall Street Journal,* Scowcroft wrote:

The shared view in the [Mideast] is that Iraq is principally an obsession of the U.S. The obsession of the region, however, is the Israeli-Palestinian conflict. If we were seen to be turning our backs on that bitter conflict— which the region, rightly or wrongly, perceives to be clearly within our power to resolve—in order to go after Iraq, there would be an explosion of outrage against us. We would be seen as ignoring a key interest of the Muslim world in order to satisfy what is seen to be a narrow American interest.

Even without Israeli involvement, the results could well destabilize Arab regimes in the region, ironically facilitating one of Saddam's strategic objectives. At a minimum, it would stifle any cooperation on terrorism, and could even swell the ranks of the terrorists.[55]

Powell and Scowcroft's views were widely shared at the CIA and among the uniformed military. Many of Bush's father's old guard shared their opinion, including former secretary of state James Baker. Ordinarily, this weight of opinion would have carried the day, but not in the Bush White House.

EXILES AND EXPERTS

There were two factors that militated against Powell and for the neoconservatives and nationalists. First, Bush himself was instinctively sympathetic to the nationalists, and he was more comfortable politically as a "war president" than as a mediator between the Israelis and Palestinians. Second, the neoconservatives finessed what should have divided them from the nationalists—their emphasis on nation-building in Iraq—through arguments from Ahmed Chalabi and the exiles linked to the Iraqi National Congress and from two key specialists, historian Bernard Lewis and political scientist Fouad Ajami. The exiles and the specialists argued that the United States could create a democracy in Iraq and the Mideast without a long and difficult occupation. It wouldn't be necessary to do the kind of nation-building the United States had backed in Somalia or the Balkans.

Like the Manila businessmen who had assured McKinley that Americans would have little to fear from Filipino nationalism, the exiles insisted, in Chalabi's words, that "the Iraqi people will welcome U.S. troops in Iraq. They will see them as liberators." The exiles, who were promoted by Perle, Wolfowitz, and the neoconservatives, met repeatedly with Bush, Cheney, and Pentagon officials. At one meeting in January with Bush, three exiles from the Iraqi National Congress told Bush, Kan'an Makiya reported, that "all Iraqis of all sects would welcome these forces from the very first moment." Makiya himself told Bush, "The Iraqis will welcome the U.S. forces with flowers and sweets when they come in."[56]

On the eve of the invasion, Cheney stressed the importance of the exiles' message. Cheney said March 16 on *Meet the Press*:

> The president and I have met with them, various groups and individuals, people who have devoted their lives from the outside to trying to change things inside Iraq. . . . The read we get on the people of Iraq is there is no

question but what they want to get rid of Saddam Hussein and thy will welcome as liberators the United States when we come to do that.

Lewis and Ajami were equally important in convincing not only Bush and the nationalists but the neoconservatives that a military victory in Iraq wouldn't entail a long period of nation-building. Both men were very well known and esteemed experts on the Mideast who had close ties to the neo-conservatives. Lewis was a professor emeritus at Princeton, and expert on the history of Islam; Ajami, a political scientist at the Johns Hopkins School of Advanced International Studies, had written several influential books on Arab politics. Lewis had been a mentor to Wolfowitz and Perle. Talking to Lewis, Perle said, was "like going to Delphi to see the oracle."[57] After September 11, Lewis conferred at length with Perle's Defense Policy Board, Rumsfeld, Cheney, and Rice. Bush read Lewis's articles. Ajami met with administrative officials and would have a particularly strong influence on Cheney.

Lewis and Ajami dismissed the arguments Powell and the internationalists made. They denied that invading Iraq, while ignoring the Israeli-Palestinian conflict, would enflame anti-Americanism. They denied that hostility to the United States in the region stemmed either from the exercise of American power or from America's ties with Israel. "In the Middle East," Lewis wrote in *National Review* in December 2001, "anti-Americanism is nourished not so much by America's power as by the sources of that power—America's freedom and plenty."[58] Anti-Americanism, Lewis argued, was a product of envy and resentment at America's success. It didn't spring, Ajami wrote, from "our ties to Israel," but "from countless other sources: a deep alienation between ruler and ruled, a rage born of the disappointments of the young, a scapegoating that shifts onto America the blame for the ills of an Arab world unsettled and teased by exposure to a modern civilization it can neither master nor reject."[59]

Lewis discounted the history of colonialism in the Mideast. "The Anglo-French interlude," he wrote in *What Went Wrong,* "was comparatively brief and ended half a century ago."[60] (In fact, colonialism in the Mideast lasted for over 150 years.) Lewis also interpreted expressions of anticolonialism or anti-imperialism as expressions of irrational envy and resentment. He dismissed Khomeini's rage at the United States: "What did the Ayatollah Khomeini mean when he repeatedly called America the 'Great Satan'? The answer is clear. Satan is not an invader, an imperialist, an exploiter. He is a tempter, a seducer, who, in the words of the Koran, 'whispers in the hearts of men.' "[61]

According to Lewis, Khomeini didn't really object to American imperialism, but to the American way of life. Americans, Lewis and Ajami contended, were not hated for what they had done in the Arab world, but for how they lived. If the United States were to tilt toward the Palestinians in their conflict with Israel, or to expend billions in foreign aid, it wouldn't make any difference. The citizens of the Mideast (and for Lewis, this meant Muslims) would still hate America and Americans. So it didn't make any sense to talk of addressing the issues that inspired support for al-Qaeda.

Instead, Lewis and Ajami proposed that the United States, in Lewis's words, "get tough" with the states in the Mideast. "For America to seek friendship or even good relations with such regimes is a forlorn hope," Lewis wrote. "But to win respect is both possible and necessary."[62] Lewis and Ajami advocated that America start to act like an imperial power. Wrote Ajami about the coming invasion of Iraq, "Where Britain once filled the void left by the shattered Ottoman Empire in the aftermath of the First World War, now the failures—and the dangers—of the successor Arab states are drawing America to its own imperial mission."[63]

If the United States were to get tough, Ajami and Lewis promised success. By ousting Saddam, it would unleash pent-up feelings of friendship rather than hostility toward the United States. Wrote Lewis, "In Iran and Iraq, with governments seen as anti-American, public opinion is pro-American. The joy displayed by the Afghan people at the ending of Taliban rule could be repeated, on a larger scale, in both these countries."[64] Ajami wrote even more emphatically, "Were we to pick up where we left off a decade ago and head to Baghdad, the tormented people of Iraq would be sure to erupt in joy. If we liberate them, they may (if only for a while) forgive America the multitude of its sins. They may take our gift and do the easiest of things: construct a better Iraq than the one that the Tikriti killers have put in place."[65] Ajami and Lewis predicted that Saddam's ouster would actually improve the conditions for peace in Israel by intimidating the radical Palestinians; and they discounted the reaction of the "Arab street."

Their views had a startling impact in the highest circles of the administration. If what they said was true, the United States did not have to worry about creating instability in the region; more important, it didn't have to worry about a difficult war and occupation in Iraq. Nation-building could be accomplished in a matter of months, not years. According to Lawrence F. Kaplan, Wolfowitz's model of how the United States would be received by the Iraqis became the French welcoming the allied troops at the end of World War II.[66] But Wolfowitz was an easy sell. What was important was that Lewis and Ajami also convinced Bush, Rumsfeld, and Cheney. When Cheney first made the case for war in a speech before the Veterans of Foreign War in Nashville in August 2002, he even cited Ajami by name. When Saddam was ousted, Cheney said,

> the freedom-loving peoples of the region will have a chance to promote the values that can bring lasting peace. As for the reaction of the Arab "street," the Middle East expert Professor Fouad Ajami predicts that after liberation, the streets in Basra and Baghdad are "sure to erupt in joy in the same way the throngs in Kabul greeted the Americans." Extremists in the region would have to rethink their strategy of Jihad. Moderates throughout the region would take heart. And our ability to advance the Israeli-Palestinian peace process would be enhanced, just as it was following the liberation of Kuwait in 1991.[67]

Over the next six months, as the administration made its case for war, the nationalists and neoconservatives worked in tandem to convince Congress and the American people that the entire operation would be, in the words of Defense Policy Board member Kenneth Adelman, a "cakewalk."[68]

IMPERIALISM IN A HURRY

As the administration begin positioning forces in the Gulf for an invasion, neoconservatives took stock of what the United States was about to do. Donnelly and Boot were no longer alone in acknowledging that the administration was engaged in an imperial strategy. Said Charles Krauthammer, "People are now coming out of the closet on the word 'empire.'"[69] *The National Interest, Policy Review,* as well as *The Weekly Standard* were now full of articles extolling the benefits of a new American empire. Stephen Peter Rosen wrote in *The National Interest,* "The notion of an American empire, far from being anomalous and ill fitted to the twenty-first century, might comport nicely with it."[70]

Liberals who backed the war also acknowledged that the United States was about to engage in imperialism. Michael Ignatieff, a professor at Harvard's Kennedy School, described the proposed war as an "imperial operation" similar to Kosovo and Bosnia. It was, Ignatieff wrote, "imperialism in a hurry: to spend money, to get results, to turn the place back to the locals and get out. But it is similar to the old imperialism in the sense that real power in these zones . . . will remain in Washington."[71] Boot had also compared the Balkans to Iraq, claiming that America had been engaged in imperialism "in places like Bosnia, Kosovo, Afghanistan, and now Iraq."[72]

Ignatieff got the fact of imperialism right, but he and Boot were completely mistaken in comparing the administration's strategy in Iraq with what the Clinton administration had done in Kosovo and Bosnia. It was like Beveridge or Roosevelt comparing America's conquest and annexation of the Philippines with the Westward migration and Louisiana Purchase. In Bosnia and Kosovo, the Clinton administration had acted in exactly the manner that Wilson had prescribed for the League of Nations.[73] The U.S. acted through NATO rather than alone; it sought to stop particular acts of aggression rather than overthrow an existing government and install a new political and economic system. Afterward, it participated in multinational peacekeeping forces. At every point, the United States sought to avoid any hint that it was trying to impose *its* will on the Balkans.

In Iraq, the United States would act virtually alone—its junior partner, Great Britain, was the former imperial power in the region. In spite of its protestations that it was acting in self-defense, it would not seek merely to destroy Iraq's weapons of mass destruction, or its ability to make them. Instead, it would use its superior might to invade and occupy Iraq and to transform it into a country that is not only "aligned with U.S. interests" but also a beacon of democratic capitalism in the Mideast. By combining neoconservatism's millennial project of global democratic transformation with nationalism's insistence on going it alone, the Bush administration had unwittingly come up with an imperial strategy that resembled that which Beveridge, Lodge, and Roosevelt had advocated in the headiest moments of 1899–1900. It was an imperialism that aspired not merely to control, but to impose an economic and political system. In his debate with Gore, Bush had said, "I'm not so sure the role of the United States is to go around the world and say, 'This is the way it's got to be.'" But this was exactly what Bush planned to say to the Iraqis and the rest of the world.

CHAPTER TEN

George W. Bush and the Illusion
of Omnipotence

History is littered with unintentional consequences. The United States undertook the annexation of Hawaii and the conquest of the Philippines for similar reasons, but with vastly different results. American officials thought that they had ensured the future of the Shah's pro-American regime by getting him to undertake a program of modernization, only to help precipitate his overthrow by an anti-American movement led by Ayatollah Khomeini.

The final result of a major international event like the American invasion and occupation of Iraq won't be known for some time. When the story of the war is written two or three decades from now, historians may find benefits from the war that were not apparent at the time. Or they may see it, like Germany's annexation of Alsace-Lorraine in 1871, as an event that set the world on a downward trajectory to a war from which it would not soon recover. But a year after the war, what was most striking was the difference between what the Bush administration claimed it was going to accomplish that first year and what actually occurred in Iraq and in the rest of the world. The difference suggested not only that the Bush administration had deceived the public, but that it had deceived itself.

SELLING THE WAR

In the speeches he gave in the fall 2002 and winter 2003, Bush presented a war on Iraq as a continuation of the war against terror and al-Qaeda that had begun on September 11. He described Saddam as "evil" and a threat to the "civilized world"—the same terms he had used to describe al-Qaeda and that his predecessors had invoked against their Indian and Mexican adversaries in the nineteenth century. In Cincinnati, on the eve of the congressional vote on the war, Bush warned of the "great threat to peace" that Americans faced from Iraq's weapons of mass destruction and its ties to terrorist organizations.[1] To make his case, he exaggerated what were already dubious intelligence findings. Bush warned that Saddam could "threaten America and the world with horrible poisons and diseases and gases and atomic weapons" and that his "alliance with terrorists could allow the Iraqi regime to attack America without leaving any fingerprints."[2] American troops would later discover neither weapons of mass destruction nor ties to al-Qaeda.

To the question of why the United States couldn't deter Saddam the way it had the Soviet Union, Bush responded that Saddam was an uncontrollable "madman"—a charge Americans had used frequently in the twentieth century against such adversaries as Fidel Castro, and that served as a strategic deus ex machina to justify intervention when insufficient provocation existed. In his State of the Union address in January 2003, Bush said, "Some have said we must not act until the threat is imminent. Since when have terrorists and tyrants announced their intentions, politely putting us on notice before they strike? If this threat is permitted to fully and suddenly emerge, all actions, all words, and all recriminations would come too late. Trusting in the sanity and restraint of Saddam Hussein is not a strategy, and it is not an option."[3]

Before the war, in a speech at the American Enterprise Institute, Bush did evoke the promise of Iraqi and Mideast democracy, but most of his speeches reflected his Hobbesian outlook on the world. His political handlers may have also believed that he could best convince Americans of the need for war by instilling fear in them. The strategy certainly worked. Most Americans came to see the war as self-defense against a looming nuclear and terrorist threat. On the eve of the invasion, a majority of Americans even believed that Saddam had been involved in the September 11 terrorist attacks.

Bush did not originally plan to take the issue of war to the United Nations, but in the summer of 2002, Powell insisted that he do so, and with the support of many of the former officials from Bush's father's administration and at the urging of British prime minister Tony Blair, he finally agreed to do so. It was a hollow victory, because Bush approached the U.N. in bad faith. He insisted that he would do what he wanted regardless of what the Security Council decided. In his September 12 speech, he didn't offer to leave the decision of war up to the Security Council. He left it up to the delegates to the United Nations to join the United States in taking a stand against Iraq: "We cannot stand by and do nothing while dangers gather. We must stand up for our security, and for the permanent rights and the hopes of mankind. By heritage and by choice, the United States of America will make that stand. And, delegates to the United Nations, you have the power to make that stand, as well."[4]

And when the Security Council entrusted U.N. arms inspectors with the task of verifying whether Saddam's regime had eliminated its nuclear, chemical, and biological weapons, the administration tried to undermine their work. Administration officials claimed to have evidence of Iraqi weapons development, but they refused to share it with the U.N. inspectors.[5] When the inspectors found no evidence of Iraqi nuclear weapons development, and when they reported progress in verifying Iraq's claims that it had no chemical or biological weapons, the Bush administration dismissed their findings.

The United States initially won the cooperation of France, Russia, and China at the Security Council, but when French officials realized, after a meeting on January 13 with National Security Adviser Condoleezza Rice, that the United States planned to go to war regardless of how the Security Council voted, French foreign minister Dominique de Villepin declared, "We will not associate ourselves with military intervention that is not supported by the international community."[6] Powell, who had assumed the role of the "good soldier," denounced de Villepin for "ambushing" him with his statement, but as Powell knew, the French were expressing a sentiment that was widespread among U.N. members. Most nations and their publics saw the war as a clear violation of the U.N. Charter, which prohibits war except in self-defense or when authorized by the Security Council to protect international peace and security.

When the United States went to war, Bush referred to the forces as "the coalition," but the actual fighting was limited to the British and Americans. Bush boasted during the war that the coalition was "larger than one assembled in 1991 in terms of the numbers of nations participating." Wrote Daalder and Lindsay, "Bush could substantiate that claim only by including such powerhouses as Macedonia, Micronesia, the Marshall Islands, Palau, and Tonga and by ignoring that the Gulf War coalition consisted of nations that actually contributed hundreds of thousands of troops and tens of billions of dollars in treasure."[7] Still, administration members were convinced that France, Russia, and other critics would eventually come around once they saw America's success in war. Appearing before the House Budget Committee in February 2003, Wolfowitz said, "I would expect that even countries like France will have a strong interest in assisting Iraq's reconstruction."[8]

PREPARING FOR WAR

As the United States prepared for the invasion that winter, most members of the military were not concerned about the conflict but about the occupation. Said one professor at a war college, "I don't think they are worried about fighting Iraq but about garrisoning it afterward."[9] In February 2003, the Army War College produced an extensive report on "Reconstructing Iraq." The report warned that "the possibility of the United States winning the war and losing the peace in Iraq is real and serious. . . . Long-term gratitude is unlikely and suspicion of US motives will increase as the occupation continues. A force initially viewed as liberators can rapidly be relegated to the status of invaders should an unwelcome occupation continue for a prolonged time. Occupation problems may be especially acute if the United States must implement the bulk of the occupation itself rather than turn these duties over to a postwar international force."[10]

The report's authors presented a dilemma. If the United States stayed too long, it risked a nationalist backlash, but if it left too soon, Iraq could become a "haven for terrorism":

> The longer the occupation continues, the greater the potential that it will disrupt society rather than rehabilitate it. Thus, important and complex goals must be accomplished as quickly as possible. However, a withdrawal from Iraq under the wrong circumstances could leave it an unstable failed state, serving as a haven for terrorism and a center of regional insecurity or danger to its neighbors. The premature departure of U.S. troops could also result in civil war.[11]

The State Department raised similar concerns in reports issued by its Iraq Working Group.[12] And in testimony before the Senate Armed Services Committee in February, General Eric Shinseki, the Army Chief of Staff, estimated that occupying Iraq would require "something on the order of several hundred thousand soldiers."

Wolfowitz, Rumsfeld, and Cheney dismissed these concerns.[13] Wolfowitz said Shinseki's figure was "wildly off the mark." It was "hard to conceive that it would take more forces to provide stability in a post-Saddam Iraq than it would take to conduct the war itself," Wolfowitz said. Rumsfeld insisted that American soldiers would be "welcomed" in Iraq. Former secretary of the army Thomas White said, "The planning assumptions were that the people would realize they were liberated, they would be happy that we were there, so it would take a much smaller force to secure the peace than it did to win the war."[14]

IMPERIAL AMBITION

On April 9, twenty days after the war with Iraq began, U.S. Marines, aided by mechanized vehicles, pulled down a statue of Saddam from Baghdad's Firdos Square. The scene, shown on television around the world, was carefully stage-managed to resemble one of the scenes from the fall of the Berlin Wall in 1989, but in fact at most several hundred Iraqis, including members of Chalabi's Free Iraqi Forces, were gathered around the statue. On May 1, Bush, speaking aboard the aircraft carrier *Abraham Lincoln* in a setting designed for television, and perhaps for the 2004 presidential campaign, proclaimed the war over. With "the images of fallen statues," Bush said, "we have witnessed the arrival of a new era."[15]

In the past, the Pentagon would have overseen the war, and the State Department would have had a large role in the occupation, but Powell was completely squeezed out of the occupation by Rumsfeld, Wolfowitz, and Feith. With the Pentagon in charge, the outlines of the administration's imperial strategy emerged even before the main fighting was over. The Pentagon flew Chalabi and his forces into Iraq on April 6 to prepare for a new government. When Rumsfeld was asked whether the United States would approve the Iraqis choosing a government of clerics similar to that of Iran, he made clear that there were limits to American support for self-determination. Said Rumsfeld, "If you're suggesting, how would we feel about an Iranian-type government with a few clerics running everything in the country, the answer is: 'That isn't going to happen.'"[16] American military officials predicted "up to four bases in Iraq."[17] Chalabi told a television interviewer that "a strategic alliance between Iraq and the United States is a good thing for both."[18]

In Baghdad, American troops protected the oil ministry, but not other government buildings, from looters. Texas oilman Philip J. Carroll was put in charge of reviving Iraq's oil industry. On May 18, Carroll gave a press conference in Baghdad where he said the Iraqi government contracts with France and Russia might not be observed and that Iraq, which was a founding member of OPEC, might want to leave the cartel. Said Carroll, "Historically, Iraq has had, let's say, an irregular participation in OPEC quota systems. They have from time to time, because of compelling national interest, elected to opt out of the quota system and pursue their own path. . . . They may elect to do that same thing."[19] Iraq's appointed oil minister said that the country would seek foreign investment to revive its oil industry. Another U.S.-appointed official, who was traveling with him, said that preference in contracts would probably be given to the United States and other countries that had participated in the invasion.[20]

In May, with the sullied Chalabi unable to establish his legitimacy as Iraq's De Gaulle, the Pentagon fired administrator General Jay Garner and replaced him with Paul Bremer. According to Garner, he was relieved of his position because he favored elections before Iraq's economy had been privatized.[21] Bremer's mandate was to carefully prepare the ground for a new Iraqi government and economy, perhaps taking several years to do so. In an interview aboard an airplane in early June, Bremer, according to *Washington Post* reporter Rajiv Chandrasekaran, "discussed the need to privatize government-run factories with such fervor that his voice cut through the din of the cargo hold." Said Bremer, "We have to move forward quickly with this effort. Getting inefficient state enterprises into private hands is essential for Iraq's economic recovery."[22]

In September, a member of the U.S.-appointed Iraqi Governing Council, with Bremer's approval, issued an order privatizing Iraqi state companies and abrogating Iraqi laws that prohibited private ownership of "national" resources and "the basic means of production" and foreign ownership of real estate.[23] Ghassan Salame, a political scientist and former senior adviser to the ill-fated U.N. mission in occupied Baghdad, commented at a London conference, "The Coalition is intent on creating a new

Iraq of its own and one should not ignore the dimensions of that truly imperial ambition."[24]

ESCALATING COSTS

By the end of 2003, however, it was apparent that the Bush administration's plans for Iraq, reminiscent of American plans for the Philippines in 1900 or for Vietnam in the late 1950s, had gone horribly awry. The American invasion and occupation revived the simmering conflict between imperialism and nationalism that went back to the nineteenth century and still lingered in the Middle East. Soon after George W. Bush's appearance aboard the *Abraham Lincoln,* attacks began to intensify on American and British troops, foreign aid workers (including those from the U.N.), foreign businesspeople and journalists, and Iraqis working in any capacity for the United States or its appointed governing council. The attacks raised the question of whether the war was really over. From March 20 to May 1, 139 "coalition" soldiers had been killed; from May 2 until May 20, 2004, 766 were killed. Estimates of American wounded over the whole period stand at 4,424.[25] Iraqi military deaths were estimated at 5,633 and civilian deaths between 9,148 and 11,005.[26]

The administration attempted to ignore the mounting casualties. Mindful of the image of the "body bags" returning home during the Vietnam War, the Pentagon banned the press from covering the return of coffins to army bases. Neoconservative Max Boot suggested that the deaths were of no significance. He wrote in October 2003, "According to the National Law Enforcement Officers Memorial Fund, 114 police officers have died in the line of duty this year, almost exactly the number of service people who have been killed by Iraqi insurgents since May 1. And more than 41,000 people are killed on the nation's highways every year, according to the Department of Transportation."[27]

The Pentagon had originally expected to need only 30,000 troops by the end of the year, but in the face of repeated attacks, the numbers hovered around 150,000—close to the number that Shinseki had originally predicted. The cost of the war also escalated. Earlier, the Pentagon had refused to estimate the cost, but Andrew Natsios, the administrator of the Agency for International Development, had volunteered that the occupation would require $1.7 billion. After spending $66 billion on the invasion, the Bush administration had asked and got from Congress another $87 billion for the occupation, and was expected to ask for a similar amount after the November 2004 election.[28]

Except in the Kurdish regions in the north, which had enjoyed autonomy for almost a decade, there was widespread hostility toward the American occupation forces. On September 17, the *New York Times* reported that

> new intelligence assessments are warning that the United States' most formidable foe in Iraq in the months ahead may be the resentment of ordinary Iraqis increasingly hostile to the American military occupation, Defense Dept. officials said today. . . . As reasons for Iraqi hostility, the defense officials cited not just disaffection over a lack of electricity and other essential services in the months since the war, but cultural factors that magnify anger about the foreign military presence. "To a lot of Iraqis, we're no longer the guys who threw out Saddam, but the ones who are busting down doors and barging in on their wives and daughters," one defense official said.[29]

These "cultural factors," which Lewis and Ajami might have attributed to resentment toward the American way of life, were in fact rooted in century-old Arab nationalism, which the invasion and occupation had awakened. Wrote Indian journalist M. J. Akbar, the editor of *The Asian Age,* "What Bush and the neocons of Washington should be worried about is Iraqi nationalism. As the British found out in 1920, Shias and Sunnis can unite seamlessly if they are convinced that their common enemy is a foreign power. The elimination of Saddam's dictatorship has created space that will be filled by nationalism, not subservience to foreign interests. No free Iraqi government will happily sign a treaty permitting American bases full of soldiers obedient to [the] Pentagon."[30] A European diplomat who served in Baghdad told *Time,* "There is a real nationalistic feeling here. It is a real country, and it has a real national feeling that it is being occupied."[31]

At the beginning of October, *The Guardian*'s Suzanne Goldenberg filed a report on her travels throughout Iraq that would be echoed in similar accounts over the next six months:

Iraq under the US-led occupation is a fearful, lawless and broken place, where murder rates have rocketed, 80 percent of workers are idle and hospital managers despair at shortages of IV sets and basic antibiotics. Police are seen as thugs and thieves, and the American and British forces as distant rulers, more concerned with protecting their troops than providing security to ordinary Iraqis. The governing council they created is simply irrelevant. A mile away from one of the richest oilfields on earth, the queues at petrol stations stretch for hours. "We completely underestimated how broken this system was," says Andrew Alderson, the financial officer of the British-led administration in Basra.

Saddam's Republic of Fear, the mechanism of iron controls that held the state together, was gone, but its replacement is a violent chaos. The void created by the defeat of Saddam's highly centralized one-party regime has empowered religious extremists, political gangs, tribal chieftains, criminals and speculators, the venal and the corrupt. These are the men profiting in the new Iraq. The knock at the door at night is no longer a member of Saddam's secret police, but it could very well be an armed robber, an enforcer from a political faction, or an enemy intent on revenge.[32]

By the end of 2003, the Bush administration was looking at the confirmation of the Army War College's dire predictions. If it were to remain in Iraq with over a hundred thousand troops and with Bremer in charge of the government's every move, it could expect continued guerrilla war. Saddam himself had been captured, but the insurgency had only grown—led now by opponents as well as proponents of the old regime. But if the United States was to begin sharply reducing its commitment, it could expect chaos and even civil war in the country, and eventually a regime hostile to what the administration saw as American interests in the region. With an American election coming in November, and public discontent with the war and occupation rising, the administration wanted to convince American voters that it was committed to leaving, but it wasn't ready to cede defeat and give up its power in Iraq.

The administration began searching for a graceful exit—perhaps through the United Nations, perhaps through NATO—but it was still unwilling to take the necessary step to find one: ceding all claims to control over Iraq's polity and oil resources while earnestly seeking the help of the countries that it had previously rebuffed. Eventually, the United States will have to abandon its ambitions in Iraq, but instead, the Bush administration sought to buy time through equivocation and further deceit. What began as "imperialism in a hurry" became imperialism by sleight of hand.

Bremer and the Pentagon put off their plans to help the Iraqis write a new constitution that could provide the basis for elections that would choose a new sovereign government. Instead, Bremer supervised the drafting of an "interim constitution," a contradiction in terms that glossed over all the most serious points of contention. The United States announced it would transfer sovereignty to an Iraqi leadership on June 30, 2004, and even allowed the United Nations a role in choosing it, but at the same time, the Bush administration took steps to retain control over the country's military and police through an American security adviser and over its economy through American-controlled commissions. The administration also wanted to prevent the new Iraqi government from passing laws. One Iraqi appointee commented, "If it's a sovereign Iraqi government that can't change laws or make decisions, we haven't gained anything."[33]

The United States continued to promote privatization of the Iraqi economy, but found relatively few takers, especially among American companies that were afraid of sabotage and assassination. The administration signed lucrative contracts with Cheney's former company Halliburton to rebuild the oil fields, but American oil multinationals were fearful of investing in Iraq's reserves. Rumsfeld took it upon himself to obscure America's intentions and to rewrite the history of the invasion. Even as the United States increased its armed presence, Rumsfeld claimed he had never favored establishing military bases in Iraq. And when a reporter reminded Rumsfeld that he had predicted that Americans would be "welcomed" in Iraq, Rumsfeld snapped back, "Never said that. Never did. You may remember it well, but you're thinking of somebody else."[34] In fact, Rumsfeld had said exactly that to interviewer Jim Lehrer on the eve of the war.[35]

The failure to discover weapons of mass destruction in Iraq or any prior connections between Saddam Hussein and al-Qaeda complicated the administration's political task by undermining what had been its main public case for going to war. In response, the administration now shifted to neoconservative arguments that the war was creating a democratic Iraq and Middle East. Speaking at the Heritage Foundation in November 2003, Bush said, "The United States will complete our work in Iraq and in Afghanistan.

Democracy in those two countries will succeed. And that success will be a great milestone in the history of liberty. A democratic revolution that has reached across the globe will finally take root in the Middle East."[36]

As the prospects for this "democratic revolution" receded even further, Bush became more vehement in asserting that the United States was carrying out its millennial mission in Iraq. In occupying Iraq, Bush claimed to be following the will of God. "I also have this belief, strong belief, that freedom is not this country's gift to the world; freedom is the Almighty's gift to every man and woman in this world. And as the greatest power on the face of the Earth, we have an obligation to help the spread of freedom. . . . That is what we have been called to do, as far as I'm concerned," Bush told a press conference in April 2004.[37] This was a heady vision, but Bush and his supporters were invoking it to obscure the dismal reality of the occupation. Like his Western forbears who invoked Manifest Destiny and the call of civilization to justify the conquest of Mexican lands and the murder of Indians, Bush was using millennialism to rationalize America's more unseemly practices.

ECHOES OF THE INDIAN WARS

By the Spring of 2004, reports of American brutality toward Iraqis began to surface. These included torture of prisoners, many of whom were not insurgents but civilians rounded up for questioning at Abu Ghraib prison, and disproportionate reprisals against Iraqis who were resisting the American occupation. These reports recalled American conduct in the Indian wars and in the Philippines and Vietnam. In these wars, Americans acted inhumanely because they saw the enemy not as an equal human being, but as "savages" or "barbarians." One British commander complained to a reporter about the American tactics in Iraq:

> My view and the view of the British chain of command is that the Americans' use of violence is not proportionate and is overresponsive to the threat they are facing. They don't see the Iraqi people the way we see them. They view them as *untermenschen* [under-humans]. . . . When U.S. troops are attacked with mortars in Baghdad, they use mortar-locating radar to find the firing point and then attack the general area with artillery, even though the area they are attacking may be in the middle of a densely populated residential

area. They may well kill the terrorists in the barrage, but they will also kill and maim innocent civilians. That has been their response on a number of occasions. It is trite, but American troops do shoot first and ask questions later.[38]

To justify these tactics, the administration and its supporters resorted to the same kind of twisted logic that Americans had used in the Indian wars and in the Philippines. They claimed they were responding appropriately to savagery, when in fact much of the savagery had been provoked by their own attacks. Historian Reginald Horsman described this logic in the Indian wars, "As the Indians desperately fought to preserve their lands they lived on from white encroachment, their 'savage' actions were used to condemn [them]."[39]

When the Iraqis, demanding an end to the occupation, resorted to suicide bombings and kidnappings to counter the American advantage in weaponry and manpower, and when citizens rejoiced over dead Americans, the administration backers claimed that these responses justified the invasion itself and the massive use of force in retaliation. After four American mercenaries were ambushed in Fallujah, and two of them hung from a bridge, Brigadier General Mark Kimmitt promised "overwhelming" force in response to the "bestial" acts. American forces subsequently shelled the densely populated city and dropped 500-pound bombs on buildings. According to an American-appointed member of the Iraqi authority, American forces killed 271 and wounded 793 in the first eighteen days of the seige.

American forces also sought to punish Shiite rebel cleric Moktada al-Sadr and his followers. American and British forces killed 305 and wounded 1,261 during the same period in clashes with the Shiites that began in April 2004.[40] Al-Sadr had opposed Saddam's regime—his father had been assassinated by Saddam—but he opposed the American occupation, and when American authorities attempted to suppress his movement, he took up arms, gaining the support of many of Iraq's Shiites who had suffered under Saddam but had grown restive under the occupation. Yet neoconservative David Brooks described al-Sadr in words that echoed older descriptions of Geronimo or Aguinaldo and their followers. "He is vicious, while his opponents are civilized. Sadr and his band terrify people, and ride on a current of blood . . . Sadr is an enemy of civilization. The terrorists are enemies of civilization. They must be defeated," wrote Brooks.[41]

During the war in the Philippines, supporters of annexation had dismissed reports that American troops were using torture against the rebels.

In 1902, a prominent clergymen, the Reverend Homer Stuntz, wrote that the Filipinos were not really being tortured "since the victim has it in his own power to stop the process, or prevent it altogether" by telling what he knows "before the operation has gone far enough to seriously hurt him."[42] In May 2004, as stories appeared about American troops using torture at Iraqi prisons, administration supporters took a similar tack. Conservative talk-show host Rush Limbaugh compared what happened to a fraternity hazing, adding, "we're going to ruin people's lives over it and we're going to hamper our military effort, and then we are going to really hammer them because they had a good time."[43] Oklahoma senator James Inhofe said he was "outraged by the outrage," and described the prisoners as "terrorists."[44] Neoconservative John Podhoretz called the torture at Baghdad's Abu Ghraib prison an "aberrancy."[45] But what was happening in Iraq was far from being an aberration. It was typical of previous American and European attempts to subjugate native peoples who had been deemed inferior. Abu Ghraib was a product of this imperial mindset.

GROWTH OF TERRORISM

On the *Abraham Lincoln,* Bush had declared that the "liberation of Iraq is a crucial advance in the campaign against terror."[47] But the invasion utterly failed to stem the growth of radical Islamic terrorism. Instead, the American onslaught against one of the original homes of Islam became a major recruiting appeal for al-Qaeda and other terrorist groups. It confirmed their charges that America was following in the footsteps of the Crusaders by trying to dominate the Mideast. In July 2003, Pakistan's *Times* reported that "jihad recruitment is on the rise" in the wake of the American invasion of Iraq.[47] The next month, the London-based International Institute for Strategy Studies reported that

> the immediate effect of the war may have been to isolate further al-Qaeda from any potential state supporters while also swelling its ranks and galvanizing its will. . . . [The] war in Iraq has probably inflamed radical passions among Muslims and thus increased al-Qaeda's recruiting power and morale and, at least marginally, its operational capability. Any conclusive failure to find WMD would only exacerbate these effects.[48]

Since May 1, 2003, al-Qaeda was implicated in major terrorist attacks in Casablanca, Riyadh (in May and again in November), Kabul, Istanbul, and Madrid, and American forces in Iraq blamed terrorist groups aligned with al-Qaeda for continuous attacks against targets like the International Red Cross.

In April 2004, Pakistani journalist Husain Haqqani wrote about al-Qaeda:

> Ideological motivation for young men to join its ranks is now more important to al-Qaeda than a state sponsor. That motivation has been provided by the haste to war in Iraq. Officials in several Muslim countries have noted a rise in recruitment to extremist groups, and even U.S. officials . . . acknowledge that "there are literally thousands of jihadists around the world." These extremists have added anti-Americanism to their causes, which in the past involved only local separatist wars in remote parts of the world such as Chechnya and Kashmir.[49]

The neoconservatives had rejected Powell's argument that the United States had to turn to Israel and the Palestinians before Iraq. Wolfowitz had said, "The road to Jerusalem goes through Baghdad."[50] But after the invasion of Iraq, the conflict between Israelis and the Palestinians failed to abate. Bush attempted to revive negotiations between the two sides during a visit to Aqaba, Jordan, in June 2003, but abandoned the effort in the face of resistance from both the Palestinians and the Ariel Sharon government. While the first Bush and Clinton administrations had attempted to appear as honest brokers between the Israelis and the Palestinians, George W. Bush sided openly with the Sharon government, refusing to talk to Sharon's elected counterpart, Yasir Arafat, and finally endorsing, during a visit by Sharon in April 2004, the massive Israeli settlements on the West Bank. The Arab press termed Bush's statement a "second Balfour declaration." Just as Britain, the first great imperial power in the region, had once guaranteed a homeland for Jews in Arab Palestine, now the United States, as Britain's successor, guaranteed that Israel's expansion into the West Bank would endure. Within Arab countries, and on the Arab street, the United States was now rightly seen as the champion of the Israeli occupation—a perception that, contrary to what Ajami and Lewis believed, was rooted in the history of imperialism in the Mideast and continued to inflame anti-Americanism and to recruit young men to international terrorism.

Wolfowitz had also predicted that France and the other dissenters on the Security Council would return to the fold after they saw Americans welcomed in Baghdad, but the war deepened the rift between the Bush administration and the governments and citizens of Europe and Asia. In South Korea and Spain, candidates critical of the war in Iraq defeated Bush allies in national elections. When Powell went to pay his respects to the new Spanish prime minister–elect, Socialist Jose Luis Rodriguez Zapatero, he was kept waiting for more than thirty minutes while the Spaniard had an "intimate tête-à-tête" with French president Jacques Chirac.[51]

Opinion polls registered distrust and disapproval of the Bush administration throughout the world. The Pew Research Center concluded from its March 2004 poll of nine European and Mideastern countries that "the war in Iraq has undermined America's credibility abroad. Doubts about the motives behind the U.S.-led war on terrorism abound, and a growing percentage of Europeans want foreign policy and security arrangements independent from the United States."[52] In the Middle East, some of the regimes began to talk reform, but their citizens were not conceiving of "reform" in a manner that the Bush administration would have preferred. A former ambassador from a western European nation to Saudi Arabia commented about Saudi Arabia to *The Economist* in March 2004, "If there were an election today, bin Laden would win by a landslide."[53] In Syria, the invasion of Iraq inspired a resurgence of conservative Islam.

The overall effect of the invasion and occupation was probably to dampen the spirit of reform not only in the Mideast but around the world. Desperately seeking allies, the Bush administration wooed regimes it had once denounced and it ignored assaults upon democratic reform. The reign of the mullahs in Iran—part of Bush's "axis of evil"—was strengthened, as the United States had to seek their help in calming a Shiite revolt in Iraq. Libya's Muammar Qaddafi was able to consolidate his rule by agreeing to be the poster boy for nuclear nonproliferation. The United States ignored the efforts by Russia's Vladimir Putin to silence his political opponents and to kill off Chechnya's independence movement. Bush, who had promised in April 2001 to defend Taiwan against a Chinese attack, criticized the Taiwanese government for holding a referendum on whether it should ask China to stop its missile threats against the island. Democratic reform may eventually come to all these areas, but it will emerge more slowly because of the administration's invasion and occupation of Iraq.

If the administration's experience in Iraq increasingly resembles past American imperial ventures, Bush's experience was remarkably similar to McKinley's in the Philippines more than a century before. Both men took office with little knowledge of the world and relied heavily on others for advice. Faced suddenly with grave challenges from abroad that could not be ignored, they went to war and, to their surprise and delight, were remarkably successful. Emboldened by their initial success at war, and prodded by a network of officials and intellectuals with unorthodox convictions, they took a far bolder and riskier step. Both men would then face difficulties of which these advisers had never warned them.

There are, however, differences between the two situations and the two men. The American conquest of the Philippines was important for Americans and for the Philippines, but was strictly a side show in the world of 1900, which was dominated by the European powers. The American invasion of Iraq may be the most important event of the first decade of the twenty-first century and could have repercussions well into the new century.

There is also a difference in what the two presidents, once in office, could draw upon for knowledge and insight. In 1900, McKinley and the United States were entering new terrain without any familiar landmarks. McKinley couldn't look back on the experience of Chester Arthur or Martin van Buren for guidance. Before McKinley, America hardly had a foreign policy outside its own hemisphere.

Bush, by contrast, had a century of American overseas experience to draw upon, including his own father's administration, but it had little impact on him. He claimed that Theodore Roosevelt was his favorite president, but like the neoconservatives, the Roosevelt he admired was the Rough Rider and the champion of the Strenuous Life, not the man who wrote Taft that the Philippines had become America's "heel of Achilles." He had no grasp of what Wilson learned in Mexico about the pitfalls of the United States trying unilaterally to impose a government on another country, even when that country was ruled by an unpopular tyrant. He had blundered into a century-old conflict between imperialism and nationalism in the Middle East, discovering to his surprise that America's intervention had provoked a nationalist backlash. Bush was ignorant, but unlike McKinley, he couldn't plead ignorance.

CONCLUSION

In the 1890s, the United States became fully aware of the struggle for imperial supremacy that had engaged Europe for two decades and was now also
drawing in Japan. Americans had to abandon their hemispheric isolation or
risk being shut out of world markets and intimidated by more powerful
navies. How to proceed? How to reconcile America's historic opposition to
imperialism and colonialism with an outward-looking foreign policy?
Over the next century, Americans developed an approach that drew upon
two world wars and the Cold War and upon disastrous wars in the Philippines and Vietnam. It was clearly outlined by Woodrow Wilson; it was repudiated during the Republican 1920s and set aside during Franklin
Roosevelt's first two terms, but revived and reshaped by Roosevelt in
World War II and by a succession of presidents during the Cold War. In the
1990s, with the Cold War's end, the ideal of collective security, rooted in a
century of bitter experience and an integrated world economy, had finally
become capable of realization. Yet as a new century dawned, George W.
Bush's administration abandoned this Wilsonian foreign policy for a toxic
mixture of nationalism and neoconservatism.

There was a common misapprehension that George W. Bush's foreign
policy was a specific response to the threat posed by al-Qaeda and to its
September 11 attack on the United States. But the foreign policy currents
that came together in the Bush administration had been swirling for
almost a decade in the pages of the *Weekly Standard* and in commissions
chaired by Donald Rumsfeld and Richard Perle. And the threat of Islamic
terrorism had first clearly surfaced in Beirut in 1983. If there was novelty
in Bush's foreign policy, it was in its embrace of a policy that preceded
Wilson's: the foreign policy of the American imperialists of the late 1890s.
Woodrow Wilson's foreign policy was meant as a corrective to the problems created by this older policy, but the lesson of this period, as well as

the years that followed, was lost on Bush and on the nationalists and neo-conservatives.

If America is to pull itself out of chasm into which Bush's foreign policy has plunged it—not just in the Mideast but in the Far East and in America's relations with Europe and Latin America—it will have to take up again where George H. W. Bush and Bill Clinton left off. Wilson's legacy, as refined over the last century, represents an understanding of world history, a strategy for peace and prosperity, and a moral and religious approach to international relations. It has not been without flaws, but, in comparison with the alternatives offered by the nationalists and neoconservatives, it has been wildly successful.

THE AGE OF EMPIRE

Woodrow Wilson and Franklin Roosevelt both understood that they were living in an age dominated and endangered by the quest for empire. But many historians today, as they look back upon the last 150 years, see an "age of empire" that lasted only from the 1870s to 1914 and was cut short by World War I, after which the world was threatened by fascism, nazism, and communism. That misses the essential continuity. Imperialism, and the age of empire, survived both world wars, and formed the subtext of the Cold War from the end of World War II until 1989. Even today, the age of empire lingers in the Mideast, South Asia, the Far East, the Caribbean, Africa, and the Balkans. In Chechnya, Tibet, or the Persian Gulf, great powers are still attempting to dominate nations either directly through colonial rule or indirectly through control of their economy and the threat of intervention against governments. In other areas, what persists are conflicts spawned by the imperial powers' earlier attempt to partition or conglomerate and rule. Foremost among these are the continuing conflicts between the Israelis and the Palestinians and between the Indians and the Pakistanis.

Within these regions, attempts by great powers to exert control still evoke the clash between imperialism and nationalism. Intervention invites a nationalist reaction. Wilson encountered this in Mexico in 1914 when he tried to unseat the unpopular dictator Huerta. Like the poet who predicted in 1845 that the Mexicans would cheer, "The Saxons are coming, our freedom is nigh," Wilson thought the Mexican people would applaud the

American intervention, but instead they resisted it as an assault on their national sovereignty. Wilson learned from this experience, but the lesson was lost upon George W. Bush. Schooled by the neoconservatives, and conned by Iraqi exiles, he assumed that because Iraq's Saddam Hussein was a murderous tyrant, Americans would be greeted as liberators. When they were not, he attributed the Iraqi's resistance to outside forces, just as British administrator Arnold Wilson had done in 1920.

Al-Qaeda and the radical Islamic movements also have to be understood as vestigial anti-imperialist movements rather than simply as the products of a fanatic religious war or a "clash of civilizations." Because the region's borders are themselves products of imperial intervention, nationalism in this region has often taken a pan-Arab or pan-Islamic form. Since the nineteenth century, when France and Great Britain began to colonize the region, anti-imperialist movements have acted in the name of Islam.[1] After World War II, the anti-imperialist leadership shifted to secular nationalists like Egypt's Gamal Abdel Nasser, Algeria's Ahmed Ben Bella, and Libya's Muammar Qaddafi. By the 1970s, a new generation of Islamic movements, led by Iran's Shiites, emerged out of the failure of secular nationalism to achieve the destruction of Israel and successful economic and social development. Many of the new Islamic militants were not clerics, but college graduates who had trained to be technicians or engineers. Wrote French sociologist Olivier Roy, "The same individuals who followed Nasser or Marx in the 1960s are Islamists today."[2]

These Islamic movements share the same animus toward the West and Israel that the older nationalist and Marxist movements did. They openly describe the enemy as Western imperialism. Where they differ from the older movements is in their reactionary social outlook, particularly toward women, and in their ultimate aspiration, which is to restore the older Muslim empire to world dominance. Standing in the way of that restoration is the United States. A recruiting pamphlet from a radical Islamic organization in Pakistan states, "Muslims have several centuries of accounts to settle. In Spain, Muslims ruled for several hundred years, and they have been pushed out. . . . All of India, including Kashmir . . . Burma, Nepal were all part of the Muslim empire. Palestine and the entire Middle East, and many important parts of Europe . . . The entire modern international order is based on injustice, and the United States is the enforcer of this order. Hence the Jihad against them."[3]

The Jihadists are committed to terrorizing Americans, destroying Israel, and replacing authoritarian and reactionary regimes with even more reactionary ones. The Clinton and George W. Bush administrations understood that they faced an implacable enemy whose objectives ran directly counter to those of the United States and who was using force to achieve them. The Bush administration's immediate response to September 11—to hunt down and destroy al-Qaeda—was the correct one. It was an act of self-defense. But officials in the White House and the Pentagon, influenced by Ajami, Lewis, and other neoconservative intellectuals, took the view that al-Qaeda's popularity lay simply in the irrational resentment of American life and not in the persistence of conflicts spawned by imperialism. The administration attacked the latest outgrowths of Islamic radicalism while ignoring the soil in which it has grown. It assumed that America's tilt to the Sharon government was irrelevant to its standing in the Mideast and that by invading Iraq America would intimidate its foes and embolden its supporters. What it did by invading Iraq was to lend credence to al-Qaeda's charge that the United States is following in the footsteps of the Crusaders, who, believing themselves the martial heirs of the Roman legions, sacked Jerusalem in 1099.* It fueled the growth of Islamic terrorist organizations.

THE BLESSINGS OF INTERNATIONALISM

Woodrow Wilson, Franklin Roosevelt, and their successors believed that through international organizations and treaties, the United States would keep the peace and promote prosperity much more effectively than it could accomplish acting alone. They were not thinking of ad hoc coalitions and arrangements, but of organizations like the League of Nations, United Nations, NATO, the IMF, World Bank, and WTO. They didn't see these

---

*Bernard Lewis and other neoconservatives had fun with bin Laden's references to Americans as "crusaders," but of course the Christian crusaders of the eleventh and twelfth centuries were mimicking the armies of imperial Rome. The Crusaders killed as many as a hundred thousand in seizing Jerusalem, which they held for a century. When the British and French began arriving in the early nineteenth century, they also professed to be bringing Christian civilization to the infidels of the area. Now it is American democracy. George W. Bush set off alarm bells, and confirmed bin Laden's use of the term, when he said on the White House lawn on September 16, 2001, that "this crusade, this war on terrorism, is going to take a while."

organizations as an alternative to American leadership, but as a way of exercising and preserving American leadership.

Theodore Roosevelt and Woodrow Wilson were the first presidents to understand that a dispute between France and Germany over who would control Morocco's police force could, if not adequately resolved, eventually threaten America's prosperity and even security. As Wilson said, "An attack in any quarter was an attack on the equilibrium of the world." But how could America make peace an ocean away? Wilson reasoned that the United States was incapable of single-handedly keeping the peace outside its own hemisphere (if even there!). He sought to create international organizations through which the United States could act. It was a simple point, and more obvious now than then, but it would lead eventually to organizations like NATO, without which the Cold War might have turned out much differently.

Wilson vested his hopes for peace in a single universal organization through which the great and lesser powers would settle disputes. The organization could also ease the transition out of imperialism through a system of disinterested mandates. But the League of Nations foundered on the great powers' continuing struggle for imperial supremacy. Although the U.N. did occasionally live up to expectations in its first four decades—for instance, in southern Africa—Franklin Roosevelt's successors experienced similar frustrations when the Cold War paralyzed the U.N. Security Council. But once the Cold War lifted, the United States was able to take advantage of what Clinton called "a network of alliances." By acting multilaterally in the Persian Gulf and the Balkans, George H. W. Bush and Clinton were able to deflect charges that they were trying to impose America's will on nations. A multilateral approach took American foreign policy out of the imperial context and removed the danger of a nationalist backlash.*

Wilson also believed that there were problems of peace and prosperity that could only be addressed through international organizations and treaties. For Wilson, these included disarmament and freedom of the seas; Franklin Roosevelt added international trade and finance and poverty;

---

*Of course, the backlash did come from al-Qaeda, but it was not caused by the American-led coalition's ouster of Iraq from Kuwait. Bin Laden himself had volunteered to help the Saudis dislodge Saddam from Kuwait. It came from the Bush administration's decision to station American troops and planes in Saudi Arabia, from which the U.S. was later to attack Iraq.

and subsequent administrations have added public health, the global environment, and international terrorism. The treaties and organizations that have addressed these problems have sometimes worked brilliantly. In 1987, for instance, the Reagan administration, from whom the nationalists and neoconservatives claim to take their cue, signed an international agreement calling for a compulsory 50 percent reduction by 1999 in the consumption of chlorofluorocarbons, which were creating a hole in the ozone layer. The goal was reached, and experts now expect the ozone layer to return to normal over the next four decades.[4]

George W. Bush's attitude toward the Kyoto agreement on climate change displayed an ignorance of the basic function of these kinds of treaties. There is simply no way to address global warming except through an international treaty. Nations and their companies will not absorb the costs of reducing pollution unless they are assured that other nations are going to share the burden. The Kyoto treaty was admittedly flawed, but Bush could have attempted to renegotiate it, or could have even let it remain unratified. Instead, he repudiated it, and in doing that, repudiated the premise of internationalism on which it was based. Future generations may regard Bush's dismissal of Kyoto in the same light as post–World War II generations viewed the attempts of Congress in the 1930s to prevent the United States from joining the struggle against Hitler.

THE PERILS OF UNILATERALISM

Wilson warned that if the United States shunned the League of Nations and tried to go it alone in the world, it would mean sacrificing the goodwill that America had acquired during the war. The world would revert to hostile trading blocs and eventually a new war would break out. Wilson's warnings may have seemed overwrought at the time, but proved to be prescient. In the interwar years, when America rejected Wilson's internationalism, its unilateral and isolationist policies didn't prevent, and may have encouraged, the outbreak of World War II.

A return in this new century to a unilateral and imperialist policy could have the kind of consequences that Wilson warned against. The first of these would be in the costs and casualties of playing what neoconservative Max Boot admiringly calls "globocop."[5] The first Persian Gulf War cost the

United States virtually nothing, and the armed forces suffered few casualities, but this war in Iraq, conducted unilaterally, could eventually cost over $300 billion and upwards of ten thousand casualties, not to mention the much greater number of dead and wounded Iraqis. These costs won't bankrupt the United States, but they will strain a budget already reeling from record deficits. America's role as globocop may not undermine America's power in the world, but it will, as Wilson warned, cripple the nation's ability to provide a rising standard of living for its citizens. They will also threaten the army's morale and its ability to attract recruits, just as the Vietnam War did.

Of course, if the alternative to the new unilateralism were a rising threat to American security, then Americans would have to make the unhappy choice of greater security over a solvent Medicare fund or enough money for their children to enjoy higher education. But there is no evidence that the Bush's unilateral approach has made Americans more secure. If anything, the opposite is the case. The war in Iraq sparked the growth of anti-American terrorism. It ensured that Americans will have to worry about homeland security well into the twenty-first century. Thanks to the Bush administration's revival of American imperialism, the age of empire will endure into the new century, but it will also be called the age of terror.

America's new imperialism and unilateralism could also exacerbate existing tensions with our would-be allies in Europe and Asia. Europe did not step forward, as Wolfowitz predicted, to help pay for Iraq's reconstruction. Disagreement over America's role in Iraq probably contributed to the paralysis in international trade negotiations. Eventually, hostility toward America could encourage rival trade and currency blocs and could even lead to attempts by other nations or groups of nations to balance America's power. In that case, the world would be back to where it was when Woodrow Wilson took office in 1913.

The key to America's long-standing leadership has been its willingness to subordinate its singular will to that of international organizations and alliances. According to political scientist Joseph Nye, "The multilateralism of American pre-eminence is a key to its longevity because it reduces the incentives for constructing alliances against us."[6] By abandoning multilateralism for the neoconservative role of globocop and for imperial power, the United States would endanger the very superiority that the neoconservatives are so intent on protecting.

THE ETHICS OF NATIONS

Before 1914, the great powers justified their foreign policies on two different grounds. First, they claimed that in subjugating weaker nations in Asia or Africa, they were contributing to the spread and enhancement of civilization by taming or enlightening barbarous peoples. Imperialism was a means of civilizing and Christianizing—to liberate savages and barbarians from their dependence on superstition. Second, they claimed that international relations rested on a balance of power that, according to the *Machtpolitik* of Wilhelm II and Clemenceau, excluded considerations of justice and right and wrong. The conquest of the weak by the strong—whether of Belgium by Germany or Morocco by France—was not subject to moral sanction.

Wilson rejected both these kinds of arguments. He believed that imperialism led to war—in effect, it brought with it a new barbarism, epitomized by World War I, that was far worse than the barbarism it purported to counteract. Imperialism was also not a means to create democratic institutions. Instead, what it immediately provoked was a unified front against the imperialist invader. It encouraged a defensive nationalism among those it sought to civilize. Wilhelm's *Machtpolitik* had had similar disastrous results. By denying a role to morality in international affairs, it denied nations a means, beyond the shifting and fortuitous balance of power, of preventing future wars. It made treaties and agreements meaningless.

Wilson believed that in order to achieve an enduring peace, the great powers would have to replace the balance of power by a community of power and *Machtpolitik* by international law. Wilson's idea of international law was an extrapolation of the Declaration's statement that "all men are created equal" to the world of nations. Wilson knew that some nations were weaker than others, just as some individuals were weaker or less talented than others, but he contended that just as the laws of a nation protected the equality of individuals, international law should protect the equality of nations.

Wilson's principles were embodied in the structure of the League of Nations and the United Nations, with their general assemblies, where each nation enjoyed a vote. These principles were also inscribed in the charter of the United Nations, which reaffirmed "faith in fundamental human rights, in the dignity and worth of the human person, in the equal rights of men and women and of nations large and small" and banned aggression by one nation against another except in the case of self-defense.[7] The U.N. Security Council could use sanctions, and did so, in response to Iraq's invasion of Kuwait, to ensure compliance with these principles.

International morality, like personal morality, is a product of experience. Two world wars made Europeans amenable to these principles, which form the basis of the European Union. It is now virtually unthinkable for one European country to undertake the conquest of another. In the world arena, these principles are less powerfully inscribed. What Wilson called the conscience of the world doesn't yet fully exist. But these principles of national equality have certainly exerted more influence over behavior than they did a century ago. Today, a tiny state like Singapore no longer feels ripe for conquest. If the United States were to defy these principles, it would encourage other countries to do so. China, for instance, might feel emboldened to force a showdown with Taiwan and Russia might feel justified in reviving its own dreams of empire. But the Bush administration has proven oblivious to these dangers.

The Bush administration's foreign policy did not rest so much on *Machtpolitik* as on the claim that America was defending civilization against the barbarians. The administration and its supporters revived the late-nineteenth-century argument for imperialism. McKinley had promised to civilize and Christianize, they promised to democratize, and the means to democracy was a new American imperialism. Wrote neoconservative Stanley Kurtz in *Policy Review*, "Imperialism as a midwife of democratic self-rule is an undeniable good."[8] But America's invasion and occupation of Iraq gave the lie to this conception of a new American imperialism. If it was a midwife of anything, it was of a nationalist backlash in Iraq and of anti-American terrorist groups.

There was also a hint of *Machtpolitik* in the Bush administration's new foreign policy. The administration and its supporters want the United States, as the chosen and most powerful nation, to be beyond the rules of behavior that govern other nations. In September 2002, it introduced a strategy for waging preemptive war, which violated the United Nations charge against waging war unilaterally except in self-defense. In October 2002, Bush's press secretary, Ari Fleischer, openly called for the assassination of Saddam Hussein—a practice that, if universalized, would have injected a new level of chaos and moral uncertainty into international relations. The Bush administration did not suggest that other countries wage preemptive war or conduct assassinations. It simply asserted its own right to do so. The administration rejected United Nations treaties largely because they would have subjected the United States to the same regulations as other countries.

In justifying this kind of approach, neoconservative Stephen Peter Rosen wrote in *The National Interest*:

> Acting in a humble manner is a ritual worth much respect, so the United States does well to consult the United Nations and the NATO councils before it acts. But such rituals will only reduce, not eliminate, the resentment toward the United States that springs from the fact that it can do what it must in any case. And what it must do, if it is to wield imperial power, is create and enforce the rules of a hierarchical interstate order. . . . The organizing principle of empire rests . . . on the existence of an overarching power that creates and enforces the principle of hierarchy, but is not itself bound by such rules.[9]

Charles Krauthammer made a similar point about international law in an era when the United States is the single dominant power. In such a situation, wrote Krauthammer, "unilateralism simply means that one not allow oneself to be hostage to others."[10] But relying simply on one's power and not a set of universalizable moral rules would return the world to the parlous conditions that led to two world wars. It would be to court anarchy in international relations, which is exactly what the Bush administration did in its invasion and occupation of Iraq.

AMERICAN MILLENNIALISM

Americans have always believed that they have a special role to play in transforming the world, and short of decline and disaster, will continue to do so. The original Puritan vision of a city on a hill has been reinforced and shaped, and given secular form, by the Revolution, the Indian Wars and the Frontier, by America's emergence as a great power, and, finally, by its emergence as the leading international power. Americans' understanding of empire and imperialism has proven to be critical to this process of redefinition.

During the 1890s, Americans, who had been preoccupied with continental expansion, looked across the seas and saw that the world they hoped to transform by example was being divided up by the European powers. How could Americans redeem the world if it belonged to others? One solution was that of Albert Beveridge and the Protestant missionaries who advocated "the imperialism of righteousness." God, Beveridge contended, has made "the English-speaking and Teutonic peoples . . . master organizers of the world. . . . He has made us adept in government that we may administer government among savage and senile peoples. Were it not for such a force as this the world would relapse into barbarism and night. And of all our race He has marked the American people as His chosen nation to finally lead in the redemption of the world."[11]

Beveridge's statement, made in the wake of America's victory in the Spanish-American War and its annexation of Spain's former colonies, rested on America eventually becoming the leading imperial power. Other imperialists, such as Josiah Strong and Brooks Adams, also shared this conviction. But by the end of the first decade of the twentieth century, this vision of American empire had faded, as America proved barely capable of retaining its hold over the Philippines.

Woodrow Wilson didn't merely change American foreign policy; he changed its underlying millennial framework. Like Beveridge, he believed that the United States was destined to create the Kingdom of God on Earth by actively transforming the world, but unlike him, he didn't believe it could be done through American imperialism. Wilson rejected the practice of imperialism, blaming it for the outbreak of world war, and the vision of inequality that underlay it. He saw America's role as creating a world in which nations didn't seek to conquer and dominate other nations.

Wilson's vision, unlike that of Beveridge, Fiske, Strong, and Theodore Roosevelt, presumed a world of equal nations sustained by liberal democratic capitalism. It represented a repudiation of the racial anthropology of the Indian wars and the conquest of the Philippines. But Wilson did not believe that the United States could by itself end imperialism and transform the world. It could only carry out this mission by working with others. Its special role would consist in creating a community of power that would dismantle the structure of imperialism and lay the basis for a pacific, prosperous world.

Wilson's successors have filled out and modified both his vision and his means of achieving it. Roosevelt envisioned a world of the "Four Freedoms," George H. W. Bush a "new world order," and Clinton a "Third Way." Clinton acknowledged that what was necessary was not a single universal organization but a "network" of organizations and alliances. Yet even before September 11, George W. Bush was uncomfortable with this Wilsonian millennialism. His was a Hobbesian, premillennial vision focused on "terror and missiles and madmen." Its origins lay in the isolationism of the 1930s and the Christian conservatism of the late twentieth century. As president, Bush would eventually supplement this darker outlook with a postmillennial vision, but it would come primarily from the neoconservatives.

The neoconservatives adopted Wilson's vision of global democracy, but they sought to achieve it through the unilateral means associated with Beveridge. They saw America as an imperial power that could transform the world single-handedly. The first step for them was Iraq; the next step would be the rest of the Middle East. Wrote Richard Perle and David Frum in *An End to Evil,* "It is only because we did insert ourselves into Iraq that the Iraqis have any hope of ruling themselves—and the same will be true in Iran and elsewhere in the Islamic world where we must fight."[12] Bush voiced similar sentiments on the eve of war with Iraq.

The neoconservatives and George W. Bush are likely to learn the same lesson in the early twenty-first century that Theodore Roosevelt learned in the early twentieth century. When America acts on its own, its ability to dominate and transform remains limited, as the ill-fated mission in Iraq or the reemergence of the Taliban in Afghanistan may have already demonstrated. America's true power has always rested not only in its economic and military strength, but in its determination to use that strength in cooperation with others on behalf of the equality of individuals and nations. When America goes out alone in search of monsters to destroy—venturing on terrain upon which imperial powers have already trod—it can itself become the monster.

NOTES

INTRODUCTION

1. Mike Allen, "Bush Strengthens Call for Help," *Washington Post,* Oct. 19, 2003. On details of Bush visit, see also David Sanger, "Bush Cites Philippines," *New York Times,* Oct. 19, 2003.
2. On the war in the Philippines, see Stuart Creighton Miller, *Benevolent Assimilation* (New Haven, 1982).
3. Cited in Margaret Leech, *In the Days of McKinley* (New York, 1959), p. 123.
4. Cited in Howard K. Beale, *Theodore Roosevelt and the Rise of America to World Power* (Baltimore, 1956), p. 80.
5. Miller, *Benevolent Assimilation,* p. 23.
6. Woodrow Wilson, "Democracy and Efficiency," *Atlantic Monthly,* vol. 87, Mar. 1901.
7. Beveridge, "The Star of Empire," Sept. 25, 1900, reprinted in Albert J. Beveridge, *The Meaning of the Times* (Freeport, NY, 1908).
8. Speech on "The Strenuous Life," in *Theodore Roosevelt: An American Mind,* ed. Mario R. DiNunzio (New York, 1994), p. 188.
9. Cited in Lewis Gould, *The Presidency of Theodore Roosevelt* (Lawrence, 1991), p. 176.
10. Cited in John Morton Blum, *Woodrow Wilson and the Politics of Morality* (New York, 1956), p. 89.
11. Cited in Derek Heater, *National Self-Determination: Woodrow Wilson and His Legacy* (New York, 1994), p. 25.
12. Condoleezza Rice, "Promoting the National Interest," *Foreign Affairs,* Jan.-Feb. 2000.
13. Max Boot, "The Case for American Empire," *Weekly Standard,* Oct. 15, 2001.
14. Press Conference, Apr. 13, 2004.

1. AN EMPIRE OF LIBERTY: THE FRAMEWORK OF AMERICAN FOREIGN POLICY

1. Foster Rhea Dulles, *Prelude to World Power* (New York, 1965), p. 120.
2. See Eric Hobsbawm, *The Age of Empire* (New York, 1987), p. 59.
3. See J. A. Hobson, *Imperialism* (Ann Arbor, 1965), p. 23.
4. A. Supan, *Die territoriale Etwicklung der Euroaischen Kolonien* [The Territorial Growth of European Colonies] (Gotha, 1906), p. 254.
5. David Healy, *U.S. Expansionism: The Imperialist Urge in the 1890s* (Madison, 1970), p. 44.
6. See *God's New Israel: Religious Interpretations of American Destiny,* ed. Conrad Cherry (Englewood Cliffs, 1971), p. 88.
7. Albert J.Beveridge, *The Meaning of the Times* (Freeport, NY, 1908).
8. *The Papers of Woodrow Wilson* (hereafter WWP), ed. Arthur Link (Princeton, 1966), vol. 45, p. 15. (Address to the AFL-CIO, Buffalo, New York, November 12, 1917.)

213

9. State of the Union Address, Jan. 29, 2002.
10. See Frank Ninkovich, *The Wilsonian Century* (Chicago, 1999), p. 52.
11. Address at the National Endowment of Democracy, Washington, Nov. 6, 2003.
12. Herman Melville, *White Jacket* (Library of America collection, 1983), chap. 36, p. 506.
13. Josiah Strong, *Our Country* (New York, 1963 [reprint]), p. 205.
14. See Nathan C. Hatch, *The Sacred Cause of Liberty* (New Haven, 1977).
15. See Paul Boyer, *When Time Shall Be No More* (Cambridge, 1992), chaps. 2 and 3.
16. Thomas Jefferson, "First Inaugural Address," Mar. 4, 1801.
17. The heart of this argument was inspired by Ernest Tuveson's *Redeemer Nation* (Chicago, 1968), although his and my account of the framework are somewhat different. Other historians and political commentators, including Loren Baritz, Garry Wills, Nathan Hatch, William McGlothlin, Ruth Bloch, and Charles L. Sanford, have similarly argued that Americans' view of the world dates from English dissenting Protestantism, but no one, to my knowledge, has made the argument as well and as thoroughly as Tuveson. I also made a similar argument in the introduction to *Grand Illusion* (New York, 1992) and in "Clinton's Great Awakening," *The New Republic*, Jan. 1993.
18. Cited in Stephen Stein, "Transatlantic Extensions: Apocalyptic in Early New England," *Journal of American History*, Dec. 1984.
19. Boyer, *When Time Shall Be No More*, p. 71.
20. See Gordon Wood, *The Radicalism of the American Revolution* (New York, 1991).
21. Hatch, *The Sacred Cause of Liberty.*
22. See Richard W. Van Alstyne, *The Rising American Empire* (Chicago, 1965).
23. Beveridge, *The Meaning of the Times*, p. 49.
24. See Peter Onuf and Nicholas Onuf, *Federal Union, Modern World* (Madison, 1993), p. 176.
25. See Tuveson, *Redeemer Nation*, p. 169.
26. Samuel Cooper, "A Sermon on the Day of the Commencement of the Constitution," Oct. 25, 1780.
27. See Albert K. Weinberg, *Manifest Destiny* (Chicago, 1963), p. 19.
28. Ezra Stiles, "The United Elevated to Glory and Honor," 1783.
29. Tuveson, *Redeemer Nation*, p. 116.
30. John Quincy Adams, "Address of July 4, 1821," reprinted in *John Quincy Adams and American Continental Empire*, ed. Walter LaFeber (Chicago, 1965).
31. See Michael Paul Rogin, *Fathers and Children: Andrew Jackson and the Subjugation of the American Indian* (New York, 1975), p. 4.
32. Ibid.
33. Ibid., chap. 10.
34. Ibid., p. 116
35. See Reginald Horsman, *Race and Manifest Destiny* (Cambridge, 1981), p. 108.
36. Cited in Philip Borden, "Found Cumbering the Soil: Manifest Destiny and the Indian in the Nineteenth Century," in *The Great Fear*, ed. Gary B. Nash and Richard Weiss (New York, 1970).
37. Horsman, *Race and Manifest Destiny*, p. 223.
38. George Brown Tindall, *America: A Narrative History* (New York, 1984), p. 534.
39. Cited by Frederick Merk, *Manifest Density and American History* (New York, 1963), p. 262.
40. Horsman, *Race and Manifest Destiny*, p. 215.
41. Rogin, *Fathers and Children*, p. 309.
42. See Weinberg, *Manifest Destiny*, p. 252.
43. Frederick C. Merk, *Manifest Destiny and Mission in American History* (New York, 1963), p. 263.
44. Ibid, p. 25.

2. AMERICA'S IMPERIAL MOMENT

1. See David Healy, *U.S. Expansionism* (Madison, 1970), p. 233.
2. Ibid., p. 131.
3. Ibid., p. 67.
4. Paul Kennedy, *The Rise and Fall of the Great Powers* (New York, 1987), p. 202.
5. Healy, *U.S. Expansionism*, p. 30.
6. Ibid., p. 165.
7. Charles A. Conant, "The Economic Basis of 'Imperialism,'" *North American Review*, Sept. 1898. On Conant's influence, see Healy, *U.S. Expansionism*, and Carl Parrini and Martin J. Sklar, "New Thinking About the Market, 1896–1904," *Journal of Economic History*, Sept. 1983. Conant's essay appeared just after the conclusion of the Spanish-American War, but from all evidence—the war is not mentioned in it, and the latest data are from 1895—was written well before it.
8. Alfred T. Mahan, "The United States Looking Outward," *Atlantic Monthly*, Dec. 1890.
9. A. T. Mahan, *The Influence of Sea Power Upon History* (Boston, 1949), p. 83. See Warren Zimmerman, *The First Great Triumph* (New York, 2002), and Jon Tetsuro Sumida, *Inventing Grand Strategy and Teaching Command* (Washington, D.C., 1997).
10. See Richard Hofstadter, *Social Darwinism in American Thought* (New York, 1944), p. 177.
11. John Fiske, "Manifest Destiny," *Harper's*, March 1885.
12. Ibid.
13. See William H. Berge, "Voices for Imperialism: Josiah Strong and the Protestant Clergy," and the introduction by Jurgen Herbst to Josiah Strong, *Our Country* (Cambridge, 1963). On the Protestant awakening, see William G. McLoughlin, *Revivals, Awakenings and Reform* (Chicago, 1978).
14. Strong, *Our Country*, p. 201.
15. Ibid., p. 206.
16. On Henry Adams's salon, see Edmund Morris, *The Rise of Theodore Roosevelt* (New York, 1979), pp. 413–415, and William A. Williams, "Brooks Adams and American Expansion," *Behind the Throne*, ed. Thomas J. McCormick and Walter LaFeber (Madison, 1993).
17. Cited in Zimmerman, *The First Great Triumph*, p. 82.
18. Ibid.
19. Address to the Naval War College, June 2, 1897, reprinted in *Theodore Roosevelt: An American Mind*, ed. Mario R. DiNunzio (New York, 1994).
20. Brooks Adams, *The Law of Civilization and Decay* (New York, 1943), p. 292.
21. Address to the Naval War College, in DiNunzio, ed., *Theodore Roosevelt*.
22. Adams, *The Law of Civilization and Decay*, p. 293.
23. See Walter LaFeber, *The New Empire* (Ithaca, 1968), chap. 2, and William A. Williams, "Brooks Adams and American Expansion."
24. E. Berkeley Tompkins, *Anti-Imperialism in the United States* (Philadelphia, 1972), p. 4.
25. See Kathleen Dalton, *Theodore Roosevelt: A Strenuous Life* (New York, 2002), p. 163.
26. Julius Pratt, *Expansionists of 1898* (Baltimore, 1936), p. 142.
27. William E. Leuchtenburg, "The Needless War with Spain," *American Heritage*, Feb. 1957.
28. Ibid.
29. See Hofstadter, *Social Darwinism in American Thought*, p. 158.
30. John A. Garraty, *Henry Cabot Lodge* (New York, 1953), pp. 144–145.
31. Ibid.
32. See Albert K. Weinberg, *Manifest Destiny* (Chicago, 1963), p. 289.
33. Denis Brogan, "The Illusion of American Omnipotence," *Harper's*, Dec. 1952.

34. Richard Hofstadter, "Goldwater and Pseudo-Conservative Politics," in *The Paranoid Style in American Politics* (Chicago, 1979), p. 133.
35. Josiah Strong, *Expansion Under New World Conditions* (New York, 1900), p. 185.
36. Ibid., preface.
37. Ibid., p. 200.
38. *The Letters of Theodore Roosevelt* (hereafter LTR), eds. Elting E. Monson, John Morton Blum, and Alfred Chander (New York, 1951–54), Aug. 11, 1899.
39. Healy, *U.S. Expansionism*, p. 108.
40. Brooks Adams, "The Spanish War and World Equilibrium," reprinted in Brooks Adams, *America's Economic Supremacy* (New York, 1947), p. 72.
41. Ibid., p. 293.
42. Stuart Creighton Miller, *Benevolent Assimilation* (New Haven, 1982), p. 18.
43. Pratt, *Expansionists of 1898*, p. 296.
44. Ibid., p. 62.
45. Healy, *U.S. Expansionism*, p. 174.
46. See Claude G. Bowers, *Beveridge and the Progressive Era* (New York, 1932), p. 63.
47. Albert J. Beveridge, *The Meaning of the Times, and Other Speeches* (Freeport, NY, 1908), p. 47–48.
48. Miller, *Benevolent Assimilation*, p. 131.
49. Albert J. Beveridge, "The Star of Empire," Sept. 25, 1900, reprinted in Beveridge, *The Meaning of the Times*.
50. Healy, *U.S. Expansionism*, p. 234.
51. Ibid., p. 237.
52. Robert L. Beisner, *Twelve Against Empire* (New York, 1968), p. 95.
53. See "Program of the American Anti-Imperialist League," 1899, available at www.norton.com/college/history/ralph/workbook/ralprs30a.htm.
54. Ibid., p. 238.
55. Williams, "Brooks Adams and American Expansion."
56. Ibid.
57. LaFeber, *The American Search for Opportunity* (New York, 1993), p. 178.
58. William McKinley, "Instructions to the Peace Commission," Sept. 16, 1898.
59. Weinberg, *Manifest Destiny*, p. 294.
60. Reprinted in Daniel Schirmer and Stephen Rosskamm Shalom, eds., *The Philippines Reader* (Boston, 1987), pp. 22–23. Some historians have disputed the accuracy of this report, which appeared in *The Christian Advocate* in 1903, but it certainly sounds like McKinley's reasoning.
61. Beisner, *Twelve Against Empire*, p. 97.
62. Ibid., p. 44.
63. William Graham Sumner, "The Conquest of the United States by Spain," reprinted in *War and Other Essays* (New Haven, 1911).
64. Beisner, *Twelve Against Empire*, p. 174.
65. Margaret Leech, *In the Days of McKinley* (New York, 1959), p. 345.
66. Miller, *Benevolent Assimilation*, p. 54.
67. Ibid., p. 93.
68. Ibid., p. 94.
69. Ibid., p. 95.
70. Ibid., p. 154.
71. Ibid., p. 73.
72. Ibid., p. 100.
73. LaFeber, *The American Search for Opportunity*, p. 150.
74. Whitelaw Reid, "The Territory with Which We Are Threatened," *Century Magazine*, Sept. 1898.

75. LaFeber, *The American Search for Opportunity,* p. 152.
76. See Jules Robert Benjamin, *The United States and Cuba* (Pittsburgh, 1977).
77. Ibid., p. 6.

3. THEODORE ROOSEVELT AND THE HEEL OF ACHILLES

1. Historian John Milton Cooper Jr., for instance, called his wonderful dual biography of Roosevelt and Wilson *The Warrior and the Priest* (Cambridge, 1983).
2. Theodore Roosevelt, *An Autobiography* (New York, 1914), p. 7.
3. Ibid., p. 9.
4. See Kathleen Dalton, *Theodore Roosevelt: A Strenuous Life* (New York, 2002), chap. 1 and 2. Dalton's book is outstanding on Roosevelt's religious background, which is slighted or even ignored in other biographies. See also Nathan Miller, *Theodore Roosevelt: A Life* (New York, 1992), pp. 31–32, on Theodore Roosevelt's philanthropic activity.
5. On this subject, see Gail Bederman, *Manliness and Civilization* (Chicago, 1995), pp. 170ff.
6. Ibid., p. 173.
7. Theodore Roosevelt, "The Strenuous Life," Apr. 10, 1899, in *Theodore Roosevelt: An American Mind,* ed. Mario R. DiNunzio (New York, 1994).
8. See Kathleen Dalton, "Theodore Roosevelt and the Idea of War," *Theodore Roosevelt Association Journal,* 7, no. 4.
9. Roosevelt, "The Strenuous Life."
10. Cited in Bederman, *Manliness and Civilization,* p. 185.
11. Roosevelt, *Autobiography,* p. 10.
12. Cited in Paul Grondahl, *I Rose Like a Rocket: The Political Education of Theodore Roosevelt* (New York, 2004), p. 21.
13. Dalton, *Theodore Roosevelt: A Strenuous Life,* p. 187.
14. Theodore Roosevelt, *Oliver Cromwell* (New York, 1900), pp. 4 and 2.
15. Theodore Roosevelt, "National Duties," Sept. 2, 1901, from *Theodore Roosevelt: American Ideals* (New York, 1926).
16. Jacob Riis, *Theodore Roosevelt, the Citizen* (New York, 1904).
17. Quoted in Julius Pratt, *Expansionists of 1898* (Baltimore, 1936), pp. 61–62.
18. On Roosevelt's idea of race, see Thomas G. Dyer, *Theodore Roosevelt and the Idea of Race* (Baton Rouge, 1980), one of the best books written about Roosevelt's thought.
19. Edmund Morris, *The Rise of Theodore Roosevelt* (New York, 1979), p. 410.
20. Theodore Roosevelt, *The Winning of the West* (New York, 1889), chap. 1.
21. Ibid., chap. 2.
22. Ibid., chap. 11.
23. Ibid., chap. 2.
24. Ibid., chap. 13.
25. Ibid.
26. Ibid.
27. See the discussion of this point in Richard Slotkin, *Gunfighter Nation* (New York, 1992), chap. 1.
28. Ibid., p. 55.
29. See Roosevelt, *Autobiography,* pp. 215ff.
30. See Margaret Leech, *In the Days of McKinley* (New York, 1959), and H. Wayne Morgan, *America's Road to Empire* (New York, 1965).
31. Cited in Miller, *Theodore Roosevelt: A Life,* p. 235.
32. Cited in Dalton, *Theodore Roosevelt: A Strenuous Life,* p. 166.

33. Cited in Howard K. Beale, *Theodore Roosevelt and the Rise of America to World Power* (Baltimore, 1956), p. 37.
34. LTR, TR letter to James Bryce, Sept. 10, 1897.
35. LTR, TR letter to William Clowes, Jan. 14, 1898.
36. LTR, TR letter to Robert Bacon, Apr. 8, 1898.
37. LTR, TR letter to Edward Oliver Wolcott, Sept. 15, 1900, statement accepting the nomination as vice president.
38. TR, "America: Part of the World; Work," from *Theodore Roosevelt: An American Mind*, op cit. p. 181.
39. LTR, TR letter to Wolcott, Sept. 15, 1900.
40. Dalton, *Theodore Roosevelt: A Strenuous Life*, p. 190.
41. LTR, TR letter to Wolcott, Sept. 15, 1900.
42. Lincoln Day speech in New York at the Lincoln Club (New York, Feb. 12, 1899).
43. Roosevelt, "The Strenuous Life."
44. Dalton, *Theodore Roosevelt: A Strenuous Life*, p. 208.
45. See on Roosevelt's foreign policy rationale, Frank Ninkovich, "Theodore Roosevelt: Civilization as Ideology," *Diplomatic History*, Summer 1986.
46. This and the following quotations are from Theodore Roosevelt, "Expansion and Peace," *The Independent*, Dec. 21, 1899, reprinted in *The Writings of Theodore Roosevelt*, ed. William Harbaugh (Indianapolis, 1967).
47. Ibid.
48. Paul S. Reinsch, *World Politics at the End of the Nineteenth Century* (New York, 1900), p. 69.
49. J. A. Hobson, *Imperialism* (Ann Arbor, 1965), p. 360.
50. Miller, *Theodore Roosevelt: A Life*, p. 102.
51. LTR, TR letter to William Howard Taft, Aug. 21, 1907.
52. Cited in Robert L. Beisner, *Twelve Against Empire* (New York, 1968), p. 44, from *Boston Evening Transcript*, Apr. 15, 1899.
53. Cited in Sarah Watts, *Rough Rider in the White House* (Chicago, 2003), p. 1.
54. Cited in Beale, *Theodore Roosevelt and the Rise of America to World Power*, pp. 303–304.
55. Cited in Walter LaFeber, *The Clash* (New York, 1997), p. 82.
56. Ibid.
57. See Lewis L. Gould, *The Presidency of Theodore Roosevelt* (Lawrence, 1991), pp. 261ff.
58. LaFeber, *The Clash*, p. 90.
59. Miller, *Theodore Roosevelt: A Life*, pp. 206–207.
60. Ibid., p. 220.
61. Ibid., p. 232.
62. LTR, TR letter to William Howard Taft, Aug. 21, 1907.
63. LTR, TR letter to Whitelaw Reid, Sept. 3, 1908.
64. See William R. Tilchin, *Theodore Roosevelt and the British Empire* (New York, 1997), p. 217.
65. See Edmund Morris, *Theodore Rex* (New York, 2001), chap. 12.
66. Cited by Gould, *The Presidency of Theodore Roosevelt*, p. 176.
67. LaFeber, *The Clash*, p. 199.
68. Cited by Dalton, *Theodore Roosevelt: A Strenuous Life*, p. 320.
69. Gould, *The Presidency of Theodore Roosevelt*, p. 252.
70. Ibid., p. 253.
71. Cited in Beale, *Theodore Roosevelt and the Rise of America to World Power*, p. 375.
72. Ibid., p. 332.
73. Cited in Gould, *The Presidency of Theodore Roosevelt*, p. 173.
74. Cited in Beale, *Theodore Roosevelt and the Rise of America to World Power*, p. 380.
75. Ibid, p. 382.

76. Cited by Gould, *The Presidency of Theodore Roosevelt,* p. 254.
77. See www.nobel.se/peace/laureats.
78. Theodore Roosevelt, "The World Movement," available on www.bartelby.com.
79. See Dyer, *Theodore Roosevelt and the Idea of Race,* pp. 26–27.
80. Dalton, *Theodore Roosevelt: A Strenuous Life,* p. 523.
81. Ibid.
82. Dyer, *Theodore Roosevelt and the Idea of Race,* p. 87.

4. Woodrow Wilson and the Way to Liberty

1. Reprinted in Woodrow Wilson, *Mere Literature* (1896; repr. Freeport, 1971), pp. 196–198.
2. Cited in John M. Mulder, *Woodrow Wilson: The Years of Preparation* (Princeton, 1978), p. 272.
3. Lloyd Gardner, *Safe for Democracy* (New York, 1984), p. 55.
4. Mulder, *Woodrow Wilson: The Years of Preparation,* p. 104.
5. See Arthur S. Link, *Woodrow Wilson: Revolution, War and Peace* (Wheeling, 1979), p. 7.
6. See Mulder, *Woodrow Wilson: The Years of Preparation,* p. 48.
7. Ibid., and *The Messages and Papers of Woodrow Wilson* (New York, 1924) (hereafter *Messages*), vol. 2, p. 700.
8. *Messages,* vol. I, p. 36.
9. See William Diamond, *The Economic Thought of Woodrow Wilson* (Baltimore, 1943), p. 138. Arthur Link also discusses this point at length in the first chapter of *Woodrow Wilson: Revolution, War and Peace.*
10. See Diamond, *The Economic Thought of Woodrow Wilson,* p. 139.
11. August Heckscher, *Woodrow Wilson* (New York, 1991), p. 95.
12. *Messages,* vol. I, p. 102.
13. On Wilson and the covenant, see Mulder's biography, which is by far the best source on Wilson and his father's religious convictions. On covenant theology, see Perry Miller, *Errand into the Wilderness* (New York, 1956), pp. 60–98.
14. John Winthrop, "A Model of Christian Charity," in *The American Puritans,* ed. Perry Miller (Garden City, 1956), p. 82.
15. Mulder, *Woodrow Wilson: The Years of Preparation,* p. 35.
16. See Woodrow Wilson, *Constitutional Government* (New York, 1911).
17. *Messages,* vol. I, pp. 593–594.
18. WWP, vol. 53, p. 541.
19. Mulder, *Woodrow Wilson: The Years of Preparation,* p. 29.
20. Ray Stannard Baker, *Woodrow Wilson: Life and Letters* (New York, 1927), vol. I., pp. 120.
21. Woodrow Wilson, "The Making of the Nation," *Atlantic Monthly,* July 1897.
22. See John Milton Cooper Jr., *The Warrior and the Priest* (Cambridge, 1983), p. 313.
23. WWP, vol., 53, p. 314.
24. Woodrow Wilson, *Division and Reunion* (London, 1921), p. 216.
25. Woodrow Wilson, *A History of the American People* (New York, 1901), vol. 5, p. 4.
26. Woodrow Wilson, *Constitutional Government in the United States* (New York, 1911), p. 14 (plurals added).
27. Baker, *Woodrow Wilson: Life and Letters,* vol. I, p. 24.
28. Lloyd Gardner, *Safe for Democracy* (New York, 1984), pp. 2–3.
29. On Feb. 4, 1917, Secretary of State Lansing writes memorandum about Wilson, "The President, though deeply incensed at Germany's insolent notice, said that he was not yet sure what course we must propose and must think it over; that he had been more and more impressed with the idea that 'white civilization' and its domination in the world rested largely on our ability to keep this country intact. . . ." WWP, vol. 41, p. 120.

30. Mulder, *Woodrow Wilson: The Years of Preparation,* p. 64.
31. WW letter to Ellen Louise Axxon, Feb. 24, 1885.
32. Woodrow Wilson, *The State* (Boston, 1889).
33. See Mulder, *Woodrow Wilson: The Years of Preparation,* pp. 233, 250, and Heckscher, *Woodrow Wilson,* p. 150.
34. See William Diamond, *The Economic Thought of Woodrow Wilson* (Baltimore, 1943), p. 88.
35. Heckscher, *Woodrow Wilson,* p. 231.
36. See Cooper, *The Warrior and the Priest,* p. 180.
37. WWP, vol. 10, p. 577.
38. Ibid.
39. WWP, vol. 12, p. 143.
40. WWP, vol. 12, p. 41.
41. Cooper, *The Warrior and the Priest,* and Kendrick A. Clements, *Woodrow Wilson* (Boston, 1987), p. 111.
42. See Walter LaFeber, *America's Search for Opportunity* (New York, 1993), p. 187.
43. Diamond, *The Economic Thought of Woodrow Wilson,* p. 134.
44. In *Safe for Democracy* (New York, 1984), Lloyd Gardner argues that Wilson had a Hobsonian view of imperialism (p. 14). I have been very influenced by Gardner's analysis of Wilson's foreign policy and in particular of Wilson's policy toward Mexico.
45. See ibid., p. 41.
46. See George E. Mowry, *The Era of Theodore Roosevelt* (New York, 1958), p. 281.
47. Historian Martin J. Sklar points out that during the Taft administration, what Democrats denounced as dollar diplomacy was also seen by bankers and diplomats as an alternative to war. See "Dollar Diplomacy According to Dollar Diplomats: American Development and World Development," in *The United States as a Developing Country* (Cambridge, 1992). See also Frank Ninkovich, *The Wilsonian Century* (Chicago, 1999), p. 27.
48. See Jerry Israel, *Progressivism and the Open Door: America and China, 1905–1921* (Pittsburgh, 1971), p. 117.
49. Baker, *Woodrow Wilson: Life and Letters,* vol. 2, pp. 71–72. Worried about Japanese imperial ambitions in China, Wilson would later reverse his decision and agree to American participation in a consortium.
50. *Messages,* vol. I, p. 35.
51. Ibid., p. 36.
52. Diamond, *The Economic Thought of Woodrow Wilson,* p. 142.
53. Arthur Link, *Woodrow Wilson and the Progressive Era* (New York, 1954), p. 105.
54. Thomas J. Knock, *To End All Wars* (New York, 1992), p. 39.
55. Heckscher, *Woodrow Wilson,* p. 299.
56. WWP, vol. 28, p. 480.
57. WWP, vol. 29, p. 229.
58. Robert E. Quirk, *An Affair of Honor: Woodrow Wilson and the Occupation of Veracruz* (New York, 1962), pp. 107–108.
59. WWP, vol. 29, p. 362.
60. Gardner, *Safe for Democracy,* p. 63.
61. Cited in Lloyd Gardner, *A Covenant with Power* (New York, 1984), p. 8.

5. WOODROW WILSON AND THE CONSCIENCE OF THE WORLD

1. August Heckscher, *Woodrow Wilson* (New York, 1991), p. 337.
2. WWP, vol. 53, p. 41.
3. "The Fourteen Points," in *The Political Thought of Woodrow Wilson,* ed. E. David Cronon (Indianapolis, 1965), pp. 443–444.
4. Ibid., p. 445.
5. Margaret Macmillan, *Paris 1919* (New York, 2002), p. 15.
6. Cited in Daniel P. Moynihan, *On the Law of Nations* (Cambridge, 1990), p. 53.
7. Heckscher, *Woodrow Wilson,* p. 510.
8. *Messages,* vol. 2, p. 712.
9. Thomas A. Bailey, *A Diplomatic History of the American People* (New York, 1950), p. 610.
10. Stockton Axson, *Brother Woodrow* (Princeton, 1993), pp. 194–195.
11. WWP, vol. 30, p. 462.
12. See Fritz Fischer, *Germany's Aims in the First World War* (New York, 1961), and a recent summary of the findings by English historian John C. G. Rohl, "Germany," in *Decisions for War 1914,* ed. Keith Wilson (New York, 1995).
13. WWP, vol. 30, p. 432.
14. See Barbara W. Tuchman, *The Zimmerman Telegram* (New York, 1958).
15. WWP, vol. 40, p. 14.
16. WWP, vol. 53, p. 351.
17. William Diamond, *The Economic Thought of Woodrow Wilson* (Baltimore, 1943), p. 163.
18. *Messages,* vol. I, p. 351.
19. See Fischer, *Germany's Aims in the First World War,* chap. 1.
20. Dominic Lieven, *Empire: The Russian Empire and Its Rivals* (New Haven, 2000), p. 47.
21. WWP, vol. 38, p. 241.
22. On similarities between Wilson and Hobson, see N. Gordon Levin Jr., *Woodrow Wilson and World Politics* (New York, 1968), p. 26.
23. Quoted by Carl Parrini, *Heir to Empire* (Pittsburgh, 1969), p. 12.
24. *Messages,* vol. II, pp. 770–771.
25. Jules François Camille Ferry, speech before the French Chamber of Deputies, March 28, 1884, available on the Internet Modern History Sourcebook, www.fordham.edu/hallsall/mod/1984/ferry.html.
26. Fischer, *Germany's Aims in the First World War,* p. 28.
27. Macmillan, *Paris 1919,* p. 23.
28. *Messages,* vol. II, p. 756.
29. Ibid., p. 379.
30. Ibid., p. 544.
31. Derek Heater, *National Self-Determination: Woodrow Wilson and His Legacy* (New York, 1994), p. 45.
32. *Messages,* vol. I, p. 475.
33. Cited by Michla Pomerance, "The United States and Self-Determination: Perspectives on the Wilsonian Conception," *American Journal of International Law,* 70, no. 1 (Jan. 1976).
34. See "Diary of William Bullitt," WWP, vol. 53, pp. 350ff.
35. See Derek Heater, *National Self-Determination: Woodrow Wilson and His Legacy* (New York, 1994), p. 63.
36. Moynihan, *On the Law of Nations,* p. 35.
37. *Messages,* vol. I, p. 355.
38. Parrini, *Heir to Empire,* p. 21.
39. Ibid., p. 12.

40. *Messages,* vol. I, p. 381.
41. Arthur Link, *Woodrow Wilson: Revolution, War, and Peace* (Wheeling, Ill., 1979), p. 77.
42. Betty Miller Unterberger, "Russian Revolution," in *Woodrow Wilson and a Revolutionary World,* ed. Arthur Link (Chapel Hill, 1982), p. 50.
43. Ibid.
44. WWP, vol. 53, p. 352.
45. Heckscher, *Woodrow Wilson,* p. 872.
46. Unterberger, "Russian Revolution," p. 73.
47. Ibid., p. 82.
48. WWP, vol. 53, p. 352.
49. Cited in Macmillan, *Paris 1919,* p. 67.
50. *Messages,* vol. II, p. 756.
51. WWP, vol. 59, p. 645.
52. WWP, vol. 53, p. 541.
53. See Thomas J. Knock, *To End All Wars* (New York, 1992), pp. 8–9.
54. Robert H. Ferrell, *Woodrow Wilson and World War I* (New York, 1985), p. 88.
55. Heater, *National Self-Determination,* p. 92.
56. Macmillan, *Paris 1919,* p. 106.
57. Ferrell, *Woodrow Wilson and World War I,* p. 150.
58. *Messages,* vol. II, pp. 1123–1124.
59. Knock, *To End All Wars,* p. 253.
60. Ferrell, *Woodrow Wilson and World War I,* p. 146.
61. Heckscher, *Woodrow Wilson,* p. 551.
62. Ibid., p. 48.
63. Theodore Roosevelt, "Self-Defense Without Militarism," reprinted in *Theodore Roosevelt: An American Mind,* ed. Mario R. DiNunzio (New York, 1994), p. 199.
64. WWP, vol. 53, p. 315.
65. John Milton Cooper Jr., *The Warrior and the Priest* (Cambridge, 1983), p. 327. Cooper's book is the best source on the conflict between Roosevelt and Wilson during the war years.
66. John Milton Cooper Jr., *Breaking the Heart of the World* (Cambridge, 2001), p. 42.
67. Cooper, *The Warrior and the Priest,* p. 331.
68. Knock, *To End All Wars,* p. 241.
69. Selig Adler, *The Isolationist Impulse* (New York, 1957), p. 49.
70. *Messages,* vol. II, p. 845.
71. Reprinted in *The Political Thought of Woodrow Wilson,* Cronon, ed., p. 507.
72. *Messages,* vol. II, p. 890.
73. Ibid., p. 833.
74. Ibid., p. 773.
75. Reprinted in *The Political Thought of Woodrow Wilson,* Cronon, ed., pp. 511–512.
76. On the controversy about Wilson's health and his political performance, see Edwin Weinstein, *Woodrow Wilson: A Medical and Psychological Biography* (Princeton, 1981).
77. Frank Ninkovich, *The Wilsonian Century* (Chicago, 1999), p. 76.
78. Heckscher, *Woodrow Wilson,* p. 634.

6. FRANKLIN ROOSEVELT AND THE FOUR FREEDOMS

1. Cited in James McGregor Burns, *Roosevelt: The Lion and the Fox* (New York, 1956), p. 69.
2. Cited in Frank Freidel, *Franklin D. Roosevelt: A Rendezvous with Destiny* (Boston, 1990), p. 39.

3. Ibid.
4. Frank Ninkovich, *The Wilsonian Century* (Chicago, 1999), p. 79.
5. Lloyd Gardner, *The Covenant with Power* (New York, 1984), p. 17.
6. Ninkovich, *The Wilsonian Century*, p. 97.
7. Richard Overy with Andrew Wheatcroft, *The Road to War* (London, 1999), p. 164.
8. WWP, vol. 53, p. 52.
9. Overy, *The Road to War*, p. 313.
10. Ninkovich, *The Wilsonian Century*, p. 121.
11. *Nothing to Fear: Selected Addresses of Franklin Delano Roosevelt* (Cambridge, 1946), p. 115.
12. Ibid., p. 253.
13. Ibid., p. 254.
14. For a discussion of Luce and his essay, see John B. Judis, *Grand Illusion* (New York, 1992), pp. 64–65.
15. Henry Luce, *The American Century* (New York, 1941), p. 23 (a reprint in book form).
16. Ibid., pp. 38–39.
17. *Nothing to Fear*, p. 352.
18. Elliott Roosevelt, *As He Saw It* (New York, 1946), p. 74.
19. Ibid., p. 115.
20. William Roger Louis, *Imperialism at Bay* (New York, 1978), p. 164.
21. Ibid., p. 155.
22. Forrest Davis, "What Really Happened at Teheran," *Saturday Evening Post*, May 13, 1944.
23. Louis, *Imperialism at Bay*, p. 161.
24. Ibid., p. 236.
25. Forrest Davis, "Roosevelt's World Blueprint," *Saturday Evening Post*, Apr. 10, 1943.
26. Ninkovich, *The Wilsonian Century*, p. 122.
27. Cited in Warren F. Kimball, *The Juggler* (Princeton, 1991), p. 44.
28. Steve Dryden, *Trade Warriors* (New York, 1995), p. 12.
29. Richard N. Gardner, *Sterling-Dollar Diplomacy* (New York, 1969), p. 8.
30. Ibid., p. 74.
31. Carl Parrini, "The Age of Ultraimperialism," *Radical History Review*, Fall 1993.
32. Ibid., pp. 129 and 131.
33. Ibid., p. 130.
34. Ibid, p. 141.
35. Ibid., p. 101.
36. Dryden, *Trade Warriors*, p. 16.
37. Cited in Townsend Hoopes and Douglas Brinkley, *FDR and the Creation of the UN* (New Haven, 1997), p. 207.

7. Cold War Liberalism from Truman to Reagan

1. See Sumner Welles, *Where Are We Heading?* (New York, 1946), p. 37.
2. For recent accounts of the influence of Russia's czarist past on the Soviet Union and the Bolsheviks, see Vladislav Zubok and Constantine Pleshakov, *Inside the Kremlin's Cold War* (Cambridge, 1996), chap. 1, and Dominic Lieven, *Empire: The Russian Empire and Its Rivals* (New Haven, 2000), Part Three.
3. Cited in ibid., p. 295.
4. Cited in Zubok and Pleshakov, *Inside the Kremlin's Cold War*, p. 37.
5. Walter Lippmann, *The Cold War* (Boston, 1947), p. 30.
6. Cited in David Caute, *The Great Fear* (New York, 1978), p. 30.

7. Address at Mechanics Hall in Boston, Oct. 27, 1948. Available in the Truman President Museum and Library Web page.
8. See John B. Judis, *Grand Illusion* (New York, 1992), chaps. 4 and 5.
9. See Evan Luard, *A History of the United Nations,* vol. 1 (New York, 1982), pp. 59–62.
10. See David Caute, *The Great Fear* (New York, 1978), p. 52.
11. Lloyd Gardner, *The Covenant with Power* (New York, 1984), p. 153.
12. Cited in John Lewis Gaddis, *We Now Know* (Oxford, 1997), p. 175.
13. See George C. Herring, *America's Longest War* (New York, 1986), p. 3.
14. William Roger Louis, *Imperialism at Bay* (New York, 1978), p. 356.
15. Gardner, *The Covenant with Power* (New York, 1984), p. 152.
16. Ibid., p. 154.
17. Cited by Stanley Karnow, *Vietnam: A History* (New York, 1983), p. 252.
18. Ibid., p. 250.
19. Gardner, *The Covenant with Power,* p. 149.
20. David Fromkin, *A Peace to End All Peace* (New York, 2001), p. 453.
21. See Nikki R. Keddie, *Modern Iran* (New Haven, 2003), pp. 123ff.
22. See Douglas Little, *American Orientalism* (Chapel Hill, 2003), p. 226.
23. See Ronald Reagan, *Ronald Reagan: An American Life* (New York, 1990), p. 561.
24. See Margaret Macmillan, *Paris 1919* (New York, 2002), p. 416.
25. See Little, *American Orientalism,* p. 110.
26. See ibid., p. 292.
27. See Stephen E. Ambrose and Douglas G. Brinkley, *Rise to Globalism* (New York, 1997), p. 334.
28. *New York Times,* Dec. 12, 1987.
29. Ronald Reagan, *Ronald Reagan: An American Life,* p. 493.

8. Bush, Clinton, and the Triumph of Wilsonianism

1. Stephen E. Ambrose and Douglas G. Brinkley, *Rise to Globalism* (New York, 1997), p. 371.
2. On this question, see David G. Becker and Richard L. Sklar, eds., *Postimperialism in World Politics* (State College, PA, 1999), in particular the essays by Richard L. Sklar, "Postimperialism: Concepts and Implications," and Martin J. Sklar, "The Open Door, Imperialism, and Postimperialism: Origins of U.S. Twentieth-Century Foreign Relations, Circa 1900."
3. During the peace talks in 1919, Etienne Clementel, the French minister of commerce and industry, drew up a plan for a "new economic order," but the United States opposed it and Britain was indifferent to it. Jean Monnet, the founder of the EEC, was Clementel's assistant. See Margaret Macmillan, *Paris 1919* (New York, 2002), p. 183.
4. George Bush and Brent Scowcroft, *A World Transformed* (New York, 1998), p. 303.
5. Cited in Stanley Meisler, *United Nations: The First Fifty Years* (New York, 1995), p. 257.
6. George H. W. Bush, "Address to a Joint Session of Congress and the Nation," Sept. 11, 1990. Note the date.
7. Bush and Scowcroft, *A World Transformed,* p. 375.
8. George H. W. Bush, "Address to a Joint Session of Congress and the Nation," Sept. 11, 1990.
9. George H. W. Bush, "Remarks to Air University Maxwell Air Force Base," Montgomery, Alabama, Apr. 13, 1991.
10. Bush and Scowcroft, *A World Transformed,* p. 489.
11. Ibid., p. 491.
12. On the aftermath of the war, see Kenneth M. Pollack, *The Threatening Storm* (New York,

2003), chap. 3, and on the administration reasoning, see John B. Judis, "Statecraft and Scowcroft," *The New Republic,* Feb. 24, 1992.

13. Bush and Scowcroft, *A World Transformed,* p. 383.
14. Sidney Blumenthal, *The Clinton Wars* (New York, 2003), p. 631.
15. On "Cold War leadership fatigue," see Stanley R. Sloan, *The U.S. Role in the 21st Century World* (New York, 1997), p. 37.
16. Cited in Douglas Brinkley, "Democratic Enlargement: The Clinton Doctrine," *Foreign Policy,* Spring 1997.
17. Speech, Federal News Service, Nov. 28, 1994.
18. Radio address, Federal News Service, Nov. 19, 1993.
19. Speech to U.N. General Assembly, Sept. 27, 1993.
20. See Anthony Lake, "Our Place in the Balkans," *New York Times,* Oct. 8, 2000.
21. "A National Security Strategy of Engagement and Enlargement," White House, Feb. 1996, available at www.fas.org/spp/military/docops/national/1996sfra.htm.
22. Ibid.
23. Thomas Lippmann, "African Crises," *Washington Post,* June 13, 1993.
24. See William G. Hyland, *Clinton's World* (Westport, 1999), p. 40.
25. Lake, "Our Place in the Balkans."
26. Speech, Federal News Service, San Francisco, Feb. 26, 1999.
27. Blumenthal, *The Clinton Wars,* p. 634.
28. Ibid., p. 652.
29. Ibid., p. 669.
30. On the politics of the Kyoto agreement, see Clyde Prestowitz, *Rogue Nation* (New York, 2003), chap. 5.
31. Berlin communiqué, "Progressive Governance for the 21st Century," White House Press Release, June 3, 2000.
32. Blumenthal, *The Clinton Wars,* p. 675.
33. See Daniel Benjamin and Steven Simon, *The Age of Sacred Terror* (New York, 2002), p. 13.
34. http://www.fas.org/irp/world/para/docs/980223-fatwa.htm.
35. See John Vinocur, "Transatlantic Visions," *New York Herald Tribune,* Nov. 22, 1999.
36. On Clinton's battles against al-Qaeda, see Richard Clarke, *Against All Enemies* (New York, 2004), chaps. 4 to 9.
37. Ibid., p. 224.

9. George W. Bush Sees Evil

1. George W. Bush, Press Conference, Apr. 3, 2004.
2. *Washington Post,* Sept. 8, 1991.
3. *Pittsburgh Post-Gazette,* May 16, 1999.
4. Ibid., Mar. 11, 1999.
5. I described these differences between "nationalists" and "neoconservatives" in "Why Iraq," *American Prospect,* Mar. 2003, and even earlier in "Beyond National Interest," *The New Republic,* June 21, 1999, but in the recent book *America Unbound* (Washington, 2004), Ivo Daalder and James Lindsay do a superior job of defining the "nationalist" foreign policy of Bush, Cheney, Rumsfeld, and Rice. Where I differ with them is in the importance I attach to the neoconservatives.
6. *Commentary,* Jan. 2000 symposium on "American Power—for What?"
7. Thomas Ricks, "Empire or Not," *Washington Post,* Aug. 21, 2001.
8. William Kristol and Robert Kagan, "Toward a Neo-Reaganite Foreign Policy," *Foreign Affairs,* July-Aug. 1996.

9. Ricks, "Empire or Not."
10. Robert Kagan, "History Repeating Itself: Liberalism and Foreign Policy," *New Criterion*, Apr. 1999.
11. See Kristol and Brooks, "What Ails Conservatism," *Wall Street Journal*, Sept. 25, 1997, and Frank Foer, "How Bill Kristol Ditched Conservatism," *The New Republic*, May 28, 2001.
12. William Kristol and Robert Kagan, "Reject the Global Buddy System," *New York Times*, Oct. 25, 1999.
13. Max Boot, *The Savage Wars of Peace* (New York, 2002).
14. See David Brooks, "Bush's Patriotic Challenge," *Weekly Standard*, Oct. 8, 2001.
15. Kristol and Kagan, "Reject the Global Buddy System."
16. Robert Kagan, "Kosovo and the Ethics of Isolationism," *New York Times*, Mar. 24, 1999.
17. Author's interview with Lawrence Kaplan.
18. See Lawrence Kaplan, "Regime Change," *The New Republic*, Mar. 3, 2003.
19. *Commentary*, symposium, "American Power—for What?"
20. Kristol and Kagan, "Reject the Global Buddy System."
21. Robert Kagan, "The Benevolent Empire," *Foreign Policy*, Summer 1998.
22. Thomas Donnelly, "The Past as Prologue: An Imperial Manual," *Foreign Affairs*, July 2002.
23. Cited in Ivo H. Daalder and James M. Lindsay, *America Unbound* (Washington, D.C., 2003), p. 37.
24. Second Presidential Debate, Oct. 17, 2000. The exchange is cited in James Mann, *The Rise of the Vulcans* (New York, 2004), p. 257.
25. See Bill Minutalglio, *First Son* (New York, 1999), p. 288, and George W. Bush, *A Change to Keep* (New York, 2001), pp. 135–139.
26. Speech at the Citadel (http://citadel.edu/pao/addresses/pres_bush.html), Sept. 1999, and at the Reagan Presidential Library, Nov. 1999.
27. See *Weekly Standard*, Apr. 16–23, 2001.
28. Associated Press, Sept. 12, 2001.
29. Daalder and Lindsay, *America Unbound*, p. 13.
30. Bush speech, Oct. 7, 2001; Bush speech, Dec. 7, 2001.
31. Quoted in Mann, *Rise of the Vulcans*, p. 308.
32. Bush speech, Dec. 7, 2001.
33. See John B. Judis, "Why Iraq," *American Prospect*.
34. The unclassified version is *Defense Strategy for the 1990s*, Sec. of Def. Dick Cheney, Jan. 1993. "We have moved from Containment to the new Regional Defense strategy."
35. See "Excerpts," *New York Times*, Mar. 8, 1992. The excerpts from the classified draft give America's interest in the region's oil more prominence than the paper that was made public in Jan. 1993. That is because American officials were sensitive to the charge that they were simply doing the oil companies' bidding. During the debate over the war in Iraq in 2002, Rumsfeld would deny that oil played any role in the Pentagon's interest in Iraq.
36. See Jane Mayer, "Contract Support," *New Yorker*, Feb. 16, 2004.
37. Cited in Douglas Little, *American Orientalism* (Chapel Hill, 2004), p. 320. The report, "Reliable, Affordable and Environmentally Sound Energy for America's Future," is available at http://www.netl.doe.gov/publications/press/2001/nep/nep.html.
38. Ron Suskind, *The Price of Loyalty* (New York, 2004), p. 85.
39. There was concern in the Pentagon that Saddam's regime had chosen to denominate its oil income in Euros rather than dollars. That could potentially strengthen the Euro and the European economy at the expense of the American. See Karen Kwiatkowski, "The New Pentagon Papers," *Salon*, Mar. 3, 2004.
40. Ibid.
41. See Suskind, *The Price of Loyalty*, p. 96.

42. Little, *American Orientalism.*
43. Interview with author (the Bush administration official asked not to be identified). See John B. Judis, "Over a Barrel," *The New Republic,* Jan. 20, 2003.
44. Interview with author.
45. See Kwiatkowski, "The New Pentagon Papers."
46. Rumsfeld would later deny this, but he recounted his intention to do so to a group of foreign and military policy experts in January 2003. Interview with Jessica Mathews. Rumsfeld's plan was also reported in the *New York Times,* Apr. 21, 2003, by Thom Shanker and Eric Schmitt ("Pentagon Expects Long-Term Access to Key Iraq Bases").
47. Mann, *Rise of the Vulcans,* p. 83.
48. Bill Keller, "The Sunshine Warrior," *New York Times Magazine,* Sept. 22, 2002.
49. John Dizard, "How Ahmed Chalabi Conned the Neocons," *Salon,* May 4, 2004.
50. Ibid., Douglas Davis, "Peace with Israel," *Jerusalem Post,* Apr. 21, 2003.
51. *Jerusalem Post,* Feb. 12, 2003.
52. Bruce Murphy, "Neoconservative Clout," *Milwaukee Journal-Sentinel,* Apr. 6, 2003.
53. Suskind, *The Price of Loyalty,* p. 85.
54. On this debate, see John B. Judis, "Some Mideast Realism Please," *American Prospect,* Jan. 13, 2003.
55. Brent Scowcroft, "Don't Attack Saddam," *Wall Street Journal,* Aug. 15, 2002.
56. Chalabi on *Good Morning America,* Feb. 25, 2003; *Al-Matamas,* the weekly newspaper of the Iraqi National Congress (INC), Jan. 24–30, 2003.
57. On Lewis's influence, see Peter Waldman, "A Historian's Take on Islam Steers US in Terrorism Fight," *Wall Street Journal,* Feb. 3, 2004.
58. Bernard Lewis, "Did You Say American Imperialism?," *National Review,* Dec. 17, 2001.
59. Fouad Ajami, "Iraq and the Thief of Baghdad," *New York Times,* May 19, 2002.
60. Bernard Lewis, *What Went Wrong* (New York, 2002), p. 153. See the review of *What Went Wrong* by Juan Cole in *Global Dialogue,* Jan. 27, 2003.
61. Bernard Lewis, "Targeted by History of Hatred," *Washington Post,* Sept. 10, 2002.
62. Lewis, "Did You Say American Imperialism?"
63. Fouad Ajami, "Hail the American Imperium," *U.S. News & World Report,* Nov. 11, 2002.
64. Lewis, "Did You Say American Imperialism?"
65. Fouad Ajami, "Iraq and the Thief of Baghdad."
66. Lawrence F. Kaplan, "Why the Bushies . . . ," *The New Republic,* May 26, 2003.
67. Richard Cheney, remarks before the VFW, Nashville, Tenn., Aug. 26, 2002.
68. Ken Adelman, "Cakewalk in Iraq," *Washington Post,* Feb. 13, 2002.
69. Emily Eakin, "All Roads," *New York Times,* Mar. 31, 2002.
70. Stephen Peter Rosen, "An Empire If You Can Keep It," *National Interest,* Spring 2002.
71. Michael Ignatieff, "The American Empire," *New York Times Magazine,* Jan. 5, 2003.
72. Max Boot, "America's Destiny Is to Police the World," *Financial Times,* Feb. 17, 2003.
73. Ibid.

10. George W. Bush and the Illusion of Omnipotence

1. In Cincinnati at the Cincinnati Museum Center, Oct. 7, 2002.
2. Spencer Ackerman and John B. Judis, "The First Casualty," *The New Republic,* June 30, 2003.
3. George W. Bush, State of the Union, Jan. 28, 2003.
4. George W. Bush, speech, United Nations, Sept. 12, 2002.
5. See Ackerman and Judis, "The First Casualty." For instance, the administration withheld from U.N. arms experts the aluminum tubes that in Sept. 2002 it claimed Iraq was trying to acquire to build nuclear weapons. When U.N. experts finally got to examine them

on the eve of the war, they concurred with American experts at the Energy Department who said they were not suitable for this purpose.

6. "War in Iraq," *The Financial Times,* May 27, 2003. See also issues of May 29 and 30.
7. Ivo H. Daalder and James H. Lindsay, *America Unbound* (Washington, D.C., 2003), p. 147.
8. Eric Schmitt, "Pentagon Contradicts General," *New York Times,* Feb. 25, 2003.
9. See John B. Judis, "Sifting Through the Rubble," *American Prospect,* Oct. 2003.
10. Conrad C. Crane and W. Andrew Terrill, *Reconstructing Iraq* (Army War College, Feb. 2003). Part of this statement is cited in James Fallows, "Blind into Baghdad," *Atlantic,* Jan.-Feb. 2004. The report is available at http://www.carlisle.army.mil/ssi/pubs/2003/reconirq/reconirq.htm.
11. Crane and Terrill, *Reconstructing Iraq.*
12. For these doubts, see Fallows, "Blind into Baghdad."
13. Schmitt, "Pentagon Contradicts General."
14. Fallows, "Blind into Baghdad."
15. George W. Bush speech aboard the U.S.S. *Abraham Lincoln,* May 2003.
16. *Associated Press,* Apr. 24, 2003.
17. Thom Shanker and Eric Schmitt, "U.S. Plans to Keep Four Bases," *New York Times,* Apr. 20, 2003.
18. Toby Harnden, "US Plans Longterm Bases," *Daily Telegraph,* Apr. 21, 2003.
19. Peter S. Goodman, "Iraq May Break with OPEC," *Washington Post,* May 18, 2003.
20. Chip Cummins, "Iraq Invites Foreign Oil-Fire Offers," *Wall Street Journal,* Sept. 25, 2003.
21. Interview with Jay Garner, BBC, Mar. 19, 2004.
22. Rajiv Chandrasekaran, "Attacks Force Retreat from Wide-Ranging Plans for Iraq," *Washington Post,* Dec. 28, 2003.
23. *Financial Times,* Oct. 29, 2003.
24. See *Middle East Economic Survey,* Nov. 17, 2003.
25. See www.lunaville.org/warcasualities/summary.aspxj.
26. See www.iraqbodycount.org and Dana Milbank and Robin Wright, "Off the Mark," *Washington Post,* Mar. 19, 2004.
27. *Los Angeles Times,* Oct. 28, 2003.
28. See www.juancole.com, Mar. 16, 2004.
29. Douglas Jehl and David E. Sanger, "Iraqis' Bitterness Is Called Bigger Threat," *New York Times,* Sept. 17, 2003.
30. Aljazeerah, Feb. 15, 2004.
31. Michael Elliott, "So, What Went Wrong," *Time,* Sept. 28, 2003.
32. Suzanne Goldenberg, "A Land Ruled by Chaos," *The Guardian,* Oct. 4, 2003.
33. Yoshi J. Dreazen and Christopher Cooper, "U.S. Tightens Grip," *Wall Street Journal,* May 13, 2004.
34. Joe Rosenberg, "Rumsfeld Retreats," Hearst Newspapers, Nov. 9, 2003.
35. "Online News Hour," Feb. 20, 2003.
36. Bush speech at Heritage Foundation Luncheon, Reagan Building, Washington, D.C., Nov. 11, 2003.
37. George W. Bush, Press Conference, Apr. 13, 2004.
38. *The Age,* Apr. 12, 2004.
39. Reginald Horsman, *Race and Manifest Destiny* (Cambridge, 1981), p. 114.
40. *ABC News,* Apr. 23, 2004.
41. David Brooks, *New York Times,* Apr. 10, 2004.
42. Miller, *Benevolent Assimilation,* p. 248.
43. http://mediamatters.org/items/20040505003.
44. CNN.com, Wednesday, May 12, 2004.

45. John Podhoretz, "Rooting for the Enemy," *New York Post,* May 14, 2004.
46. George W. Bush, speech, May 1, 2003.
47. *Pakistan Times,* July 29, 2003.
48. International Institute for Strategy Studies, *The Military Balance: 2003–4* (London, 2003).
49. Husain Haqqani, "Rise of the Baby Al Qaidas," *Salon,* Apr. 7, 2004.
50. See John B. Judis, "The Road to Aqaba," *American Prospect,* July 1, 2003.
51. "Powell Kept Waiting," *Financial Times,* Mar. 25, 2004.
52. Pew Global Attitudes Project, "A Year After Iraq War," Mar. 14, 2004.
53. *The Economist,* Mar. 6, 2004.

CONCLUSION

1. See Rudolph Peters, *Islam and Colonialism* (The Hague, 1979). For instance, in 1882, clerics issued a Jihad to expel the British from Egypt: "Wake up from your heedlessness, O sons of this land, and free yourselves from shame and ignominy. Cause the English to taste a painful punishment and prepare for them whatsoever force and cavalry ye are capable of gathering" (p. 80).
2. Olivier Roy, *The Failure of Political Islam* (Cambridge, 1994), p 4.
3. "Why We Do Jihad," Abu Salam Ben Mohammed (pseudonym), Center for the Call of Righteousness (the Army of the Pure), translated by Husain Haggani.
4. See Prestowitz, *Rogue Nation,* pp. 115–117.
5. Max Boot, "America's Destiny Is to Police the World," *Financial Times,* Feb. 17, 2003.
6. Joseph Nye, *The Paradox of American Power* (Oxford, 2002), p. 159.
7. Preamble, "United Nations Charter."
8. Stanley Kurtz, "Democratic Imperialism: A Blueprint," *Policy Review,* May 2003.
9. Stephen Peter Rosen, "An Empire If You Can Keep It," *National Interest,* Spring 2002.
10. Charles Krauthammer, "The Unipolar Moment Revisited," *National Interest,* Winter 2002–2003.
11. Quoted in Ernest Tuveson, *Redeemer Nation* (Chicago, 1968).
12. Richard Perle And David Frum, *An End to Evil* (New York, 2004), p. 277.

ACKNOWLEDGMENTS

In May 2002, I was at a seminar at the American Academy in Berlin, where an American political scientist was explaining George W. Bush's foreign policy to an audience of German academics, American embassy officials, and Academy fellows. The American political scientist, exasperated by the Germans' criticisms of the Bush administration, asked one of them, "What would *you* have us do?" She replied, "I would have you follow the example of your President Wilson." As she was explaining what that meant, one of the American embassy officials interrupted her. "Do you mean that you would have us use our superior power to create a world in which it was irrelevant?" he asked.

In the spring of 2003, with this exchange still fresh in mind, I wrote an essay for *The New Republic* on the relevance of Wilson to the debate over the Bush administration's foreign policy. I am grateful to Peter Beinart, the editor, for encouraging me to write it, especially since I did not share the magazine's support for the invasion of Iraq. After the article appeared, I asked Lisa Drew, who edited my last book at Scribner, whether she would consider doing a longer version as a book, and she was enthusiastic. I am very grateful to Lisa for her support of this book and for her editorial advice, and to Samantha Martin for shepherding the book to publication. I also got welcome encouragement from Eric Nelson, who is now an editor at Wiley.

I couldn't have done this book without support from Bill Moyers and the Florence and John Schumann Foundation. This is the second time that Moyers and Schumann have made the difference for me. I couldn't have finished it without the support of Jessica Mathews and the Carnegie Endowment for International Peace. Carnegie is one of those institutions in Washington that is still faithful to the progressive ideal of disinterested policy research. I wasn't asked to toe a line or to please funders, and I was able to discuss my ideas with people who knew considerably more about the world than I did. I got enormous help from Carnegie's librarians. Kathleen Higgs, Jill Fox, and Chris Henley procured materials that I could never have found on my own or that I would still be looking for. Greg Minor and Veronica Arrington helped me adjust to life at a think tank.

I called on many people for advice and comments. I talked through key ideas of the book with Eli Zaretsky, Walter LaFeber, Husain Haqqani, James Gilbert, and William Burr. I got ideas and advice from Art Eckstein, Rose-marie Zaggari, Michael Kazin, Sidney Blumenthal, Walter Laqueur, Derek Chollet, Spencer Ackerman, Anatol Lieven, Ed Lincoln, Karen DeYoung, Lawrence Kaplan, Jacob Heilbrunn, Ruy Teixeira, Ronald Radosh, Marina Ottaway, Alice Martin-Adkins, and Arnold Krupat. Jorgen Dragsdahl spotted an embarrassing mistake in the introduction. Bill Burr read the first draft, and Spencer Ackerman the final draft. I'm sure there are still errors, but there are considerably fewer because of their generous assistance. Rafe Sagalyn negotiated my contract and provided advice and encouragement. And my wife, Susan Pearson, and daughters, Hilary and Eleanor, kept me believing that life was worthwhile even during this difficult period in America's history.

INDEX

multilateralism of, 6, 7, 8, 89, 128,
150–51, 169, 204–6, 208–9, 211–12
Pan-American Pact of, 89
at Paris peace conference, 81, 95–96,
104, 107, 108–11
peace without victory policy of, 99–100,
106, 112
and Philippine independence, 2
racial beliefs of, 80, 83
religious beliefs of, 77, 79, 109
Russian Revolution and, 106–8
Theodore Roosevelt compared with, 78,
80–81, 85
Turner's influence on, 81, 82–83
on U.S. imperialism, 4, 5, 86
war views of, 81
World War I and, 95–104, 106
writings of, 75, 81, 83, 84–85
Winning of the West, The (Roosevelt), 35,
37*n*, 56–57
Winthrop, John, 16
Wiseman, William, 107
Wittman, Marshall, 169, 171
Wohlstetter, Albert, 168
Wolfowitz, Paul, 9, 168, 171, 171*n*, 173,
175, 178, 181, 183, 189, 198–99, 207

Wood, Leonard, 48
Woodrow, James, 77
Woodrow, Thomas, 77
Woolsey, James, 173
World Bank, 127–28, 129, 151, 160, 165,
204
World Court, 122
*World Politics at the End of the Nineteenth
Century* (Reinsch), 63
World Trade Center, 163
World Trade Organization (WTO), 7, 151,
156, 158, 159, 165, 204
World War I, 5, 12, 49, 76, 89, 95–104,
150, 202
causes of, 100–104
World War II, 6, 16, 19, 116, 120–23, 131,
141, 150
causes of, 124–25
Wurmser, David, 168, 171, 171*n*

Yalta Conference (1945), 133, 135
Yuan Shih-k'ai, 88, 92
Yugoslavia, 149, 159

Zimmermann telegram, 99
Zionism, 37*n*

ABOUT THE AUTHOR

JOHN B. JUDIS is a senior editor for *The New Republic* and a visiting scholar at the Carnegie Endowment for International Peace. He was educated at Amherst College and at the University of California at Berkeley, from which he received an M.A. in philosophy. He was a founding editor of *Socialist Review* and the foreign editor of *In These Times*. His articles have appeared in *The American Prospect, The New York Times Magazine, The Washington Post, Foreign Affairs, Foreign Policy, Washington Monthly, The Wilson Quarterly, GQ,* and *Dissent.* His books include *The Emerging Democratic Majority* (with Ruy Teixeira), *The Paradox of American Democracy: Elites, Special Interests, and the Betrayal of Public Trust, William F. Buckley: Patron Saint of the Conservatives,* and *Grand Illusion: Critics and Champions of the American Century.*